Socializing Democratic Norms

# Socializing Democratic Norms

## The Role of International Organizations for the Construction of Europe

Edited by

Trine Flockhart
*Associate Professor, Institute for History, Social and International Studies*
*University of Aalborg, Denmark*

palgrave
macmillan

First published in 2005 by
PALGRAVE MACMILLAN
Houndmills, Basingstoke, Hampshire RG21 6XS and
175 Fifth Avenue, New York, N.Y. 10010
Companies and representatives throughout the world.

PALGRAVE MACMILLAN is the global academic imprint of the Palgrave Macmillan division of St. Martin's Press, LLC and of Palgrave Macmillan Ltd. Macmillan® is a registered trademark in the United States, United Kingdom and other countries. Palgrave is a registered trademark in the European Union and other countries.

ISBN-13: 978–1–4039–4521–1
ISBN-10: 1–4039–4521–7

This book is printed on paper suitable for recycling and made from fully managed and sustained forest sources.

A catalogue record for this book is available from the British Library.

Library of Congress Cataloging-in-Publication Data

Socializing democratic norms : the role of international organizations for the construction of Europe / edited by Trine Flockhart.
p. cm.
Includes bibliographical references and index.
ISBN 1–4039–4521–7 (cloth)
1. Europe, Central – Politics and government – 1989– 2. Europe, Eastern – Politics and government – 1989– 3. International agencies – Europe. 4. Democratization – Europe – International cooperation. 5. Political socialization – Europe – International cooperation. I. Flockhart, Trine.

JN96.A58S65 2005
320.947—dc22 2004058674

10 9 8 7 6 5 4 3 2 1
14 13 12 11 10 09 08 07 06 05

Printed and bound in Great Britain by
Antony Rowe Ltd, Chippenham and Eastbourne.

*In memory of my mother*
*Birgit Inger Hansen*
*1934–1978*

# Contents

# Figures and Tables

## Figures



## Tables

# Contributors

**Petr Drulák** is Deputy Director of the Institute of International Relations in Prague. He publishes on the theory of international relations and the enlargement of the European Union. His articles have been published in *Journal of International Relations and Development* and in *Journal of European Public Policy* as well as several book chapters.

**Trine Flockhart** is Associate Professor at the University of Aalborg, Denmark. Her publications include *From Vision to Reality: Implementing Europe's New Security Order* (Westwiew, 1998), and articles published in *European Security: Perspectives on European Politics and Society, Co-operation and Conflict, International Relations*, as well as several book chapters. She is currently working on a book on the Europeanization of Europe.

**Jean Grugel** is Professor in the Department of Politics, University of Sheffield, UK. Her research interests and publications focus on democratization, citizenship and global governance. She is presently engaged in an ESRC-funded project on new regionalism and transnational collective action in South America.

**Lucie Königová** is a research fellow with the Institute of International Relations, Prague, Assistant Editor of *Mezinárodní vztahy* (International Relations), and lecturer at the Department of Political Science in the Faculty of Arts, Charles University. Her PhD project is focused on institutional identity transformation within the process of enlargement.

**Elena A. Korosteleva** is Lecturer at the Department of International Politics, University of Wales, Aberystwyth. She received her doctoral degree in political science from the University of Bath, Department of European Studies, and subsequently became a British Academy Postdoctoral Fellow at the University of Glasgow. Her research interests include democratization and the quality of new East European democracies, party systems and government formation, and civic disengagement across Europe.

**Sonia Lucarelli** is Adjunct Professor of International Relations at the University of Bologna at Forlì. Her areas of interest include IR theory, European security and EU foreign policy. She has published books with Kluwer Law International, Taylor & Francis, Routledge, as well as articles and book chapters.

**Michael Merlingen** is Assistant Professor at Central European University, Budapest. His research focuses on international organizations, European security and IR theory. His publications have appeared in journals such as *Cooperation and Conflict, Journal of Common Market Studies, Security Dialogue, Journal of International Relations and Development* and *Zeitschrift für Internationale Beziehungen.*

**Sally Morphet** is a former Research Analyst for the British Foreign and Commonwealth Office (retired) and currently Visiting Professor at the University of Kent at Canterbury. She has published articles and chapters in books on UN civil administration, the environment and NGOs, foreign policy groups at the UN, peacekeeping and the Security Council. She is currently contributing to a book on Southern politics.

**Rasa Ostrauskaitė** is with the Policy Planning and Early Warning Unit of the General Secretariat of the Council of the EU. She is also a PhD student in the Department of International Relations and European Studies at Central European University, Budapest. Her articles have appeared in the OSCE Yearbook and *Populacao e Sociedade.*

**Bill Park** is a Senior Lecturer with the War Studies Group, King's College, London University, at the Defence Studies Department (DSD) at the Joint Services Command and Staff College, Watchfield, and is Research Associate at the Centre for Defence Studies (CDS), also at King's. He has lectured, broadcasted and advised on Turkish foreign and security issues, and in addition to book chapters has published in journals such as *World Today, Jane's Intelligence Review* and *Middle East Review of International Affairs.*

**Clelia Rontoyanni** obtained her PhD from the University of Glasgow (2001), and has since worked as a Research Fellow at the Russia and Eurasia Programme of the Royal Institute of International Affairs. She currently works for the Delegation of the European Commission in Moscow. The views expressed in her contribution to this volume are her own and do not represent the official position of the European Commission.

**Marek Rybář** is Assistant Professor at the Department of Political Science, Comenius University, Bratislava, Slovakia. He has published several articles and book chapters on political parties in Slovakia and on EU–Slovak relations. His current research focuses on Europeanization of national political institutions of the new EU member states and on party politics in East Central Europe.

**Frank Schimmelfennig** is a Fellow of the Mannheim Centre for European Social Research at the University of Mannheim. His work has been published, among others, in *European Journal of International Relations*, *International Organization*, *Journal of Common Market Studies* and *Journal of European Public Policy* and by Cambridge University Press.

**Mette Skak** is Associate Professor of Peace and Conflict Research at the Department of Political Science, University of Aarhus, Denmark. She holds a PhD in Political Science and MA in Russian language and history. She has published widely in both Danish and English on Russian post-communist foreign policy, Central Europe and on the Baltic states.

# Abbreviations

| | |
|---|---|
| AKP | Justice and Development Party |
| AMG | Advisory and Monitoring Group |
| ANP | Annual National Programme |
| APC | Association Parliamentary Committee |
| APEC | Asia-Pacific Economic Community |
| CEE | Central and Eastern Europe |
| CEECs | Central and East European Countries |
| CEFTA | Central European Free Trade Area |
| CIA | Central Intelligence Service |
| CIS | Commonwealth of Independent States |
| CLRAE | Congress of Local and Regional Authorities of Europe |
| CoE | Council of Europe |
| CSCE | Conference on Security and Co-operation in Europe |
| ČSSD | Czech Social Democratic Party |
| EAPC | Euro-Atlantic Partnership Council |
| EC | European Community |
| ECHR | European Court of Human Rights |
| ECU | European Currency Unit |
| EEC | European Economic Communities |
| EIDHR | European Initiative for Democracy and Human Rights |
| ENP | European Neighbourhood Policy |
| EU | European Union |
| FTAA | Free Trade Area of the Americas |
| FYROM | Former Yugoslav Republic of Macedonia |
| GNP | Gross National Product |
| HCNM | High Commissioner on National Minorities |
| HZDS | Movement for a Democratic Slovakia |
| ICCPR | International Covenants on Civil and Political Rights |
| ICESCR | International Economic Social and Cultural Rights |
| IPE | International Political Economy |
| IR | International Relations |
| KOZ | Trade Union Confederation |
| LTMs | Long-term field Missions |
| MAP | Membership Action Plan |
| MERCOSUR | Common Market of the South |

| | |
|---|---|
| NACC | North Atlantic Co-operation Council |
| NAFTA | North American Free Trade Association |
| NATO | North Atlantic Treaty Organization |
| NATO–PA | North Atlantic Treaty Organization–Parliamentary Assembly |
| NGO | Non-governmental Organization |
| NSC | National Security Council |
| ODA | Civic Democratic Alliance |
| ODIHR | Office for Democratic Institutions and Human Rights |
| ODS | Civic Democratic Party |
| OECD | Organization for Economic Co-operation and Development |
| OF | Civic Forum |
| OH | Civic Movement |
| OSCE | Organization for Security and Co-operation in Europe |
| PACE | Parliamentary Assembly of the Council of Europe |
| PCA | Partnership and Co-operation Agreement |
| PDU | Police Development Unit |
| PfP | Partnership for Peace |
| PHARE | Poland–Hungary: Actions for Economic Reconstruction |
| PKK | Kurdish Worker's Party |
| PTDP | Phare and Tacis Democracy Programme |
| SDK | Slovak Democratic Coalition |
| SIT | Social Identity Theory |
| SMK | Party of Hungarian Coalition |
| SNS | Slovak National Party |
| TACIS | Technical Assistance for the Commonwealth of Independent States |
| TRNC | Turkish Republic of Northern Cyprus |
| UDHR | Universal Declaration on Human Rights |
| UN | United Nations |
| UNDP | United Nations Development Programme |
| USSR | Union of Soviet Socialist Republics |
| WEOG | Western European and Other States Group |
| WEU | West European Union |
| WTO | World Trade Organization |
| ZRS | Association of Slovak Workers |

# Socialization and Democratization: a Tenuous but Intriguing Link

*Trine Flockhart*

This book seeks to understand one of the important processes of change taking place in the 'New Europe' in its process of enlarging the circle of states whose shared identity and core values of democracy, human rights and the rule of law, makes them a value-based community with some very specific qualities – most notably peaceful and co-operative relations. In its focus on the processes of change in the relations between states, the book is very much located within International Relations. However, a key assumption of the book is that we cannot separate the 'international' from the 'domestic', and that both form a mutually constitutive relationship. As a result, we must direct our attention at *both* the 'international' and the 'domestic', thereby locating the book at the intersection between International Relations, Comparative Politics and Democratization Studies. The assumption is that in our quest for explaining the processes of change *between* states in the post-Cold War world, we must also look in more detail at the processes of change *within* states, because as suggested by Ian Clark, 'the change is relational to both rather than particular to either' (Clark, 1999: 5).

The specific focus of this book is ideational change at the domestic level and its consequences at the international level and vice versa. Interest is focused on the adoption of one of the key norms and shared values underpinning the Euro-Atlantic community – liberal democracy. Therefore the question that is addressed in this book is how and why a democratic norm set seems to have been adopted relatively easily in some Central and East European (CEE) states, but with considerable difficulty or not at all in other similar states, despite the appearance of similar structural and practical circumstances. It assumes that what is entailed in these states' transition from an authoritarian political system to a democratic one is a form of identity construction through the adoption of a new norm set, which has been socialized by a number of external agents, in the case of this volume, a number of international organizations.

The chapters in the volume roughly follow the same theoretical perspective located within the 'broad church' of social constructivism, and more specifically related to the theoretical framework called 'Complex Socialization' presented in Chapter 2. They do not, however, follow any similar pattern in how the contributing authors have chosen to apply the theoretical model, nor in which aspects of the very complex model they have chosen to focus. In that sense each chapter represents an individual interpretation of the Complex Socialization model and its application to the different empirical areas covered within the pages of this book. Most of the contributing authors have a background in International Relations, but a few are drawn from the ranks of Democratization Studies or Comparative Politics, or somewhere in between. All agree that the intersection between International Relations and Comparative Politics/Democratization Studies may well be the place for answering the questions addressed here, and that there is a need for a systematic integration of international factors into the comparative analysis of democratization processes (Schimmelfennig, 2002: 4). It is therefore hoped that the volume may be a starting point for further much-needed research drawing on the particular insights of *both* disciplinary perspectives utilized in this volume.

This introduction will start out with an outline of the 'separate lives' of the two disciplines: International Relations and Democratization Studies. Following on from that and in recognition that readers with a background in Democratization Studies or Comparative Politics may not be familiar with the debates within International Relations on either the importance of democracy for security, or on the specific conceptual and theoretical considerations utilized in this volume, the introduction will provide a brief survey of these debates and related conceptual and theoretical issues. For those unfamiliar with democratization, Chapter 1 provides a similar function as Jean Grugel discusses the 'international' in democratization. Finally, of course, the introduction will present the individual chapters.

## The 'separate lives' of International Relations and Democratization Studies

Where does democracy come from, and why does it seem to move along in waves from one country to another (Huntington, 1991)? In truth, and perhaps not surprisingly, the answer to these questions is likely to depend on who is answering, and perhaps also *when* the answer was sought. Had the question been directed at democratization scholars in the 1970s and 1980s, the likely answer would have been that democratization was simply a process of regime change following (almost automatically) after the end of authoritarianism. In other words, a process-oriented approach, which focused exclusively on the domestic conditions for a transition to take place. On the other hand, had the question (also in the 1970s or 1980s) been directed to an International Relations scholar, the answer would probably have been to refer the question to someone more qualified to talk about the mysteries of the 'internal workings of states'. Apart from an interest in the making of foreign policy within the sub-field of Foreign Policy Analysis, the domestic level was of no concern to International Relations. Since then, however, both disciplines have had to reconsider their stance on the 'international' and the 'domestic' respectively in recognition of the point put forward by Ian Clark that, 'it is precisely in the synergy between the two that the dynamics of change is to be located' (Clark, 1999: 5).

Within the field of Democratization Studies, the fact that not all the collapsing authoritarian regimes of the 1980s and early 1990s were transformed into democracies, but instead imploded with civil war and an increase in non-democratic practices as a consequence, seemed to challenge the process-oriented view of democratization of the 1970s and 1980s. The challenge was made all the more robust when it became clear that following the initial, perhaps successful transition to democracy, consolidation might not occur, but instead leave the transforming society lingering in a situation of persistent instability and malfunctioning, between transition and consolidation, with a considerable danger of 'sliding' back into an authoritarian regime type. Added to this was the fact that the collapse of authoritarianism in Central and Eastern Europe (CEE) occurred at more or less the same time following similar democratizations across the world in what Huntington (1991) called 'the third wave'. This seemed to suggest not only a single common cause for the collapse (Grugel, 2002: 198), but also that the cause had to be located *externally* to the democratizing state, and not as hitherto presumed rooted within particularities of individual nation states (Grugel, 2002: 7). As this re-evaluation of disciplinary assumptions coincided with the onset of the globalization debate and a realization that the contemporary context of democratization *is* globalization with its ever-deeper forms of interconnectedness and subsequent transnationalism

(McGrew, 1997), Democratization Studies were ready to consider the 'international' in the analysis of trying to understand why and how democratization takes place, and why it is sometimes successful and sometimes not.

International Relations scholars also had to reconsider their aloofness in relation to the importance of the domestic affairs of states. The internal changes in the Soviet Union in the 1980s clearly had major repercussions in the international sphere since it led to structural change in the international system. Also the rediscovery of Immanuel Kant in Michael Doyle's seminal articles from 1983 suggested a specific link between democracy and peace and brought new-found (or re-found as it was essentially a reformulation of Wilsonianism) interest in democracy and other domestic issues to the IR discipline. Alongside the rediscovery of Wilsonianism, the IR community also became interested in globalization, and in the process discovered the importance of International Political Economy (IPE) and that the discipline's hitherto downgrading of 'death by economics' as opposed to 'death in armed conflict' was both morally and practically untenable (cf. Smith, 2003). The result was that (some) acknowledged the need to include issues hitherto deemed to fall outside the scope of International Relations on an equal footing with (security) relations *between* states. Alongside the reconsiderations of what constituted suitable areas of interest for a discipline, whose main theoretical foundations were perceived (by some) to have been severely challenged by the end of the Cold War and the subsequent systems level changes, the discipline also went through a vigorous meta-theoretical debate, which saw the birth of the so-called 'constructivist turn', emphasizing ideational rather than material factors. The result has been that from its narrow focus on states and military security in the 1980s, the 1990s saw the birth of an IR discipline with a much broader empirical *and* theoretical reach, in which 'anything goes'. It seems that the IR discipline is now ready to proceed from its focus on the meta-theoretical level with its focus on ontological and epistemological questions, to an explicit first-order theory level dealing with the understanding and explanation of specific issues. The present volume is part of that enterprise.

By the beginning of the 1990s, both sub-disciplines had reason to reconsider some of their own key assumptions and areas of interest. Democratization Studies realized the importance of the 'international' whilst International Relations realized the importance of the 'domestic'. It would appear that the foundations for a fruitful relationship between the two were in place. However, despite such congenial circumstances for debate and co-operation, and the occasional plea for co-operation (Smith, 2000), the actual contact between IR and Democratization Studies has been somewhat limited. This may, of course, be because of the absence of any fundamental disagreement between the two on where democracy comes from, and what determines its success – after all *disagreement* is the foundation for debate. Therefore debate may be absent because the two sub-disciplines simply seem to see different things, and hence 'never the twain shall meet'. Indeed, what is remarkable about the debate and co-operation between IR and Democratization Studies is the profound lack of it until Huntington's book in 1991 identified global rather than domestic factors as the principal cause of contemporary democratization (Grugel, 2002: 8). Apart from a handful of studies (cf. Smith, 2000; Grugel, 1999, 2002; Pridham, 1991; Pridham and Vanhanen, 1994; Huntington, 1991; Whitehead, 1996 [2001]; O'Donnell et al., 1986) a specific connection between Democratization Studies and International Relations has been conspicuous by its absence rather than its vigour. The exception, apart from the above, is on the connection between Globalization and Democracy, which has provided a shared focus of interest and attracted scholars from both IR and Democratization Studies (cf. Held, 1995; Held et al., 1999; Robertson, 1992; Scholte, 2000). However, the lack of debate does not necessarily mean that there are no areas of common interest between IR and Democratization Studies; it may simply mean that they have yet to be discovered. By viewing the two levels as mutually constitutive, such an area seems to have not only been discovered, but to be of central importance for the understanding of processes of change at both levels.

The topic under investigation in this volume may well provide such a link between Democratization Studies and International Relations. The assumption of the volume is generated from research within International Relations, that shared values – in this case democratic values – are likely to lead to peaceful and co-operative relations between states. It is therefore important to know how and why authoritarian regimes become democratic ones, and what factors determine their failure or success in that endeavour – in other words a key interest for Democratization Studies. The theoretical perspective is very much located within some of the key theoretical debates of International Relations from the last decade or so. Located squarely within the social constructivist 'camp', the attempt here is to provide an explanation for how and why democracy seems to have taken root in a number of CEECs; why has this process failed in some instances, and lagged behind in others? Hence the focus is on the external influences on democratization through the promotion/socialization of a specific norm set espousing a commitment to a 'Western' conception of liberal democracy, human rights, the rule of law and a market economy, and how the results of the processes of change at the domestic level 'loop back' to the external level with structural change. The process that is under investigation is conceptualized as a process of socialization, leading to the construction of new identities and membership of new social groups. In that sense the current interest within International Relations in 'socialization' is linked up with the current interest within Democratization Studies on 'democracy promotion'. By combining the two it is hoped that the result will be new insights into not only how democracy is promoted/socialized by external agents, but also how their efforts are received in the countries that are being socialized/subjected to democracy promotion, and how that in turn leads to altered relations at the international level. What is more, it is hoped that the specific theoretical framework presented in this volume will open up a comparative research programme, allowing for systematic comparison across the many similar, yet very different cases of democratization/democratic norms transfer.

## Democracy in International Relations in theory and practice

Democracy and its promotion clearly hold a prominent position in current foreign policy. Hardly a day passes by without news analysis related to the prospects for the Bush Administration's goal of establishing democracy in post-war Iraq,[1] which is intended to lead to a so-called democratic 'tsunami' in the Middle East (Pei et al., 2004). Democracy promotion was also a major part of the Clinton Administration's foreign policy, where the president in his 1994 State of the Union address stated that 'the best strategy to ensure our security and to build a durable peace is to support the advance of democracy elsewhere'. Indeed, similar statements abound in the Bush Administration, especially in relation to 'building democracy' in the Middle East.

It seems that the inspiration for the Clinton Administration's foreign policy emphasis on democracy promotion, to a large extent has come from the academic community, where the 'democratic peace thesis' was under vigorous discussion in the early 1990s. Certainly Madelaine Albright had taken part in a Rand Corporation Conference on the support of East European Democracy and Free Markets in 1990 (Wolf, 1991: vii). This is not the place to rehearse the democratic peace thesis as that is amply covered elsewhere in the literature. Suffice to acknowledge here that there is a clear connection between liberal democracy and peace, and that its effects have been considerable at the level of practical policy-making.

## The rise and fall of the fortunes of democracy in International Relations

Democracy has to some extent, and despite appearances to the contrary, always had a prominent position within International Relations both in theory and practice. The 'idealists', also sometimes known as 'Wilsonian liberalists', who dominated the discipline in the first twenty years of its existence, attached a great deal of importance to democracy, as it was seen as a safeguard against warring leaders. The logic went that as 'the people' would not want war, they would not elect leaders that were likely to take them to war. Therefore by ensuring that states were democratic, one would also ensure that only 'sensible' and non-warmongering leaders were elected. This albeit very normative theoretical position found a practical application in the peace treaties following the First World War, which were greatly influenced by President Wilson. Apart from ensuring that the successor states had democratic constitutions, Wilson's fourteen points also included a commitment to free and open negotiations and to the establishment of international organizations through which diplomacy could work in open channels with all states present.

There are many reasons why these noble ideas did not fare well in the events that followed the end of the First World War, an analysis of which is well beyond the scope of this introduction.[2] For now it can just be noted that the proposed policies were extremely poorly implemented and probably based on an insufficient understanding on how democracy is consolidated following the initial constitution-writing phase. The point is that the conditions included in the Wilsonian form of liberalism in the first quarter of the twentieth century may not have been as naïve and ill-conceived as they have often been presented. What is also worth noting is that the ideas espoused by Wilsonian liberalism were remarkably similar to the ideas espoused by Immanuel Kant in his pamphlet *Towards Perpetual Peace* (1795). Like Wilson, Kant presented a three-legged argument, which in a (late) twentieth-century, neo-Kantian perspective can be summarized as consisting of:

1. Liberal democracy: referred to by Kant as states sharing 'republican constitutions';

2. Interdependence: referred to by Kant as 'cosmopolitan law' embodying ties of international commerce and free trade;[3]
3. International organizations: referred to by Kant as a 'pacific union', which is established by treaty in international law among republics.

The result of the establishment of these conditions would be a condition referred to as a *Perpetual Peace* where the states within the 'zone' live in peaceful relations, although on the outside conflict may well prevail. Kant did not envisage that the process towards perpetual peace would be easy or straightforward, but predicted that the process would be gradual, taking place through different stages, and that success would not be achieved straightaway. Indeed, he foresaw the possibility that some 'republican states' might revert back to their previous non-republican stage.

The Kantian peace perspective has been extremely influential in practical politics throughout the twentieth century. Its influence can be seen in, for example, the preamble to the Rome Treaty, as well as in the practical politics of Wilson, Schumann and Monet, Carter and Bill Clinton. During the Cold War, however, the link was not only downplayed (with the exception of President Carter, who at the time was ridiculed for his emphasis on democracy and moral foreign policies), but was clearly not adhered to in the assumption that authoritarian states formed the best bulwark against Communism. In theoretical terms, the link between democracy and peace did not have to be downplayed as it seemed to have been all but forgotten after the discrediting of idealism in IR theory in the 1930s and 1940s. Apart from some aspects of integration theory (which mainstream IR largely ignored at the time), the link between peace and democracy remained something that was taught in universities as 'the fallacy' of idealism, and remained so until Michael Doyle's seminal articles on 'Kant, Liberal Democracy and Foreign Affairs' appeared in 1983 and caused the IR community to 'rediscover' the writings of Immanuel Kant on the relevance of democracy for peace. Since then a true avalanche of 'democratic peace thesis' literature has appeared (cf. Doyle, 1983, 1986; Russett, 1993; Lake, 1992; Owen, 1994).

In the process of rediscovering Kant, the IR scholarly community also rediscovered another almost forgotten author: Karl Deutsch, and his concept 'security community'. A 'security community' was one of the concepts developed by Deutsch and his associates within their theoretical work on transactionalism. A 'security community' can be said to be equal to the situation envisaged in *Perpetual Peace* when all three legs of the Kantian peace perspective have been achieved. A security community can be said to be in place when a group of states have been integrated to such a point that they have developed a sense of community and a will to settle their disputes by peaceful means, effectively suggesting that the member states of the security community have overcome the problems posed by the security dilemma, and have achieved dependable relations characterized by peaceful change and a sense of 'we-ness' (Deutsch et al., 1957; Adler and Barnett, 1998).

At the time of publication, the work by Deutcsh et al. received some interest, but it soon faded into obscurity, perhaps because the IR discipline at the time really was not comfortable with such fuzzy concepts as 'community' and a 'we-feeling'. As expressed by Emanuel Adler and Michael Barnett in the introduction to *Security Communities*:

> Scholars of International Relations are generally uncomfortable evoking the language of community to understand international politics. The idea that actors can share values, norms and symbols that provide a social identity, and engage in various interactions in myriad spheres that reflect long-term interest, diffuse reciprocity, and trust, strikes fear and incredulity in their hearts. (Adler and Barnett, 1998: 3)

Although 'fear and incredulity' may still be felt by some mainstream IR scholars, the beginning of the 1990s saw a growing interest in social constructivism, and along with that a growing acceptance of the 'fuzzy' concepts. Furthermore, the rediscovery of Kant as well as the burgeoning 'democratic peace' literature meant that interest in security communities was revived. The importance of the concept for this volume cannot be overstated. The 'in-group' referred to in this volume, and which is conceptualized as the Euro-Atlantic community, *is* a security community, and given that membership of it implicitly provides security, it constitutes a very attractive in-group, providing some very attractive and tangible benefits to its members. It is therefore important to understand what it is that makes an alliance or other institutionalized relations between states of more than just functional importance, but of emotional and ideational importance as in the case of a security community. Secondly, the processes utilized in the development and subsequent expansion of the security community, most notably socialization and social learning, suggest how membership of the security community is achieved, whilst maintaining the 'dependable expectations of peaceful change'. Finally, by identifying the Euro-Atlantic community as a security community, we are also provided with the reason for why the existing security community is willing to expand, which in the case of this volume explains why new members are admitted to organizations, despite the fact that expansion of membership may initially weaken their organizational structure and efficiency.

**Towards a democratic security community in Europe**

In a Deutschian sense, the Euro-Atlantic Community[4] is a security community and has been to an increasing degree since some time in the 1950s, and now in an enlarged version, which includes the new NATO and EU members. The primary 'glue' of a security community is shared values, mutual trust and collective identity (Adler and Barnett, 1998: 38) rather than collective functional tasks, although the development of shared values, trust and collective identity may have developed partly in consequence of having undertaken collective functional tasks. The fact that a security community is based on 'soft' concepts such as values, trust and identity, does not, however, mean that power relations or the distribution of knowledge is distributed evenly or that all members of the security community fulfil similar roles. On the contrary, both power and knowledge (here understood as the knowledge of the community's shared knowledge and understandings) are concepts that are central for understanding the development of security communities (Adler and Barnett, 1998: 39). The more powerful and the more knowledgeable members of the community are likely to form its centre, to set its agenda and to act as a magnet on those states that are on the fringes of the security community. As expressed by Deutsch: 'larger, stronger, more politically, administratively, economically and educationally advanced political units were found to form the cores of strength around which in most cases the integrative process developed' (Deutsch et al., 1957: 38 quoted in Adler and Barnett, 1998: 39). Furthermore, power within the security community may be understood as the authority to determine what constitutes the shared meanings that the security community is built around, hence in practice having the power to define what constitutes the basis of the 'we-feeling' of the community, and thereby also on who gains access to the security community (Adler and Barnett, 1998: 39).

In the case of the Euro-Atlantic security community, it is quite clear that 'some are more equal than others' even within the institutional expressions of the security community such as NATO, where at least officially, consensus is the ruling principle. Becoming a 'member of the club' therefore may mean that in organizational terms all members are equal by having equal rights, but as members of the security community and their ability to define and understand the shared values, they are not. In practice this means that the strong centre performs an educational role through socialization and teaching, whereas the less powerful and new members of the security community go through a process of social learning. Such processes of socialization and social learning are likely to be performed continually, and especially to take place in the start-up period of the security community, when it is essential that the knowledge and understanding of the community's shared values and identity are understood (and shared) by all. Likewise this socialization and social learning process plays an important role when new members are either in the process of being 'vetted' for membership, or have recently become members of the community. The processes of socialization and social learning perform a key function within the security community in ensuring that the values and the identity of the members are indeed shared, and that trust between the members is maintained. In that sense socialization and social learning are processes that are all the more necessary in times of change or expansion of the security community, because it is what ensures that expansion can take place without losing the essential aspect of a security community – its 'dependable expectations of peaceful change'.

As the inclusion of new members of a security community clearly may have the unintended consequence of making 'expectations of peaceful change' less dependable, as a consequence of new members not completely sharing the values and norms determining acceptable behaviour, one may ask why security communities would want to run the risk of enlarging membership? The answer to this question is simply a trade off between the desire for a well-functioning organizational structure and calculations on threats to the security community as a whole, from external sources of conflict and instability. Clearly the more states that can successfully be admitted as members into the security community, the less risk there is of conflictual relations with those states. By incorporating potentially troublesome outsiders into the community, and through the process of socializing transforming them into insiders sharing basic values and adhering to shared codes of conduct, a net gain in security is achieved. It is therefore in the interest of the security community to expand in order to reduce the number of potentially hostile relationships with the outside. However, every security community will have a boarder zone demarcating a line between those on the inside and those on the outside, which is where threats to security are likely to be located. As a result, security communities have three essential tasks in order to maintain overall peace and security:

1. To continually ensure that the values and identity of the security community remain shared and adhered to by all.

2. To be as inclusive as possible to new members who are willing and able to adopt the shared values, code of conduct and identity of the community.
3. To maintain non-conflictual relationships with those on the outside of the security community, for some with a view to later expansion.

It is action undertaken in the process of fulfilling these tasks that to a large extent characterizes the processes of change at both the domestic and the international level under investigation in this volume. As suggested earlier, what takes place at the domestic and international level is part of a mutually constitutive relationship in as much that the processes of socialization and internalization of norms taking place at the domestic level will constitute the nature and strength of the relationship of those states within the security community, with significant further repercussions at the structural international level. In order to understand those processes it is necessary to look at the micro-processes of socialization and the concepts of importance for those processes.

## Norms, socialization and social learning

Within the social constructivist literature, the concepts of norms and socialization as well as social learning play a key role in all identity construction processes. Identity, on the other hand, plays a key role in social constructivism, because one of the main assumptions is that interests and preferences are not fixed, but are determined by the agent's identity, since 'an actor cannot know what it wants until it knows who it is' (Wendt, 1999: 231). However, this of course only begs the question of how agents have arrived at a particular identity. To this question constructivists agree that ideas, norms and rules constitute meanings, which construct actors' identity, interests and subsequent actions (Klotz, 2001: 226). The concern of this volume is precisely about how specific identities are constructed through the process of socializing a specific norm set that defines acceptable codes of conduct and attitudes for those who belong to a certain social group with a given identity. The problem is that identity is one of those concepts whose meaning can be said to be at once self-evident and non-problematic and at the same time to present a conceptual morass with a seemingly never-ending layer of different and increasingly abstract definitions (Lapid, 1997: 7). In its simplest form identity relates to how we think of ourselves as people and how we think about other people around us, and indeed how we think they might think about us (Kidd, 2002: 7). That means that identity is essentially rooted in an individual's self-understanding, with the important qualification that for the identity to actually be an identity (as opposed to a delusion) it must be represented by other actors in the same way (Wendt, 1999: 224). In that sense identities are intersubjective. For example, as shown in Chapter 10, the administration of Belarus clearly has a self-perception of Belarus as a democratic state, based on the fact that the government is supported by the majority of the population. However, outside observers do not concur with this view, which (from the point of view of the 'West') makes Belarus' self-perception a delusion on the part of the Belarusian administration. In other words (and as will be further elaborated in Chapter 2) 'identity' is by its very nature relational in that it is always constructed by looking outside the self, and is constituted by both internal and external structures. What is of particular interest is the *content* of identity, which can be described as a changing set of beliefs, ideas or norms that reflexive selves follow (Locher and Prügel, 2001: 79). Here the interesting question about identity is how it came about and how it came to have its particular content.

For the purposes of this volume, what is of interest is not only the considerations and processes in which the individual engages in trying to define 'the Self', but also processes of collective identity formation. Collective identity on the one hand fulfils the same purpose as individual identity in as much as it defines the 'social we', where the 'social we' defines itself by delineating its boundaries against the others (Risse et al., 1999: 9). In the model presented in Chapter 2 this is conceptualized as a process of self- and other-categorization. However, collective identity formations also have to do with what Alexander Wendt calls 'frequency dependency effects' (Wendt, 1999: 365), which means that collective identity formation will depend on the frequency of individual identity changes taking place at the same time. It could be said that the role of socialization of specific norms, such as a democratic norm set, is an attempt to increase the frequency dependency effect and hence make collective identity formation based on a particular norm set more likely.

## Norms

The concept of norms, like 'identity', is a concept, which can be said to be at once 'self-evident and non-problematic' and yet at the same time to pose a number of conceptual problems. However, in this volume norms are seen as intersubjective beliefs about the social world, which have behavioural consequences (Farrell, 2001: 71). Norms define a collective standard as to what constitutes proper behaviour of actors with a given identity. Norms are different from principled ideas which, although they also distinguish between right and wrong, do not make behavioural claims on individuals. An acceptance of a social group's norm set, and behaviour in accordance with that norm set, is usually a minimum requirement for admittance into a social group and for continued acceptance within the social group. Consistent disregard of the norms of the social group will not invalidate the norm set because norms are 'counterfactually valid' (Ruggie, 1998: 97), meaning that no single or several counterfactual occurrences can refute the norm set, although continued disregard of the norm set may put the offending actor's continued membership of the social group at risk. Norms are different from rules or laws because they are obeyed, not because they are enforced, but because they are seen as legitimate and hence define 'what ought to be' and what constitutes proper behaviour.

The claim in this volume, and indeed generally within constructivist literature, that norms have an explanatory value, is based on the belief that norms can assume the character of structures and become embedded in international institutions where they may shape states' behaviour and even constitute actor identities and interests. As suggested by Martha Finnemore and Kathryn Sikkink, 'shared ideas, expectations and beliefs about appropriate behaviour is what gives the world structure, order and stability' (1998: 894). Indeed, 'norm shifts are to the ideational theorist what changes in the balance of power are to the realist' (Finnemore and Sikkink, 1998: 894). Through their embeddedness in structures, norms also determine actors' practices. As political change occurs through actors' practices, 'fundamental international change can occur, when actors through their practices change the rules and norms constitutive of international interaction' (Koslowski and Kratochwil, 1995: 128). Such change happens 'when beliefs and identities of domestic actors are altered, thereby also altering rules and norms that are constitutive of their political practices' (Koslowski and Kratochwil, 1995: 128). In other words the mutually constitutive relationship between the 'international' and the 'domestic' holds a prominent position in the social constructivist discussion on norms.

The specific norm set under investigation in this volume is the one that is seen as constitutive for the Euro-Atlantic community. This is a norm set that has been defined and redefined in increasing detail since the end of the Cold War, when it was no longer sufficient to define the Euro-Atlantic norm set in terms of *what it was not*, i.e. Communist, but had to be defined in positive terms of *what it is*.[5] This was a process of separating out and strengthening what was seen as the good norms underpinning the value community until then known as 'the West', and jettisoning those norms that were no longer relevant for the new security environment. The key statements defining both the core constitutive norms and values of the Euro-Atlantic community, and the entrance requirements for membership of the value community, are contained in the Charter of Paris for a New Europe from November 1990, which was hailed at the time as the 'Magna Carta' of Europe. The signatories to the document undertook to 'build, consolidate and strengthen democracy as the only system of government'. Furthermore, the document contained a commitment to respect human rights and fundamental freedoms, a commitment to the rule of law and a commitment to the basic principles of the market economy (Charter of Paris, 1990). These four areas have subsequently become known as the CSCE (OSCE) Commitments, and can be regarded as the key statement on what constitutes the shared norm set of the Euro-Atlantic community. The commitments are echoed in all of Europe's organizational institutions, in their defining documents and in their membership criteria, with individual variations for an organization's specific area. Of these, possibly the most significant are the so-called 'Copenhagen Criteria' agreed at the Copenhagen European Council in 1993. In many ways the Copenhagen Criteria contain the strictest entrance requirements, even to such an extent that it is doubtful that all existing members are fully able to honour the conditions stated in the document. As pointed out by Bill Park in Chapter 11, Turkey may be justified in its claim that the Copenhagen Criteria can be seen as 'moving the goal posts during the game'.

## Socialization and social learning

The method for diffusing the norms of the Euro-Atlantic security community among its aspiring members is a process of socialization and social learning. This volume adopts the same definition of socialization as that used by Risse et al. (1999) in their seminal volume on the socialization of human rights norms, which sees socialization as the 'induction of new members ... into the ways of behaviour that are preferred in a society' (Barnes et al., 1980: 35). By using this definition of socialization, two presuppositions are implicitly acknowledged. First of all, the relationship between socializer and socializee is an unequal one where the socializer either has, or believes itself to have, a greater knowledge or understanding of the norm set than those that are being socialized, and that it has the power to judge whether the required norm changes have been undertaken satisfactorily. Secondly, the definition used here clearly presupposes the existence of a society. What is being sought is entry into an existing 'club' in which the rules and norms for proper conduct are already well entrenched and understood by existing members. The aim of the socialization process is for those who are being socialized to adopt and internalize the norm set to such an extent that external pressure is no longer needed to ensure compliance (Risse et al., 1999: 11). In terms of the workings of the security community, this means that the aim of the socialization process is for the intersubjective understandings of the security community to become taken for granted by the socializee (Johnston, 2001: 495).

Successful socialization will always result in some level of behavioural change on the part of the socializee, preferably to such an extent that external pressure is no longer needed and preferably in a 'deep' way that has actually altered attitudes and beliefs in the socializee. There is, however, no way of knowing when 'deep' socialization has occurred, as the observable changed behaviour may simply have been undertaken for strategic reasons to gain entry to the community, or to gain other promised benefits. Hence all we can observe is whether agents who have been socialized *comply* with the norm set in question (Checkel, 2001). The concept of and strategies for socialization are further elaborated in Chapter 2.

The process that takes place at the level of the socializees in response to socialization is known as 'social learning'. Adler and Barnett define social learning as 'an active process of redefinition or reinterpretation of reality ... Social learning represents the capacity and motivation of social actors to manage and even transform reality by changing their beliefs of the material and social world and their identities' (Adler and Barnett, 1998: 43–4). As such, empirically social learning is somewhat problematic. Nevertheless, social learning is presented by Adler and Barnett as playing a crucial role in the emergence of security communities as it explains how transactions and institutional actions encourage the development of mutual trust and collective identity. According to Adler and Barnett, socialization and social learning (1) involve communication about 'self-understandings, perceptions of reality and normative expectations'; (2) takes place within institutional settings, where institutions promote the diffusion of meanings; and (3) the learning taking place within the institutional setting is connected to functional processes that lead to a general improvement in the state's overall condition (Adler and Barnett, 1998: 44). It is precisely such processes that are examined in this volume – processes that are located at the domestic level, but which have major repercussions for, and originate from, the international level.

## The structure of the book

This volume combines theory and practice in its analysis of how the socialization of democratic norms in the New Europe has been undertaken by a number of international organizations, and how those efforts have been received in a number of individual countries all at a differing ideational distance from the socializing in-group. The countries discussed here are all examples of the four different 'out-groups' defined in Chapter 2, although Turkey is slightly anomalous in that it doesn't really fit into any of the identified out-groups.

Part I – 'Theoretical and Conceptual Considerations' – opens with a conceptual chapter by Jean Grugel which describes how 'the international' has come to be an important element within Democratization Studies. Grugel examines the growing literature within International Relations concerned with norms and social learning, and suggests that this may constitute a fertile basis for related democratization issues such as global governance and democratization. She also assesses the extent to which debates about the transnationalization of politics and norm diffusion more generally may shed light on processes of democratization. Chapter 2, by Trine Flockhart, is also of a conceptual/theoretical nature, presenting the theoretical framework for the later chapters. The framework is called 'Complex Socialization', as a result of the realization of just how complex these processes are, and just how many variables one needs to take into account when analysing the transfer of international norms to the domestic realm. The framework builds on other similar models for socialization (cf. Risse et al., 1999; Finnemore and Sikkink, 1998; Marcussen, 2000) but differs in its emphasis on self- and other-categorization processes between socializer and socializee as the main influence on the likely outcome of the socialization process. What seems to be indicated from the model is that socialization, and by extension externally generated democratization, is only likely to be successful where socializer and socializee start out with positive self- and other-categorization processes in place at both the domestic elite and mass level.

Part II – 'Promoting Ideas through International Organizations' – contains chapters by Sally Morphet on the UN, Sonia Lucarelli on NATO, Frank Schimmelfennig on the EU and Michael Merlingen and Rasa Ostrauskaitė on the OSCE. The chapters outline how those specific international organizations have undertaken to socialize the democratic norm set outlined in the CSCE commitments with particular emphasis on which strategies for socialization each organization has utilized. It is evident from these chapters that all organizations have their own particular 'take' on the socialization of the shared norm set, ranging from the UN's rather indirect and general norm-defining approach, NATO's mixed approach of persuasion, teaching and social influence, to the EU's robust emphasis on reinforcement by material reward, and the OSCE's much more gentle emphasis on strategies of persuasion. What is clear from all the chapters is that norm socialization is a conscious and goal-oriented process on the part of these organizations, which has resulted in the setting up of specific institutional structures for dealing with the demands of norms transfer.

Part III – 'Receiving and Internalizing Ideas in Transforming Societies' – contains chapters by Petr Drulák and Lucie Königová on the Czech Republic, Marek Rybář on Slovakia, Mette Skak on Russia, Clelia Rontoyanni and Elena Korosteleva on Belarus and Bill Park on Turkey. Drulák and Königová analyse socialization of the democratic norm set into the Czech Republic, which in relation to the complex socialization model is an example of an out-group 1 country, where the expectation is a robust process of adoption and internalization of the promoted norm set. Indeed this assumption is fully supported by the evidence presented in the chapter along with the specific conditions for socialization of the democratic norm set within the Czech state/elite and nation/people level. The analysis is continued in the chapter by Marek Rybář on the out-group 3 country, Slovakia. As in the case of the Czech Republic, the example of Slovakia exhibits precisely the socialization path suggested by the model. During the period of Vladimír Mečiar's rule, the socialization strategies open to the socialization agencies were limited to negative influence vis-à-vis the state/elite level with social influence being mainly directed towards the nation/people level and the parliamentary opposition. As suggested by Rybář, these socialization efforts seem to have been successful, as the otherwise rather fragmented opposition united in their effort to prevent a return by Mečiar to government, which would have unleashed the ultimate of negative social influence tools – non-accession to NATO and the EU.

Chapters 9 and 10 present analyses of Russia and Belarus. Russia is here presented as an example of an out-group 2 country, although as in most circumstances Russia does not fit easily into standard categorizations. In many ways Russia is itself an influential player in the construction of the New Europe, and therefore sits uncomfortably in the position of being both an agent of socialization and an object for socialization. The chapter focuses mainly on Russian domestic structures and their embrace of the new 'winds of change' in Russia's development towards democracy. In Chapter 10, Clelia Rontoyanni and Elena Korosteleva present a very detailed analysis of the situation in the out-group 4 country case: Belarus. As suggested by the complex socialization model, countries such as Belarus are not easily, if at all, socialized by outside agents. Not only are attempts at socialization viewed as 'interference in internal affairs', but the empirical material presented also suggests that the Belarus people have an extremely poor understanding of democracy, its workings and core values, and certainly no desire for change towards democracy. Successful socialization of Belarus seems therefore not likely in the immediate future, unless a major event occurs to jolt Belarus in a different direction.

Finally, in Chapter 11, Bill Park looks at the interesting case of Turkey's prospects for socialization of the constitutive norm set underpinning the Euro-Atlantic community, and particularly the thorny issue of EU membership. As Bill Park shows, the issue at hand is much more complicated than simply being a question of different cultures based on different religious outlooks, although that too is problematic. Rather, the fundamental issue relates to the friction between the very characteristics that have constituted modern Turkey as a secular, Kemalist state and the accession conditions contained in the Copenhagen Criteria. Indeed, the eternal question of 'being, or becoming, European' seems set to continue for a while longer.

Like most projects of this kind, the road from idea to a finished book has been long (and sometimes stony) and has involved help from many sources. Thanks are due to the contributing authors for their patience in the long process from conception to completion, and in complying with my sometimes very tight deadlines and (probably) annoying comments on chapter drafts. It is also a real pleasure to be able to thank Tim Dunne, Martin Marcussen, Tim Shaw, Ray Taras, Poul Thøis Madsen, Andrew Williams and Li Xing for their comments and early involvement in the project. A special thank-you goes to Iben Kierkegaard whose computer wizardry in setting up the manuscript and bibliography was immensely helpful. Thanks are also due to the Danish Social Science Research Council and to the Danish Institute for International Studies (former COPRI) for generous financial support and to the Institute for Historical and International Studies at Aalborg University for granting research leave and administrative back-up. Finally, of course, I must thank my family – John, Emilia, Alexander, Helena and Phoebe – for putting up with me spending far too much time in front of the computer instead of spending it with the people who *really* matter.

## Notes

1. A major, perhaps impossible, challenge given the findings of this volume, as the minimum precondition for such norms transfer (positive self- and other-categorization processes) are manifestly absent. See also Flockhart (2004b).
2. The fact that democratic constitutions were simply written up without any further support for the establishment and consolidation of democracy goes some way in explaining why only Czechoslovakia remained democratic until the German occupation. Also, the fact that the United States did not itself become a member of the key institutional innovation of the League of Nations is a factor that weighs heavily on the failure of the system. For a more thorough discussion of this point see Flockhart (2001); Cox et al. (2000).
3. It should be noted that the concept of 'cosmopolitan law' is rather obscure as Kant does not explain it fully himself. Therefore the present-day link to interdependence must be said to be rather circumstantial.
4. The exact extent of the security community is a little difficult to pin down, since some countries clearly do not take part in organizational expressions of the Euro-Atlantic community such as NATO and the EU, yet clearly shared values and mutual trust are present, as is dependable expectation of peaceful change. In that sense the security community is likely to have a number of 'fuzzy' edges and ambiguous relationships with some states – for example Sweden during the Cold War, Switzerland and Turkey.
5. A positive definition of the Euro-Atlantic community's shared values and constitutive norm set was not possible during the Cold War because of the inconsistency of not only tolerating states with a decidedly undemocratic norm set, but in some instances also supporting them and working with them in alliances. Although such practice still continues (for example the US–Saudi relationship) it has increasingly become a source of political embarrassment, suggesting that change is imminent.

# Part I

# Conceptual and Theoretical Considerations

# 1

# The 'International' in Democratization: Norms and the Middle Ground

*Jean Grugel*

The locus of Democratization Studies was for a long time squarely within comparative politics. Scholars of comparative politics tended to adopt agency-centred theories in which democratization was treated essentially as a function of the political behaviour, coalition-building and pact-making of actors from inside nation-states.[1] Until the end of the 1990s, scholarship that paid attention to the role of international factors in democratization was relatively scarce. More recently, the international dimension in democratization has merited sustained and considered attention and a broad range of scholars now recognize that the international matters in a very fundamental way (Grugel, 2003). Nevertheless, there is no agreement on the circumstances under which it is salient or how the international and domestic link together. There is not even a clear consensus as to what, precisely, is meant when we talk of 'the international' in processes of democratization.

To an important extent, these debates reflect wider ontological and epistemological debates between sub-disciplines of politics and international relations, in particular between Comparative Politics, Development Studies, International Political Economy and mainstream International Relations. The gulf between (and even sometimes within) comparative politics and international relations perspectives, broadly understood, has frustrated attempts to generate hypotheses and data that are recognized as useful by all parts of the academic community, in so far as democratization is concerned. This chapter cannot pretend to overcome these divisions. Instead, it seeks to make a balanced assessment of the main contribution of some of the initial approaches before engaging with the interdisciplinary work emerging around norms and social learning, currently fertile areas for research into 'soft' issues of global regulation, including rights, global governance and democratization. To some extent, then, the chapter maps, albeit briefly, the chronological development of the democratization debate. It examines how the international was conceptualized in a field dominated by comparativists; how it was understood in the 1990s by a diverse range of scholars for whom the international/global system lies at the centre of the social and political order; and finally discusses the extent to which contemporary debates around the transnationalization of politics and norm diffusion can shed light on processes of democratization.

## The emergence of the debate between the 'international' dimension and the comparative approach

Regime changes in the 1970s in Southern Europe, followed by the end of the dictatorships in Latin America in the 1980s and the dramatic collapse of the Soviet-style dictatorships in Eastern Europe after 1989 led to the emergence of what Whitehead (2002: 1) terms the 'mini-industry' of democratization studies:

> As the variety of democratizations has multiplied, so has the scholarly and analytical literature proliferated. Empirically-minded social scientists have vied with normative political theorists and constitutionalists, with practitioners of comparative historical analysis, with area studies specialists and with single country experts to cover all this new terrain. (Whitehead, 2002: 2)

The first attempt at theorizing these exciting events took place within comparative politics. Area studies scholarship, however rich or sensitive, was simply not broad enough to frame the emerging scholarship that embraced deep comparisons between events taking place in different cultures, with different class structures and with varying levels of development. The difficulties and the pitfalls of comparison of this type are many and well known (Collier and Mahoney, 1996; Whitehead, 2002: 198–202). As a result of the methodological difficulties associated with cross-regional comparisons or large N studies and as the number of cases that were included increased and the findings became more generalizable, the comparativist approach to democratization adopted excessively narrow understandings of what democracy and democratization meant. In particular, institutionalist and electoralist definitions of democracy were employed, as much due to the need to facilitate comparison as the real difficulties of defining operationally what democracy means. Attention also focused on the role of (mainly elite) actors in the process of regime change.[2]

Comparative studies of democratization thus offered a significant, but partial, window on the process of democratization. Democratization was understood to comprise the transformation of the political system from non-democracy towards accountable, representative and elected government, accompanied by a gradual increase in liberal freedoms. An important distinction was made between the transitional stage, the beginning of the movement towards democracy during which politics is fluid and outcomes unclear, and consolidation, when democracy becomes 'the only game in town' (Linz and Stepan, 1996: 5). Initially, academic emphasis focused on the sequential changes within democratization (O'Donnell et al., 1986); later, interest shifted towards identifying those factors that make new democracies endure and those that, conversely, make for fragility or weakness. Here, research focused alternatively on political culture (Diamond, 1999), economic management (Haggard and Kaufman, 1995) and institutionalism (Remmer, 1997).

A great deal was learned through the paradigm of comparative democratization about the mechanisms through which transitions were engineered and the pitfalls associated with consolidation, but not very much about the significance of the international. It would not be true, however, to suggest that the comparative approach paid no attention to the significance of international factors in democratization. In fact, as I have argued elsewhere, the comparative approach is largely responsible for the suggestion that the complex process of regime decay and political change in apparently dissimilar countries such as Spain, South Africa, El Salvador, Brazil, Turkey, Poland, Albania, the Philippines and China are different manifestations of the same phenomenon (Grugel, 2002). As a result, perhaps paradoxically, it is inherently responsible for the global scope of Democratization Studies (Grugel, 2002: 62–3). Moreover, the role of the international was consciously examined; even the early comparative collection by O'Donnell et al. (1986), which became the founding text of the comparative approach, contained a thoughtful early examination of the significance of the international arena for understanding when and how democratization occurred. In his contribution to the study, Whitehead assumed his trademark long-term approach to democratization in order to discuss the extent to which the international climate and the activities of states external to the process of democratization were able to intervene in support of it in Latin America, the Caribbean and in Europe.

In the 1990s, this kind of work expanded to include research that aimed to uncover the significance of geopolitics and region-building initiatives as drivers of democratization. Attention mainly focused on the role of the European Community/European Union (EC/EU) in support of democratization in first the Southern European cases of Spain, Portugal and Greece, followed by those of East and Central Europe (Pridham, 1991, 1993, 1999a). Still closely associated with the comparativist approach, this body of work tended, on the whole, not to theorize why and how macro-regions (Europe or the Americas, for example) move towards models of democracy with common features but rather to concentrate on the roles of particular actors, such as political parties or regional bureaucracies, in support of processes that are still seen as primarily internal to states. Pridham (1993) argued that European political parties were key architects of the European policy of promoting democracy abroad. Youngs (2001) analysed the role of the EU in particular in the promotion of democratization within the Mediterranean. Grugel (2000) has shown how European civil society actors have consistently been concerned to offer material and moral support to key actors within Latin American transitions. Thus it was, ironically, that work from within comparative politics, and even indeed on one of the mainstays of the sub-field – the political party – constituted the first real attempt to overcome the limitations of the comparativist frame. I return to the question of regionalism and democratization again below, but here what should be noted is that this work constitutes the first serious attempt to conceptualize and grapple with the Janus-faced complexity of democratization as a process with both domestic and international dimensions. As such it provided an important bridge with emerging concerns first articulated from within International Relations.

## Democratization and globalization

As questions of globalization were placed ever more centrally on the agenda of social scientists, whatever their sub-field, it became more difficult to justify leaving the study of democratization to comparative politics. Whitehead (2002: 263) explains:

> The comparative study of democratization can hardly continue to focus on the self-contained national political system as its exclusive unit of analysis at a time when ... so much leverage over economic issues is clearly shifting away from Ministries of Economics and budgetary committees of individual countries, and when intergovernmental

> cooperation between democracies is leading to an evident pooling of sovereignty in multiple arenas, legal, regulatory and indeed on many more strictly political questions.

Once democratization was recognized as a prominent feature of the global agenda, it could no longer be seen as a set of unconnected and discrete events in different and closed nation-states. But making the connection between processes of democratization and trends within global politics did not mean that a convincing account of how and why democratization occurred or whether it succeeded could easily be produced (Mayall, 2000: 62). After all, democratic ideals had been part of the intellectual baggage of international politics for a long time; they had been bolted on, even, to the principal ideas ordering international society during the Enlightenment. Yet, as realists were quick to point out, the democratic ideals that states in the West endorsed rhetorically only rarely guided their own behaviour. Of course this had been especially true during the Cold War, when support for democratization was reduced to the status of a decorative motif on an otherwise self-interested agenda. But even after 1989, when democracy, respect for human rights and the importance of the rule of law were enthusiastically reconfirmed as discursive ordering principles for the international system, it seems that Western states have consistently been ambiguous in terms of endorsing democracy within international society. How much had really changed, then, and how could the nuances and complexities of both global discourses and practices of democratization be captured and conceptualized?

Globalization was the starting point and a number of potentially rich avenues were suggested. It was easier to generate questions and offer suggestive hypotheses, however, than supply empirically grounded answers. Is democracy linked to the spread of global capitalism? Is it the result of a global *zeitgeist* of democracy and the absence of other powerful and unifying ideologies (Huntington, 1991; Fukuyama, 1992)? How are ideas about democracy transmitted through an increasingly globalized polity? Does globalization empower democrats within nation-states to 'win' internal struggles for power or does it foist democracy on unwilling or unready societies? Is it, in other words, a form of westernization? What model of democracy and what kind of democracies are emerging under conditions of globalization? What became immediately obvious is that any hope of answering these questions sensibly required first a clarification of what globalization itself meant. Greater analytical clarity, in other words, about the transformations taking place within the global order was the first stage to elucidating how the new 'global inter-connectedness'

(Held et al., 1999) might contribute and frame the dissemination of the idea and the practice of democracy.

The first theoretically informed explanation linking globalization and democratization came from within International Political Economy (IPE). Because of its focus on the interface between the market, politics and society, IPE has tended to probe the extent to which the division between the domestic and the international as the crucial principle for understanding the social world still makes sense. It offers a focus on globally generated trends and politics within nation-states that emphasizes the ways the global and national mesh together and reinforce each other (Underhill, 2000). Moreover, contemporary IPE scholarship starts from the view that '[i]f there is a global polity, certainly its dominant ideology, now, is liberal, both economic and political' (Murphy, 2000: 792). IPE locates all discussion of democratization in the context of the linkages between the market and states/societies and the recognition that ideational change is rooted, in some fundamental way, in the material world. Susan Strange (1992), the pioneer of new IPE, was amongst the first to suggest that post-1989 democratization should be understood quite simply as a reflection of the formation of an increasingly liberal global political economy. Here, globalization is taken to mean the global expansion of liberal capitalism; democratization thus becomes the outcome of the market and the hegemony of the capitalist West. As a result, democratization becomes simply part of the architecture of a liberal global political economy and deepening global capitalism. Democracy – understood as the introduction of a set of formal procedures for elected government and the gradual diffusion of liberal values – is functional for capitalist growth and, as such, should be seen as its corollary. Democratization thus becomes a symbol of the triumph of free market capitalism; it is part of the 'seemingly monolithic conformity' that emerged in the world order in the 1980s and 1990s that Cox (1987) calls 'hyperliberalism'. Not surprisingly, many IPE scholars regarded this form of democratization as a form of elite control and a manifestation of the hegemony of the liberal Atlantic West.

The new globalized capitalism appeared to strengthen the authority of footloose financial and multinational capital at the expense of both national producers and labour, thereby weakening states, and making welfare policies difficult, if not impossible, to implement. In the much-quoted formulation of Robert Cox, under conditions of global capitalism, states become 'conveyor belts' for decisions taken elsewhere (Cox, 1997). Put crudely, the threat from the Left decreases and a weak version of thin liberal democracy becomes possible everywhere. The question, then, became how to explain the trend towards democratization in a context dominated by a relative shift in authority towards capital and away from labour. The answer was to link democratization with the spread of global capitalism. Democratization was conceptualized as part of an attempt to establish a stable political framework through which to bind the poor into competitive nodes of a globalized capitalist economy. It became, in other words, almost straightforwardly a cover for economic liberalization. Perhaps not surprisingly, this scholarship mainly focuses on how democratization has been introduced in the developing world, where there is an abundance of evidence linking the introduction of weak and limited democratic regimes with liberal economic reform. The result is that democratization was interpreted simply – and only – as part of what Gill (1992) refers to as 'the new constitutionalism' of liberalism that governs the market-led globalized polity.

Clearly, this approach offers a historical materialist account of democratization. Of course, not all IPE-influenced work on democratization takes as materialist a line as I have identified here (Grugel, 2004a). Some studies emphasized instead the agency of subaltern groups in resisting the imposition of liberal capitalism from below (Abbott, 2001; Morton, 2002). Nevertheless, emphasis is generally placed, in terms of explaining why democratization happens, more on economic transformation than on political will. Agency was ascribed to a new transnational elite (or class) that, it is argued, has emerged with global capitalism. The reach and the concerns of these groups are global, not national. And it is precisely these individuals and their organizations that are usually conceptualized as the 'bearers' of the project of liberal, or neo-liberal democracy (van der Pijl, 1995).

More than perhaps anyone else, Robinson (1996, 2000, 2002) has attempted to ground empirically the idea of democratization as a project of global capitalism transmitted by globalized elites. Using examples drawn from Latin America, Robinson offers an in-depth analysis of how transnational elites – composed of actors from within the US state and international financial institutions – promote a twin agenda of 'polyarchy and neoliberalism'. Robinson's view is strengthened by the emergence of a substantial body of research on sub-Saharan Africa, frequently carried out by academics who do not themselves draw on the theoretical baggage of either Marxism or IPE, that also points to the imposition of democratization as a tool of economic management (Clapham, 1996; van Cranenburgh, 1999; Harbeson, 2000). Nevertheless, this research begs the question of whether the findings are fully generalizable. After all, the work points to the continuance of relations of dependence and domination between the developed world and the underdeveloped periphery. Latin America and sub-Saharan Africa, in different ways, both represent areas of the world where forms of dependence have traditionally been acute. Could this interpretation apply elsewhere, in East and Central Europe and Asia, for example?

Moreover, there is another problem with this literature. Suggestive and significant as these accounts are, they tend to be overly structuralist and predetermined. They pay little detailed attention to the role of actors (other than transnational elites) in processes of democratic creation and diffusion. Attention is firmly – and exclusively – at the macro-level of the global polity. There is little room for questions of how exactly democracy is embedded in societies that were previously resistant to them and how global ideas transmute in local contexts; whether what is meant by democracy is subject to change or contestation; or whether the globalization of democracy leads to the long-term creation of stable, if limited, democracies. Neither is there any interest in conceptualizing and explaining how different meanings attach to the term democratization in different contexts. Overall, there is something of an assumption that, where mass political activism takes place, it will be not to welcome but to reject the limited and partial democratization that global capitalists endorse (Gills, 2000).

Other approaches from within International Relations have attempted to address some of the deficiencies identified above. One important line has tackled the question through a discussion of the transnationalization of public spheres of authority. This, it is argued, has led to the increased policing of the global system by multilateral agencies (Cammack, 2002). In particular, evidence has gradually emerged to substantiate the notion that agencies such as the IMF and the World Bank have incorporated the promotion of democracy into their policy repertoire. In the 1980s, these once 'technical' organizations shifted focus to include more obviously political criteria and goals, subjecting dependent or developing states to an agenda of good governance, which included the implementation of democratic reforms. While the global governance approach to democratization probes some important questions about the spread of the discourse of democracy globally, it offers little that is convincing as to the detail of how democracy is brought about and why it succeeds or fails. Another significant line of research has been to question the extent to which globalizing democracy leads necessarily to limited and elitist democracies. Held (1995) has pioneered work on cosmopolitan democracy which he understands as a process of genuine liberalization and inclusion, although it should be noted that criticisms of this approach abound (Sandel, 1996; Thaa, 2001).

Meanwhile, it has also been noted that pro-democracy policies do not simply float in the ether; they are underpinned by strong support from key states. The US and the EU also shifted towards formalizing and institutionalizing pro-democracy policies, thereby reinforcing the democratic 'turn' at the multilateral level. Carothers (1991, 1994, 1996) has done most to document empirically the range of pressures that emanate from Washington in favour of spreading democracy abroad, while the EU has embraced policies of support for the introduction of basic freedoms and political reform in Africa, Latin America and, of course, the East and Central European states. Some scholars of international aid, meanwhile, noted that aid-giving had become a weapon in the struggle to promote democracy internationally (Burnell, 1997). As a result of these well-documented interventions, democratization gradually came to be seen as a core element of an international agenda, pushed and implemented by powerful states and multilateral institutions. Many pro-democracy interventions, it is recognized, are supported by a range of international and domestic NGOs (O'Brien et al., 2000). Its spread to the developing world can, to some degree, at least be explained as a consequence of the leverage of the multinational agencies and their increased capacity to incorporate at least some elements of local and international civil society into their agendas and their decision-making processes.

Above all, one feature of democratization has gradually become clear: namely that there is a growing disjuncture between the international endorsement of democracy and the processes on the ground. For, while some new democracies are reasonably stable and meet at least basic democratic criteria in terms of a range of liberal freedoms – Chile, Brazil, the Czech Republic and Poland, for example – others are excessively limited, crisis-ridden and thin. The depressing evidence is that, despite a greater interest in democratization, democracy, especially in many developing regions and countries, is fragile and weak (see for example Abrahamsen, 2000). In this the evidence comes as much from middle-income countries as from the very poorest and most dependent. In Latin America, where the trend has on the whole been established since the 1980s, periodic reversals, populism and corruption undermine the new political systems, despite continuous support from outside. Moreover, tensions over democracy have occurred in Venezuela and Argentina, the richest of the Latin American countries, as well as Peru, Bolivia, Guatemala and Haiti. External support, in other words, seems to be only one more variable such as per capita income or literacy. It can make a limited contribution to projects of democratization, but it cannot create successful democratizations where other factors are missing.

Crawford's (1997) findings support this. He registers the extent to which democracy promotion is dominant within Western foreign policy in the developing world, but notes at the same time that it is largely ineffective. Some scholars argue that this failure to develop genuine and sustaining democratization is the result of economic globalization. Martin and Shumann (1997) argue that economic globalization produces greater income inequality and class polarization, thereby weakening the chances for democracy in the process: a return to the IPE arguments identified above, in other words. Other scholars suggest that the subjection of states that is inherent within globalization is where the problem lies. Without effective and independent states, nascent democracies find it impossible to satisfy internal demands; states work, in fact, not to shore up democracy but to impose limitations on it (Gill, 1995). A third argument focuses on the destabilizing impact of globalization on societies and communities of rapid cultural change and the subsequent loss of national identity (Robertson, 1992).

In sum, a range of literature places globalization at the head of the failure of the democratic project. Nevertheless, it might be more accurate to recognize that globalization has created demands for democracy, as well as imposing greater controls over states and societies. Democracy appeals to ordinary people as well as to elites, albeit for different reasons. Globalization and democratization are both multilayered and contradictory processes that place visions of what might be alongside systems of social and state reorganization. Democracy is beyond any doubt an aspiration for whole swathes of the globe that had previously seen themselves as excluded from it. Yet it is also clear that democracy is exceptionally fragile and some models of democracy – especially those that depend on strong redistributive states – are very difficult to sustain, especially in the developing world.

## Finding the middle ground

Research around the linkages with globalization rescued democratization from the narrow and tightly bound agendas of comparative politics. It placed the international dimension centrally within the problematic of democratization and opened a range of important avenues for research. Studies of globalization and democratization take very different views not only as to the drivers of democratization but also as to what kind of democracy is possible under conditions of globalization.

Suggestive as this research is, it suffers from a major defect: it is too broad-brush. While the comparativist line of research focused narrowly on politics within nation-states and disregarded the global level, the literature on democratization that takes globalization as its starting point views outcomes in national societies as mainly uninteresting and does not differentiate between them. Differences between experiments in democratization are lost.

A way forward, I want to suggest, is to conceptualize the relationship between globalization and democratization rather differently from the scholarship discussed so far. Globalization can be understood not only as a set of macro-structural changes that derive from the global economy or the growing interconnectedness of cultures but also as the incremental process by which the local, the national and the global become interlinked. Globalization produces a transnationalization of how actors conceive of themselves, the universe in which they act and the nature of relationships that they develop. It widens contacts, leads to the emergence of new networks and produces multiple sets of relationships that stretch over and around national state boundaries. While this process of transnationalization is greater for elites, it can also incorporate non-elite groups because the costs of connecting are relatively low, can be shared and may be financed from outside. Moreover, this process of transnationalization, even of non-elites, may not be a choice but a consequence of the very processes of economic globalization, as Munck (2000: 5) explains:

> Workers still live in Buenos Aires, Bombay and Birmingham, they work in those places and their aspirations are in relation to these places. Globalisation is not just 'out there' in cyberspace but exists, operates and is contested in these local places. Globalisation has prompted new identities and new interests within local, political processes. Local politics in the global era has not been shut down, rather it has been transformed and ... reinvigorated by the multiple identities and fluid processes of the current era.

One advantage of conceptualizing globalization as transnationalization is that it directs attention to the importance of agency within the global order and hence to sites of political activity or fault-lines where political activism can cluster (Mittleman, 2000; Rupert, 2000). Transnationalization, it is important to note, does not imply the formation of one global civil society. Rather it supposes that people still live, act and are concerned with events in their own locality and community and how their own societies and communities behave and engage with the wider world. But their understanding of what constitutes their community may change and they may choose – for strategic or for ideational reasons – to mobilize beyond state boundaries in order to influence outcomes. It recognizes that all social groups, elite and non-elite, have access to resources from outside the nation-state.

Transnational political activity may be motivated by rational self-interest, principles and beliefs or a complex combination of the two. It may take the form of co-operation between technocratic groups, politicians, labour unions, NGOs, interest networks, churches and so on. The view that political activity in the contemporary period inherently tends towards transnationalization has, in fact, a long pedigree and predates discussions of globalization. Forerunners of the debate on transnational political activity include liberal interdependence theorists such as Keohane and Nye (1971). However, the importance of transnational political activity has received more attention lately through its revival as an appropriate frame for the study of agency in global politics (Keck and Sikkink, 1998; Risse et al., 1999). Here attention has focused less on the activities of elite groups or epistemic communities – the groups that theories of liberal interdependence would see as central to the process – and more on how NGOs and groups motivated by ideas organize and understand their role in global and national politics. In particular, transnationalism has become an important lens through which to understand the operation of networks, social movements and principled groups in the global order. As a result, transnationalism has lately become associated with issue areas that can be framed by general and principled claims, such as democracy, human rights, labour rights and so on. So far, most research into transnational political activity has assumed that it occurs through globalized networks – that is, that the territory the activity is designed to affect and the place of origin of the groups are not important for motivating participation or mobilization (Keck and Sikkink, 1998; Risse et al., 1999). This is true, up to a point. However, as I argue below, regions may play more of a role in understanding transnational activity than is always recognized. Regional identities are growing in importance and the region is an important – and rather neglected – meso-level site of globalization processes.

This leads to another important point: how to define democratization. The difficulties around how we understand democracy have increased as more and more countries have engaged in some process of regime change or reform. Initially, the comparative approach tended to draw on the experience of established democracies and tended to conceptualize democracy in procedural terms. More recently, the number of regimes for which democratization claims are being made has led to a loss of analytical clarity and given rise to a rather arcane debate 'over the choice between a dichotomous or graded approach to the distinction between democracy and non-democracy' (Collier and Adcock, 1999: 537). Studies of democratization through the lens of globalization, on the other hand, have tended not to be interested in fine questions of regime definition and have tended to regard democracy either as the introduction of institutions that regulate and reproduce liberal capitalism, or an idealistic project of cosmopolitan inclusion or anti-capitalist revolution from below. In all cases, definitions were sweeping and suggestive, but imprecise and largely unhelpful when it came to distinguishing democratic progress on the ground.

It makes sense to see democratization neither as a set of processes driven by macro-structural change at the global level – in which all experiments are inherently the same – nor as an experiment in institutional change behind the closed borders of the nation-state – in which case fine distinctions about what is, and is not, democracy predominate. Democratization is an open-ended and contested process of social transformation within (usually national) communities. Many different kinds of actors, elite and non-elite, national and otherwise, are caught up in it and become involved in the ongoing struggle to define what democratization should and can mean and the appropriate roles of institutions, the state and society in democracy. Put differently, democratization can be understood as a struggle over the norms that govern society and how decisions are taken within that community. Processes of democratization are essentially conflictual and unfinished, for while, superficially, the norms that constitute democracy appear straightforward, in practice the social upheavals in which these debates are placed are ones of struggle (Beetham, 1992). These social struggles frequently come to be expressed through debates around whether democracy is appropriate for particular societies and, if so, how much democracy is appropriate, what kind of democracy should be created, how can it be institutionalized, what is the role of a democratic state, who has rights to citizenship and how should democratic citizenship be brought into existence and exercised. This is what Jelin (1996: 168) means when she talks of democratization as a 'struggle about who is entitled to say what in the process of defining common problems and how they will be faced', for the package of norms contained within the concept of 'democracy' is inherently contested. The transnationalization of politics means that the processes of defining and redefining the norms understood to constitute democracy are debated in states and societies permeable to external influence, and outcomes are affected by actors from outside the nation-state.

## Democratization as norm transformation

Norms have become central to how we conceptualize the international order and their study is an important component of the discipline of International Relations. Much of this is due to the insights into how the global order works garnered through constructivism. In contrast to the realist emphasis on material power and the liberal insistence on rationally determined preference, constructivism emphasizes the role of ideas and identity. According to Schmitz and Sikkink (2002: 521):

> Constructivist theories highlight the independent role of norms and ideas in affecting international and domestic policy outcomes ... Norms and principled ideas are assumed to have constitutive effects on the identity formation of actors, rather than simply intervening between interests and behaviour. Reflecting a shift towards a sociological perspective, constructivists see agents embedded in a set of norms and rules often described as 'world culture'.

Realists and liberals also recognize that norms can matter, but they see them as essentially derivative of hegemonic interests (realism) or contingent on rational state preference (liberalism). Constructivists, in contrast, argue that, in certain circumstances, ideas can resonate with independent meaning and they see ideas as potential catalysts of change. Some constructivists, including some contributors to this volume, suggest that the spread of ideas can lead actors to adopt new social rules and that these can go on to become part of the identity of actors through a process of socialization (Risse et al., 1999; Flockhart, this volume).

Norm change, then, is a dynamic social process and social transformations can be understood as a shift in the norms that govern a community. But, in the present global order, where there are real inducements for states and other actors to behave in accordance with Western norms, how can we tell if norm change is skin-deep or profoundly embedded? After all, actors have considerable incentives to accept new rules because they are not powerful enough to contest them. Accepting new rules because there is no alternative may not mean that a fundamental process of rethinking has taken place. In these cases, lapses in democratic behaviour are likely. When state actors superficially endorse new norms in this way, Meyer et al. (1997) attribute it to the need to conform to established scripts of statehood. Such scripts are written by a combination of Western states and global agencies. Inducements to read from scripts of this kind have undoubtedly increased in the post-Cold War order as tolerance of divergence from Western norms has decreased. Simmons (2003) has explained how external pressure leads even authoritarian states to sign up to international treaties on human rights. She points out that while signing up to international law indicates an apparent transformation of the norms that govern these states and may lead to some important changes taking place within them, in fact sustained and self-motivated change, at least where authoritarian states and human rights are concerned, is far more limited. In other words, apparent norm change on rights does not lead to a cascading process of more widespread internal reform. There is a very limited process of 'lock in' of reform, understood more widely. In cases such as these, it is unlikely that apparent norm changes will lead to embedded or 'locked-in' processes of political change, and once external vigilance is relaxed or international interests shift elsewhere, then reversals to previously held beliefs are likely.

The motivational power of ideas is far more straightforward in the case of non-state actors, who play a growing role in global politics through relationships with governments and through the establishment of effective transnational advocacy networks (Keck and Sikkink, 1998). In the latter case, principled ideas – about rights, gender, justice, the environment and so on – act as the glue binding together activists from distinct communities. Such networks have existed for a long time (Colas, 2001), but they have become empowered through globalization for reasons that have to do with the transformation of state sovereignty, the increasing dependence of government actors on civil society for the delivery and design of policies, the time–space compression that is the result of technological change and the ideological cataclysm of the Communist collapse which has left the West with no serious rival, at least until September 2001. As a result of these developments, a research agenda has emerged devoted to the study of transnational social movements and non-state actors. This body of research recognizes the importance of states in global politics and tends to adopt an interactionist perspective, which identifies two-way patterns of influence and authority between states and non-state groups. Moreover, this kind of research has identified the ways in which local and national politics have tended to be caught up in processes of transnationalization. Local contexts, in other words, are rendered porous to influence from outside. Political spaces can no longer be shaped exclusively by (local) state actors and are invaded by groups, ideas and networks from outside the nation-state.

The power of principled ideas is most obviously expressed in the contemporary push for a global ethic of human rights. This, more even than the ambiguous search for democracy to which the question of rights is related, has motivated non-state activists. Risse et al. (1999) trace responses to human rights violations in eleven comparative cases. The findings suggest that mobilization by transnational networks can – sometimes – work to introduce sustained improvement in human rights records. They suggest that what happens in successful cases is that, over time, and taking advantage of a favourable international climate, successful non-state groups are able to create sufficient internal and external pressure to force state leaders, first to acknowledge that there is a problem of human rights violations and then to introduce some tactical concessions. In turn, this may empower domestic groups (connected into transnational networks and using resources that contacts abroad give them) to mobilize and push for further reform (Schmitz and Sikkink, 2002). In the most successful cases, new norms are constructed through activism and the successful politics of persuasion. Finnemore and Sikkink (1998) describe processes such as these as a 'norms cascade', that is the gradual unfolding of change within a critical mass of relevant domestic actors. Nevertheless, it is important to recognize that Risse et al. (1999) do not suggest that pressure *always* leads to change and recognize that the reasons that explain success and failure are complex and sometimes obscure.

Risse et al.'s research suggests one important path to the introduction of new norms: external pressure gradually leading to state reform, underpinned by a change in the beliefs of sufficient domestic actors who both support and police the process of state transformation. Can this model be applied to questions of democratization, an issue area that is cognate in many ways with the question of human rights? Certainly in theory, it could. There is a range of transnational networks engaged in monitoring and campaigning for processes of democratization, some of whom connect into relationships with governments, multilateral agencies and local civil society movements. But the difficulty resides in the fact that democratization is in reality an umbrella term for a package of reforms and a broad range of policies, that can include rights, state reform, legal and constitutional reform, policies of accountability and transparency and socio-economic change. Furthermore, as explained above, democratization is a political, not a technical process, limited to legal or constitutional change. What it consists of is contested – actors who claim to be in favour of democratization, international and domestic, do not necessarily agree on what it means and which policy changes should take place. Many groups that lay claim to be pro-democracy are, in fact, hostile to each other. As a result, tracing the operation of democratization networks is a particularly complex task. Researchers are forced critically to evaluate the ideas of, and claims made by, transnational actors – what kind of norms do they understand by democracy – as well as to develop a methodology for the analysis of how they operate and whether they are successful.

The most visible and authoritative of those organizations that are attempting to write the script of what democratization should mean are (Western) states and multilateral agencies. Not surprisingly, they pattern their pro-democracy policies through an often idealized understanding of the operation of Western governments. The norms they support are drawn less from abstract ideas about democracy than from a particular understanding of Western democratic politics – separation of powers, free elections, decentralization, freedom of the press and so on. Other non-state actors also act as democratic 'norm entrepreneurs', although their understanding of democratization may be very different. There is the very real potential for conflict and disagreement, then, when it comes to measuring progress towards democracy and interpreting the actions of external players in democratization processes. In the case of the activities of both states and non-state actors, democratic norm diffusion is also very easily derailed. Democracy-building easily elides into a process of domination and a rejection of cultures and norms that are regarded as un- or anti-Western. Actors from outside frequently send unintended mixed messages, due to cultural distance, insensitivity, a failure to understand societies other than their own and the general complexity of interests and belief patterns, their own included. Good intentions, then, do not necessarily make for success, in so far as democratization is concerned. Moreover, commitment to democratic norm diffusion can sometimes be thin or subordinated to other interests. Geo-strategic concerns, for example, frequently override European and US commitment to democracy in much of Asia, including China, Africa and the Arab world.

These difficulties do not only apply to state actors engaged in trying to spread and determine the nature of democratic norms. Non-state actors, despite their apparently principled intentions, may act inappropriately and their attempts to encourage norm change may easily be perceived as westernization (Schmitz, 2002). All of this, in sum, points to the fact that norm diffusion is fraught with perils and obstacles. It is not always clear what 'democratic norms' consist of, or how they can best be diffused. In so far as elite actors are concerned, even relatively successful pressure very probably will only induce thin processes of change, at least in the short term, unless there is also an internal and self-sustaining process of transformation. Creating a transformation on a mass scale of values, meanwhile, will almost certainly take a very long time and be difficult to measure. Moreover – and this too is important – while norm diffusion is important and is a *sine qua non* of democratization, it is not always enough. To believe sincerely in democracy and to want to live in a democratic society will not, on their own, suffice to bring it about. Democracy-building requires confrontation with embedded sources of power. The introduction of democracy can easily be hampered, or even prevented, by such embedded authoritarian enclaves or by structural or material constraints. For Yashar (2002), indeed, the danger of the norms approach is precisely that it runs the risk of ignoring such questions of power.

## Norms, democratization and regions

The transnational approach to politics assumes that networking takes place globally, irrespective of the particular geographic location of actors and activists. Space, time and distance matter less than ever. In fact, regions are becoming more important social and economic sites of activity as globalization proceeds. They are significant meso-levels within a globalizing order. Far from producing a borderless world, globalization seems to be leading to the proliferation of institutions and sites of belonging above and alongside the state. This reconfiguration of both identity and sovereignty is leading to the strengthening of regions within global politics, as states opt to pool sovereignty in order to respond more effectively to the challenges posed by new security threats, the globalization of finance flows, the power of multinational corporations and transnational crime syndicates, demographic upheavals and so on. New regionalist formations that have become stronger in recent years range from the enlarged European Union, the development of an Americas-wide project of free trade integration through the North American Free Trade Association (NAFTA) and the Free Trade Area of the Americas (FTAA), the Common Market of the South (MERCOSUR) in South America and the Asia-Pacific Economic Community (APEC).

Regions constitute an important space for the socialization of groups and individuals. They also allow groups to co-ordinate their activities and to exchange views. As a result, regions can serve as 'the fulcrum of transnational contention' (Tarrow, 2001). In an important study of democratizing networks in Asia, Piper and Uhlin (2003) argue that the region acts as the most effective space for the generation and co-ordination of transnational non-state action. They emphasize the importance of shared cultural codes and notions of community and the possibility of more effective communication taking place at the regional level. As a result, they argue that more effective mobilization can take place at the level of the region. These arguments can be extrapolated to other regions. The EU, for example, is an important site for the co-ordination of both state and non-state activity. Over time, states within regions are moving towards similar models of governance through macro-economic integration and, in the case of the EU, harmonization of social policies. Non-state actors in regional blocs are also moving towards policies of advocacy co-ordination in aid, the environment, trade and so on. In sum, regions act as sites of identity change and reproduction and ideational regulation. Regional norms about how societies should be governed and the role of government gradually come into being.

When new members are brought into existing regional blocs, or new regionalist associations formed such as the North American Free Trade Association (NAFTA) or the Free Trade Area of the Americas (FTAA), new channels for the diffusion of norms and beliefs are established and new incentives for their adoption created. Where new regionalism maps onto significant power asymmetries – as in the case of EU enlargement, NAFTA and the FTAA – it is reasonable to suppose that regional institutions act to diffuse the norms that emanate from the resource-rich actors. In the case of democratization, this suggests, within NAFTA and the FTAA, that there will be pressure for Latin American states and societies to adopt, at least superficially, the norms that are understood to constitute democracy by US state and non-state actors. With the process of EU enlargement, the norms associated with Western Europe become more likely in the new member states. Models of regionalism, in other words, generate opportunities for different governance projects and different concepts of what democratization means (Grugel, 2004b). At the same time, participation in new regional associations makes it more difficult for political elites to appeal to discourses of nationalism or difference. Region-building, in sum, can act as a homogenizing clearing-house for ideas, creating networks and communities bound by ideas and interests.

## Conclusion: rethinking democratization

This chapter has sought to review the different ways in which the international can be understood to influence and shape processes of democratization. It has identified the strengths and weaknesses of the two dominant approaches, namely that of comparative politics and the more recent literature on globalization and democracy. Instead, it has proposed a middle way. Globalization should be understood as transnationalization, allowing for more actor-centred analysis. Democratization should be defined as an ongoing process of norm transformation, alongside social struggles over how to define the norms that constitute democracy. Democratization should be understood as a complex and conflictual site of struggle, in which the kinds of democracy that are thought to be desirable and the degrees of democracy that are thought to be possible are continually negotiated and renegotiated between differently motivated and differently situated actors internal and external to states. This leads to a view that we need to study in depth the different processes of norm diffusion that take place. One window on this process, I have argued, is through an analysis of the politics of region-building. Different regionalist formations create different opportunities for norm diffusion, empower different sets of actors and have histories of thinking differently about social conflict and the 'good society'. Ultimately, they may lead to different models of democracy. Moreover, interventions in the name of democracy, however limited the intention, can sometimes lead to unexpected consequences through changes in collective expectations – a process that Flockhart terms 'complex socialization'. Nevertheless, it should be remembered that norm diffusion can be resisted or only superficially adopted. Explaining how and why some instances of norm diffusion work and others fail is the task of the empirical chapters in this book.

## Notes

1. For a full discussion of approaches to democratization, see Grugel (2002).
2. On the role of elites in transitions see, for example, Higley and Gunther (1992); Vanhanen (1997).

# 2
# Complex Socialization and the Transfer of Democratic Norms

*Trine Flockhart*

This chapter is an attempt to offer a structural framework for explaining the transfer of norms through processes of socialization which, if successful, may lead to changes in the behaviour and possibly in the identity and basic values of the socializee. In the case of this volume, the specific socialization process of interest[1] is the transfer of democratic norms, where the socializing agents are international organizations, and the socializees are the Central and East European (CEE) states, which started out on their journey towards democracy following the end of the Cold War. It is claimed that the specific utility of the framework is its ability to account for the significant variation in the extent to which states in similar circumstances and in response to initially similar socialization efforts on the part of the socializing agents, have nevertheless resulted in very different outcomes. Put simply, why has socialization of democratic norms been successful in the Czech Republic but not in Belarus, when arguably both started out from a totalitarian past, experienced a similar ideational shock (Marcussen, 2000) in the shape of the end of Soviet domination and the de-legitimization of Communism, and were initially offered similar socialization 'deals' by the West?

Generally, there has been agreement within the social constructivist literature (cf. Checkel, 1999; Marcussen, 2000; Risse et al., 1999; Finnemore and Sikkink, 1998) that socialization best takes place following a critical juncture (Finnemore and Sikkink, 1998) or a destabilizing ideational shock (Marcussen, 2000) which has severely undermined the existing norm set, leaving the agents in an ideational vacuum (Marcussen, 2000) or state of anomie or 'normlessness'. There is also agreement that norms do not just 'float freely' into agents' heads (Risse-Kappen, 1994), but that they must be promoted by someone and that certain conditions are more conducive for norm promotion and reception than others.

Here the social constructivist literature is also in agreement in identifying a number of factors that are likely to influence the outcome of the socialization process, focusing in particular on how socialization takes place, which strategies are utilized, how salient the socialized norm set is with the receiver of socialization (Cortell and Davis, 1996) and the extent to which the socializing agent is able to access the domestic political system of the socializee and able to build 'winning coalitions' that can ensure the adoption of the new norm set in terms of policy and daily behaviour (Risse-Kappen, 1994). However, so far no model has been offered which is able to take all the significant factors that influence the outcome of socialization into account, and which is also able to account for the common occurrence of variation across apparently similar cases. In this chapter it is proposed that by utilizing a combination of agent level theories from social psychology and social learning, a model can be constructed, which not only allows for comparison across different cases, but which also has a significant degree of predictive and explanatory value. What makes this model different is that self- and other-categorization processes are seen as the primary factor for determining the outcome of the socialization process, with all other variables in this complicated process being dependent on the initial self- and other-categorization process. With self- and other-categorization processes as the starting point, a model can be constructed which takes into consideration all other secondary factors such as socialization strategies, the nature of domestic structures, political processes and political culture at the domestic elite and mass levels, as well as the prospects for creating 'winning coalitions' at both levels, albeit that it is an extremely complex model.

The Complex Socialization model consists of four constituent parts:

1. Social Identity Theory (SIT) particularly the importance of self- and other-categorization processes for the receptiveness to socialization and the willingness on the part of the socializer to socialize. Self- and other-categorization processes constitute the model's first 'filter' between the international and domestic levels.
2. Socialization strategies taken from within the field of 'social learning', here conceptualized as persuasion and social influence strategies.
3. Domestic structure where the traditional division between a mass and elite level is reconceptualized as two separate 'we-concepts', a state/elite and nation/people level, which may have different self- and other-categorization processes and different conceptions about what constitutes a critical juncture.

4. The domestic level 'filters', conceptualized as political structures and processes at the state/elite level, and political culture and participation traditions at the nation/people level.

The result is a model (see Figure 2.1), which operates with four different so-called out-groups, that are all likely to behave differently vis-à-vis the socializing agent (the in-group). It has three different levels separated by 'filters' through which the socialization process must proceed, and it has two different strategies for socialization, which will both be influenced by the first 'filter' (self- and other-categorization processes) and which will themselves influence the outcome of the process.

In the following, I will proceed by first describing the model's constituent parts, followed by a presentation of the model as a whole with particular emphasis on its utility as an explanatory and predictive model. Finally I will indicate very briefly how the model may be utilized in comparative analysis of democratic norms transfer in the New Europe. In the following chapters individual contributors to this volume

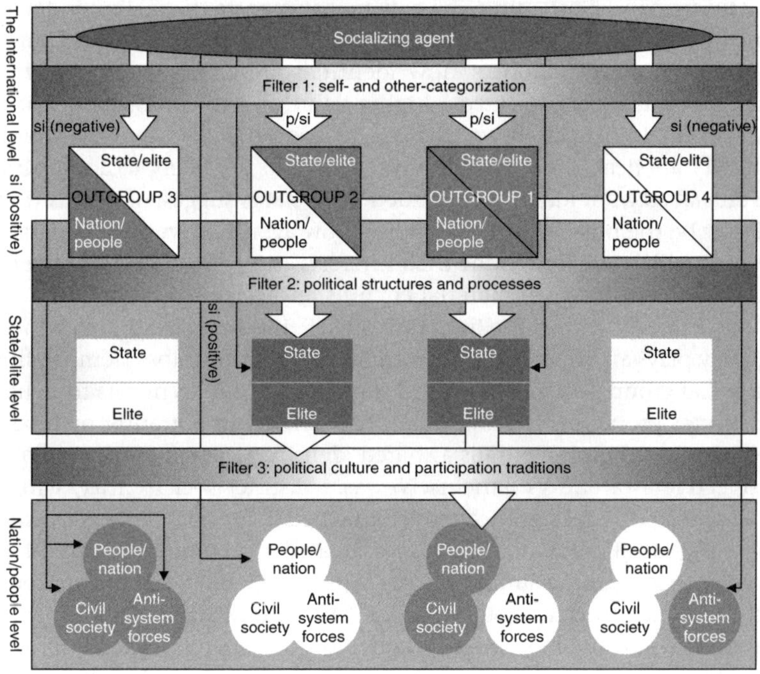


*Figure 2.1* Complex socialization

will utilize aspects of the model in their analysis of both socializers (selected international organizations) and socializees (individual countries categorized into the different out-groups).

## Social identity theory

It is suggested in this chapter that theories from social psychology have a great deal to offer for the understanding of norm change, and indeed for social constructivism generally. This is because SIT, in its emphasis on explaining why individuals find certain social groups and their norm set (and identity) more attractive than others, and as a result are willing to undertake significant behavioural change to comply with the norm set of a specific social group of which membership is desired, may in fact also offer social constructivism a general agent level assumption on par with rationalist theories' assumption about agent behaviour as determined by rationality. As has been noted by several scholars (Checkel, 1998; Harvey, 2000; Lose, 2001) social constructivism does not have such an agent level theory, which causes problems when social constructivist analyses attempt to go beyond the mantra that action is determined by preferences which are determined by identity. This of course simply begs the question of how identities are constructed and why some identities seem to have a higher value and thus more attraction than others. It is precisely on this key question that SIT seems to offer a generally applicable assumption on how agents are likely to act during the crucial stage of identity construction. What is suggested here is that SIT may be the missing link explaining how agents arrive at a particular identity, which will determine their interests and preferences, and hence their behaviour in given material circumstances.

A key concept within the literature on SIT[2] is the 'social group', which arguably plays an important role in *all* human relationships. Membership of a social group provides rules and standards as well as norms for what constitutes proper behaviour and attitudes. Most importantly membership of a 'social group' entails a shared identity, where individuals have a collective awareness of themselves as a distinct social entity, where value and emotional significance are attached to group membership and where the social group is constantly evaluated and compared with other social groups within a similar realm (Tajfel, 1978: 63). Membership of a highly ranked social group provides the individual member with self-esteem, and the more highly valued the social group, the better the self-esteem of its individual members is likely to be. In that sense membership of a social group becomes a means for higher self-esteem, and for individuals to organize their world cognitively and to place themselves within it (Druckman, 1994).

Theories from social psychology offer an interesting insight into the importance of the social group for actors, and how, once membership of the social group has been achieved, members of the group will be motivated to positively distinguish their own group above other groups (Tajfel, 1978; Tajfel and Turner, 1985), and how they will engage in a process of categorizing themselves as members of distinct social groups and will through the self- and other-categorization process define their relationship and distance from other social groups within a similar realm, thereby creating a layered hierarchy of different social groups. What this adds to the common understanding of identity construction is that certainly identity constructions are always relational (Hopf, 2002: 7), but they are not constructed purely in terms of 'the other', but equally, perhaps even more so, in relation to other 'we' entities. Hence what is important in the self- and other-categorization process is both 'the other' which defines what 'the self' *is not*, but also the 'significant we' or ' in-group', which defines what 'the self' *is striving towards*. What characterizes the hierarchical system of different social groups within a similar realm is that they are likely to share a definition of what constitutes 'the other' and what constitutes the 'significant we'. As the desire of individuals will always be to have as positive a self-esteem as possible, it is possible to hypothesize that individuals will strive towards membership of the social group, which they have categorized as the 'significant we' – the 'in-group'.

As is well known to social constructivists, norm sets are highly stable structures because norm change and change of identity are costly processes. Therefore norms and group identities are only likely to change following significant events that somehow undermine or delegitimize the existing norm set, hence preventing individuals from continuing to positively distinguish themselves and maintaining a satisfactory level of self-esteem.[3] However, once such an event has taken place, and assuming that the 'in-group' is open to new members, a socialization and learning process can start in preparation for membership of those out-groups that are able and willing to undertake the necessary norm change for obtaining membership of the 'in-group'. In this process it is clear that it matters for the success of socialization to what extent the actor being socialized identifies with the norm promoting actor and vice versa, and the extent to which such identification (or non-identification) extends to the domestic level. What is therefore suggested by SIT is that the norms that are likely to be the most salient to the individual will be those norms that are found within the individual's social group, and that the preferred social group will be the group that is categorized as the most highly valued social group within a given realm. From that one can assume that action is determined, not by simple material rationality, but by an equally rational desire for belonging to a social group, which provides the desired feeling of positive self-esteem and cognitive comfort.

In the Complex Socialization model, the process of self- and other-categorization is conceptualized as the first 'filter', which will divide the different social groups into a system of hierarchically ordered out-groups. In other words what emerges is different 'layers' of out-groups, whose relationship with the in-group will determine methods of socialization available to the norm promoter, and openness for socialization on behalf of the socializee. In the next section the model's second constitutive element, socialization strategies, will be presented.

## Socialization strategies

Although socialization is often seen as simply being a learning process teaching 'novices' how to behave in a new group, it is important to stress that different forms for socialization exist, where the socialization strategy itself may have significant implications for the result achieved. The claim made here is that the chosen (or available) socialization strategy will in large measure depend on the structural position of the out-group being socialized.

At present the literature on social learning and socialization operates with two different strategies, one that is referred to as 'social influence', which elicits pro-norm behaviour through the distribution of social rewards and punishments, and one that is referred to as 'persuasion', which encourages norm-consistent behaviour through a social process of interaction that involves changing attitudes without use of either material or mental coercion (Johnston, 2001: 499; Flockhart, 2004a). The 'social influence' method of socialization tends to utilize a variety of social and material rewards ranging from psychological well-being through increased status or a sense of belonging or having a close relationship with a positively valued social group such as the Euro-Atlantic community, to promises of material reward. The social influence method is likely to use the well-being, which it is assumed that aspirant in-group members will get from receiving public praise for achieving identified goals in the process of norm change, or as suggested by Schimmelfennig (this volume) by utilizing conditionality reinforced by material rewards to be distributed *after* all conditions have been met. In cases where there are no options for positive social influence, the method of socialization will utilize punishment such as public shaming, opprobrium, exclusion or demeaning, or the withholding of promised material rewards, in other words the denying of either material or psychological well-being (Johnston, 2001: 499).

Persuasion, on the other hand, is a process that reaches deeper than social influence, and as such is also likely to have more profound effects in terms of changing attitudes and deeply held beliefs, although only under certain conditions. Certainly the proclaimed aim of persuasion as opposed to social influence strategies is that it aims at changing beliefs and attitudes in the persuadee, rather than simply changing behaviour. Persuasion may take place in a variety of different forums, but will always involve transmission of a message from the persuader to the persuadee, and will not rely on either material or social reward or punishment. As such, persuasion can take place in private settings, where social influence to a large extent relies on a public forum, since well-being with regards to status or shame are mainly confined to the public sphere. In that sense persuasion is a process of *convincing* someone through argument and principled debate. For persuasion to have any effect, however, a number of specific conditions need to be fulfilled. Jeffrey Checkel has suggested that persuasion is most likely to be successful if the persuadee is cognitively motivated to analyse new information, has few prior ingrained beliefs that are inconsistent with the views of the persuader's message, and when the persuader is someone the persuadee holds in great esteem or is a member of an in-group to which the persuader wants to belong. Furthermore Checkel suggests that persuasion is more likely to be effective if serious deliberative argument is used as opposed to lecturing or demanding, and the process takes place in a private setting among individuals who share common professional backgrounds and meet repeatedly (Checkel, 1999: 545–60; Checkel, 2001: 543). What that seems to suggest in relation to the presented model is that persuasion strategies are more suitable at the state/elite level than at the nation/people level.

Whether or not the strategy chosen is persuasion or social influence or a combination of both, the actor being socialized must as a minimum identify with the social group to which the norm promoter belongs, and the actor must have a desire for inclusion in the group. This clearly has repercussions for the strategies available to international organizations, where no strategy of actual socialization is available for dealing with states, which manifestly do not wish to belong to the in-group, except to try to make the state re-evaluate its own falsely perceived positive 'distinguishness' by exposing the state's failures and utilizing shaming and opprobrium. On the other hand in the case of social groups that are close to the in-group, and clearly want to join the in-group, the number of available strategies is much greater as is the number of issue areas where socialization can take place, as well as channels for socialization. As a result a successful outcome is much more likely in cases where there is a small ideational distance between in-group and out-group.

## Domestic structure

As the object of the presented model is to explain the transfer of international norms from one agent (in this case an international organization) to another agent's (a state's) domestic setting, it is clearly necessary to consider the landscape into which the norm is being diffused. The transfer of norms from one international actor to another is only likely to have any effect if the norm is diffused into the domestic society at large, at a minimum at the governmental level, but for most norms (and certainly for democratic norms) also eventually to the general mass public level. Therefore a promoted international norm should ideally achieve the status as a 'relevant structure' at the whole domestic level of a given society to ensure stability through institutionalization (Berger and Luckmann, 1966: 97–9). For that reason a detailed 'map' of what happens at the domestic level is necessary for explaining norm transfer to the domestic level, which makes it useful to conceptualize the domestic level in a way that allows for some degree of parsimony, but still has the possibility of explaining variation between different domestic settings. This has traditionally been done through the approach generally identified under the rubric 'domestic structure' (Evangelista, 1997: 203; cf. Krasner, 1978; Katzenstein, 1976; Risse-Kappen, 1992, 1994).

In the Complex Socialization model, however, the domestic level is conceptualized as consisting not only of the formal and informal structures and political processes included in the traditional domestic structure sense, but as also including the possibility of two very differently constructed social groups; one located at the state level and mainly consisting of the elite and government structures, and one located at the nation level and mainly consisting of 'the people', traditionally described as the mass.[4] By understanding the societal division as arranged around a nexus between state/elite and nation/people, it is possible to conceive of the domestic level as two distinct social groups, or as Lene Hansen and Ole Wæver (2002) suggest, as 'we-concepts', which not only have been differently constructed, and which therefore may be undergoing different self- and other-categorization processes, possibly leading to very different conceptions of interests and political preferences, but also which social group is perceived as the in-group and what constitutes a critical juncture. By dividing the domestic level into these two different 'we-concepts' it is possible to work with a bifurcation of causal dynamics, where different causal factors will be relevant at each level. Indeed, precisely such a bifurcation has been observed by Maxine Isaacs (1998) as the formulation of opinions about American foreign policy by American elites and masses can be said to involve entirely different reference points and logics (Stiles, 2003: 3). This corresponds well with the view put forward by Ulf Hedetoft (2003), who has suggested that it is possible to identify a 'state culture' as well as the widely accepted 'political culture'. This is despite the fact that 'state culture' has not traditionally been seen as a separate analytical concept, basically because the state and its actors (the elite) are not supposed to close culturally around themselves, but are supposed to operate within the overall 'political culture', representing the nation. Yet as suggested by Hedetoft, 'everybody has a hunch that states and their political elites have cultural peculiarities of their own' (Hedetoft, 2003: 7).

This is not to say that the existence of two 'we-concepts' in the form of state and nation will always be two separate, even conflicting cultures, consisting of *different* discourses and *different* self- and other-categorization processes, but is merely to suggest that this *might* be the case on certain issues and in relation to certain norm sets, and that such a constellation would have a significant influence on the prospects for successful socialization of particular norms at the domestic level. In fact in countries where the two levels have the same orientation in terms of what constitutes the relevant in-group and where the discourses and self- and other-categorization processes are likely to be similar, the prospects for successful socialization are very good, in comparison to countries where the two levels remain separate. By conceptualizing the domestic level as consisting of a nexus between state/elite and nation/people, it is possible to divide countries undergoing a process of socialization in relation to a specific norm set into four different types of out-groups according to the self- and other-categorization processes taking place between the socializer and the socializee.[5] Each type of out-group is likely to undergo very different processes of socialization, with very different prospects for success.

## The domestic filters of socialization

The socialization process discussed within International Relations is chiefly concerned with the socialization of *states*. Yet the actual processes of changes of behaviour, identity and attitudes take place at an individual or small group level consisting of persons directly associated with the norm promoting agency. At the state/elite level these are likely to be relatively small groups of professionals who may loosely be described as epistemic communities (Haas, 1992) whose specific expertise is a thorough understanding and acceptance of the norms being socialized. As pointed out by Ken Wang (2003) however, the elite level has hitherto received by far the most attention in the socialization literature. Yet socialization of a norm set into the state/elite level may well be the easiest form for socialization, and will certainly say very little about the prospects for successful socialization at the nation/people level, where entirely different salience structures, cultures and participation traditions may be in place. In recognition of this, the Complex Socialization model operates with two separate filters through which successful socialization must proceed. These are conceptualized as: (1) domestic elite,[6] political structures and processes, and (2) domestic mass political culture and participation traditions.

### Filter 1: domestic elite political structures and processes

The adoption and internalization of a new norm set at the domestic level can generally take place through actions and interests of state and societal actors and/or through the incorporation of the new norm set into national laws (Cortell and Davis, 1996: 454). Either way the norm promoting agency and/or the epistemic community with expertise of the new norm set, must succeed in getting decision-makers to accept the norm set and act accordingly either through legislation or changed behaviour and procedures within the political system. If such diffusion into the domestic decision-making level is not possible, then the norm will not be successfully adopted, despite perhaps eager acceptance in the epistemic community. It is therefore essential that the promoted norms are directed towards individuals who are able to reach into the decision-making process or strategically important segments of the political elite. Thomas Risse-Kappen (1994) has clearly demonstrated that whether or not an idea set is adopted as policy will depend on whether those promoting the new idea set are able to gain access to decision-makers in the political system and whether they are able to build winning coalitions. Whether such access can be gained and winning coalitions can be built is likely to depend on the specific domestic structures in the country in question, and on the salience attached within the country's elite to the specific norm set. The more alien the norm set to the state culture in question the more difficult it will be to establish support for it. Easy access to decision-makers in the political system is not, however, necessarily an advantage for getting the norm set accepted within the decision-making political elite, since other competing norm sets will also have easy access and hence constitute competition at the decision-making level. It is therefore crucial for the successful adoption and institutionalization of the norm set that those promoting the norm set from the international level have a thorough understanding of the specific domestic political structures and processes in the state in question.

Apart from the political structures and processes at the domestic elite level, the process of socialization will also be dependent on self- and other-categorization processes, which for the outsider may be almost impossible to detect. The political elite in most countries cannot be viewed as one homogeneous mass, but is clearly constructed of different groups, which at a closer inspection are likely to constitute different 'social groups within the social group'. These groups are likely to be in competition with each other and to attach a different degree of value to the norms being promoted. For example, the culture and identification processes with outside actors and their norm set can in some cases be very different depending on whether one speaks with members of the elite from a foreign ministry or a defence ministry, from a left-wing party or from a right-wing party, from a nationalist/patriotic newspaper editor or a critical/independent newspaper editor etc. What is more, where some of these may be of importance for the diffusion of the norm set within the political elite, it may be other members of the elite who are important for diffusing the norm set into the nation/people level. In other words, what emerges is a process which is extremely complex and which demands a thorough understanding of the prevailing domestic conditions.

## Filter 2: domestic mass political culture and participation traditions

In many ways it is the same conditions for socialization that are important at the domestic mass level as are important at the elite level. That is, successful diffusion of the norm set will in large measure depend on the norm promoting agents' ability to gain access to strategically important members of the mass domestic public, and the salience of the norm in question. However, although the ingredients are the same as in the case of the state/elite level, the process and the requirements for successful norm diffusion may turn out very different at the nation/people level. At the state/elite level access depends on the ability to make an appointment and arrange meetings with members of the elite that can be identified through their role and position within the elite. This is not the case at the nation/people level – here the key factor is interest in the topic or salience of the norm being promoted. In other words, successful norm diffusion at the nation/people level depends in large measure on the existence of an 'interested audience', which again depends on the norm having undergone a process of 'politicization'.[7] If nobody turns up to the public hearings about democracy, if nobody reads the relevant articles in the newspapers, engages in the political process, takes part in everyday institutional and associational life such as school boards and the local football club, then diffusion and institutionalization of a new norm set such as democracy is a very difficult and slow process. A domestic culture where participation in the political process is traditionally low is likely to be much more difficult to socialize than one where there is a strong and vibrant civil society through which norm diffusion may take place.

As suggested earlier, both levels have peculiarities of their own, which are likely to require very different socialization strategies and to have very different prospects for success, at least in the short term. Where elites may be 'easier' to convince about a specific issue through either persuasion or social influence, attitudes at the mass level tend to be more firmly rooted in nation-specific culture and traditions and therefore less open to persuasive argument. The result is that socialization at the nation/people level is likely to be a more long-term process than socialization at the state/elite level. Yet in the case of the diffusion of a democratic norm set, the institutionalization and internalization of the norm set at the nation/people level is important and yet wrought with difficulties and pitfalls, which require much more attention than is possible within the scope of this chapter. However, what seems clear is that the nation/people level cannot be ignored, leaving research on the transfer of norms into a domestic setting with emphasis resting mainly on diffusion of norms to the state/elite level. Successful diffusion of norms to the state/elite level may say little about the capacity of the elites in turn to influence the nation/people level.

## Towards a Complex Socialization model

The socialization of a specific norm set from an externally located socializing agent into a domestic setting is clearly a very complex process, which involves multiple processes and different agents. What is at stake is not merely a process of A teaching B something, but rather a process of constructing new identities through membership of other social groups than was previously the case. Hence what is under investigation may be conceptualized as a process of social group change from out-groups with varying distance to the in-group into members of the in-group, which in the case of democratic norm socialization in the New Europe can be viewed as the Euro-Atlantic community.

In the case of the socialization of democratic norms in the New Europe it is possible to conceptualize four different out-groups, based on the specific in-group orientation at the two domestic levels state/elite and nation/people. For the purpose of conceptualizing the different out-groups in relation to adoption of a 'Western' democratic norm set, I have followed Frank Schimmelfennig[8] (2000) in his assessment that two factors seem to matter most for successful socialization – 'the strength of western orientations in society [nation/people level] and the ideology on which the government [state/elite level] has based its claim to authority after the collapse of communism' (Schimmelfennig, 2000: 132). With a simple combination of these two factors one is left with the possibility of four different out-groups with differering distance to the in-group. These four different out-groups in increasing distance from the in-group are:

- Out-group 1 – countries with a strong domestic Western orientation and a liberal government.
- Out-group 2 – countries with a weak domestic Western orientation and a liberal government.
- Out-group 3 – countries with a strong domestic Western orientation and a non-liberal government.
- Out-group 4 – countries with a weak domestic Western orientation and a non-liberal government.

As the first stage of the socialization process in this case[9] takes place in a top-down manner directed at the state/elite level, the most important factor for determining distance to the in-group is regarded as the government being of a liberal democratic persuasion, and hence wishing for inclusion in the in-group, which is characterized by liberal democratic credentials. Therefore those countries that have liberal democratic governments in place will be regarded as closest to the in-group, with the combination of liberal democracy and strong domestic Western orientation as the out-group clearly closest to the dominant in-group.

The two middle out-groups – those with a liberal democratic government, but weak Western orientation in society and those with a non-liberal government and strong Western orientation in society – are both at a roughly similar distance from the in-group, but the strategies for dealing with their socialization are likely to differ significantly. Finally, in the case of the out-group with a non-liberal government and weak Western orientation in society, the socialization strategies available for the socializing agencies is extremely limited, except directed towards anti-system forces to facilitate conditions that are likely to bring about a re-evaluation of the country's self-perception from positive to negative, and hence motivate a desire for change in social group identity.

What is important is that it is the positioning of a state into one of the four out-groups, that to a large extent will be the determining factor for the further process of socialization, both in terms of socialization strategies, in terms of whether the process will be top-down or bottom-up, and in terms of which societal groups can be reached by the socializing agencies in the socialization process. As such the initial self- and other-categorization process is a key determinant for the further outcome of the process. The process of self- and other-categorization is undertaken both by the in-group in its assessment of the overall out-group and categorization of it into different layered out-groups, and by the out-groups themselves which continually will assess their distance to the in-group relative to the distance of other members of the overall out-group. The norm promoting agency is likely to respond to its own evaluation of the different out-groups by utilizing a differentiated strategy of socialization, where different methods of socialization will be employed depending on the perceived closeness of an out-group and the existing channels of communication with the different out-groups, which will consolidate and further exaggerate the differentiation. As suggested by Lucarelli (this volume) a process of increasingly differentiated socialization can be clearly seen in, for example, the case of NATO, where the socialization process started out through NACC/EAPC, which are institutions that at least informally distinguish between actual and self-perceived differences between its members. However, soon after the establishment of NACC in 1991, mainly in response to pressure from some of the NACC members themselves who regarded themselves as 'closer friends', the socialization process changed to a differentiated socialization process utilizing PfP and MAP, where not only differentiation was recognized, but where self-categorization and self-definition of distance to the in-group on the part of the socializees was actively encouraged. Indeed in the Madrid Declaration on Euro-Atlantic Security and Co-operation it is stated that, 'on the basis of inclusiveness and self-differentiation Partner countries will thus be able to draw closer to the Alliance'.[10] A similar initial lack of categorization is suggested by Merlingen and Ostrauskaitė (this volume) in the case of the OSCE, which initially saw 'the East' 'as one big, more or less undifferentiated landmass characterized by instability and human insecurity'.

The claim made here is that different strategies of socialization will be employed by the socializing agent, depending on an assessment of the position of the country being socialized in the hierarchical system of out-groups. As the choice of strategy is likely to have a significant impact on the effectiveness of the socialization process, the choice of strategy and the options available to the socializer are extremely important.[11] However, the position of states in particular out-groups is not static as seen in, for example, the case of Slovakia and Croatia as countries that have moved from out-group 3 to out-group 1, with a resulting change in the socialization strategies available to the socializer, leading to a veritable quantum leap in terms of reducing the distance between those countries and the in-group. Indeed, there is room within the model for a significant degree of variation between members of the same out-group (as illustrated by the significant difference between, for example, Hungary and Romania both of whom until recently were members of out-group 1[12]). However, by using the Complex Socialization model, it is easier to identify causes of slow or rapid socialization by checking which of the model's four constituent elements is the cause of success or failure. To use the rather difficult example of Romania as a member of out-group 1 again, Romania's low level of development of mature and stable democratic institutions, low or patchy level of political participation traditions, and persistent problems of corruption and social exclusion clearly slow down the process of socialization and movement towards full in-group membership. Yet having been categorized by the in-group as a prospective in-group member, openness to socialization has greatly increased and the strategies available and channels that are open for socialization are clearly factors that influence the prospects and speed of the socialization process in a positive direction. In that sense, therefore, by employing the Complex Socialization model in the analysis of norms transfer from an international to a domestic setting, it becomes 'less impossible' to get an overview of what processes are at work in similar, yet different, and certainly very complex socialization processes.

Apart from its utility as an ordering device within a field that is characterized by a bewildering number of independent variables, the model also has some very useful predictive qualities. By having identified the ideational distance between socializer and socializee, and having placed the socializees into one of the available out-groups, a significant measure of prediction is possible. The key determinant for a successful and robust socialization process is clearly ideational closeness between socializer and socializee at both domestic levels. As can be seen in Figure 2.1, the socialization process is only likely to have available avenues into both levels in a robust manner, understood as utilizing both external and internal (socialization taking place from the state/elite level to the nation/people level) socialization avenues, in out-group 1. From that it seems possible to conclude that only socializees that fit into out-group 1 are likely to undergo successful socialization, understood as obtaining in-group (novice) membership.[13] The prospects for socialization of other out-groups are not, however, entirely bleak, as a possibility exists for movement from one out-group to another either as a result of gradual change through social influence and persuasion strategies through the albeit limited available avenues for socialization, or through the occurrence of a new critical juncture leading to a fundamental re-evaluation of the existing norm set.

## Complex socialization and democratic norms transfer in the New Europe

Within the New Europe and the ongoing promotion/socialization of democratic and liberal norms and values, the processes outlined in the framework can be clearly seen. As indicated by the model, socialization efforts in countries where the political system is not based on a liberal democratic ideology are wrought with difficulty because opportunities for socialization at the state/elite level are very limited with only few access points within the opposition and at the public level. An example of such a state where access is extremely limited is Belarus, where socialization efforts have been abandoned by several socializing agencies, but where there is also an acute awareness of not isolating Belarus to such an extent that the relationship worsens (see Rontoyanni and Korosteleva, this volume). Similarly in the case of states with a strong domestic Western orientation but a non-liberal government such as Slovakia under Mečiar or Croatia under Tudjmann, the strategies open for socialization through international organizations are limited at the state/elite level to methods of social influence at the negative end of the spectrum to deprive the non-liberal government of domestic support and legitimacy, and hence to facilitate a re-evaluation of its own self-perception from positive to negative, and thereby motivate change, or through links with the parliamentary opposition. In these cases other avenues of socialization available go through direct contact with members of the opposition and civil society. Indeed in such circumstances the less high-profile organizations such as NATO-PA, CoE, or OSCE can play a valuable role, as they do not deal exclusively with the governmental political elite. As suggested by Rybar (this volume), this was the case during the period of Vladimir Mečiar's rule in Slovakia, where socialization efforts by NATO and EU were confined to public shaming and withdrawal of rewards, whereas socialization efforts were increased through methods of persuasion vis-à-vis the opposition through other less high-profile organizations.

In contrast, in the case of states whose self- and other-categorization places them at a shorter distance from the in-group, such as out-groups 1 and 2, the socialization strategies open for international organizations are much more varied. In fact, as suggested by Frank Schimmelfennig (2000), it may even be that in the case of the closest groups the desire to be included in the in-group as full members is so strong that they are in effect 'self-socializing'. In practice, though, even in highly motivated states there will always be areas where improvement is possible because the ongoing self-categorization process will induce actors to search for differences between the self and the other with the sole purpose of adopting as many norms, customs, procedures and values associated with the in-group as possible. In such an environment socialization methods within the persuasion approach are likely to be effective, as persuasion methods work best within limited and specific issue areas, such as specific bureaucratic working practices, specific standards for evaluation, specific issues around legitimacy and transparency of government, etc.[14] Furthermore, even in the case of out-group 1, institutionalization and internalization of the norm set at the nation/people level are likely to be slow processes, placing high demands on the ability of both internal and external socializers in getting their message across in the deeply rooted political culture found at the nation/people level.

In practice strategies of both persuasion and social influence (as suggested by Schimmelfennig (this volume), especially conditionality reinforced by material reward), are utilized in relation to the out-groups with liberal democratic governments. The positive spectrum with rewards rather than punishments seems to be preferred, although the public shaming and punishment approach was utilized in the case of Estonia and its citizen rules vis-à-vis its Russian minority as well as in the case of the Hungarian treatment of Romas. Furthermore, as was evident in the case of Slovakia during 2002, the 'big stick' in the form of severe punishment was always a possibility, as it was made abundantly clear that a government, which included Vladimir Mečiar, would result in denial of the ultimate reward – membership of NATO and EU. As suggested by Rybář (this volume) the message was clearly received within both the political elite and a majority at the domestic level in Slovakia.[15]

In the case of countries where a liberal democratic government is in power, but where the domestic Western orientation is weak, the strategy to be followed should concentrate on efforts that are seen as changing the orientation at the domestic public level. In these countries persuasion at the elite level is a possibility because of the close ties between the political elite and the international organizations of the Euro-Atlantic community, but it is less clear to what extent it has a positive effect once brought back home to be diffused at the domestic political elite level, and even less so at the public mass level, where Western attitudes and procedures are likely to meet a hostile environment. In the mixed case of liberal governments with domestic publics with a weak Western orientation, it is more likely that a socialization strategy based on material rewards that can be seen and felt at the public level will have positive effects. However, as the two prime cases of such mixed out-groups, Russia and Ukraine, show, material rewards have a rather limited effect. In Russia the effect of material reward is likely to be limited due to its sheer size, where Western material rewards are likely to have the effect of a drop in the ocean. Furthermore, although the governments in place either have been or are moving in a liberal democratic direction, the political systems are still immature, and marred by high levels of corruption, which makes the practical management of material rewards highly problematic. This is, however, an area that is as yet under-researched, but which certainly promises to be an interesting research topic.

Apart from the four types of out-groups presented here, there is of course the perennial problem of where a country such as Turkey would fit in. As an example of a country where the form of government is not entirely liberal democratic, and where the orientation of society is deeply divided, the socializing strategy open for European international organizations appears to be to work towards a consolidation of liberal democracy and a Western orientation of society. However, as suggested by Bill Park (this volume), the specific characteristics of Turkish political and state culture do not easily lend themselves to such an approach. If socialization is achieved (and certainly the motivation at the government level seems to exist), then Turkey would clearly move into the out-group with the shortest distance to the in-group, but with the complicating factor of a significantly different 'cultural other'. The cultural difference is likely to give rise to different self- and other-categorization processes, which are likely to present a different picture than those outlined above.

## Conclusion

The aim of this chapter was to present the Complex Socialization model, which it is believed will allow for a more fruitful analysis of how new norms are socialized in a transnational setting, specifically in relation to the socialization of democratic norms in the New Europe. The motivation for constructing such a framework has been a degree of frustration with the apparent inability of sociological/constructivist approaches using agent-level theories that have been borrowed from social psychology to put forward explanations for norm change that are valid across different cases. Furthermore, the motivation has been to provide a framework which can introduce a degree of order into the otherwise quite overwhelming number of possible micro-level explanatory tools available, once one opens up the 'black box' and looks at the domestic mass and elite level. From the brief application of the framework provided in this chapter, and more so from its application in subsequent chapters, it would seem that the framework offers grounds for optimism that it is indeed possible to utilize the tools available from social psychology and social learning in a way that can significantly help our understanding of the complex socialization process involved in the transfer of democratic norms in the new Europe.

### Notes

1. The framework is a general framework and can be used for analysing the transfer of a variety of norm sets between a variety of different norms transferring and norms receiving agents. See for example Flockhart (2003) in which the Europeanization process in Denmark is analysed. See also Flockhart (2004b) in which the socialization of democratic norms in post-war Germany is compared with the socialization of democratic norms in present-day Iraq.
2. There is a very large body of literature on Social Identity Theory. See, for example, Tajfel and Turner (1979, 1985); Tajfel (1978, 1982); Turner (1987); Worchel and Austin (1985); Herman and Kegley (1995).
3. There is a wealth of evidence from psychological experiments which suggests that individuals will go to great lengths in order to categorize their own group in more positive terms than other groups, even when there manifestly are no distinguishing features between groups that have been created completely at random (Tajfel, 1978).

4. The term 'people' is preferred because that denotes a we-feeling, which the term 'mass' does not.
5. The constellation of the two levels is not a country-specific constant, but will vary according to the norm set in question. For example, the constellation of state/elite and nation/people level in Denmark is split on the question of Europeanization, but fused on Human Rights.
6. I use the term 'political elites' according to Almond's (1950) definition which distinguishes between four types of foreign policy elites: political; administrative and bureaucratic; interest; and communication elites. However, as socialization will also be directed towards the military elite, I have adapted Almond's definition to also include the military elite.
7. I borrow the terms 'audience' and 'politicization' from Buzan et al. (1998).
8. Although Schimmelfennig's categorization is constructed in relation to enlargement of the EU, there is sufficient overlap between the two processes to adopt the same categorization.
9. In a bottom-up version of the model, out-groups 2 and 3 would have reversed priority, as the nation/people level would weigh heavier than the state/elite level. A more detailed presentation of the model can be found in Flockhart (2004c).
10. Article 10 of the Madrid Declaration on Euro-Atlantic Security and Co-operation 1997.
11. The choice of strategies available to the socializer is illustrated in Figure 2.1 by 'SI' (social influence) or 'P' (persuasion), whilst the number of socialization avenues open to the socializer is illustrated by the width of the arrows.
12. With the accession to both the EU and NATO as the key defining organizations for in-group membership, Hungary (and the other new members of NATO and EU) must be regarded as members (albeit novice ones) of the in-group.
13. The fact that only socializees that fit into out-group 1 are likely to display successful socialization is clearly a cause for concern in the case of the current attempt at democratic norms transfer in Iraq. See Flockhart (2004b).
14. The suggestion from the empirical research conducted so far seems to indicate that persuasion is most likely to take place in small seminar-like gatherings where a specific issue or problem is being discussed with the clear intended outcome being that what has been learned is incorporated into working practices at home. In fact this is precisely the kind of activity that organizations such as NATO, NATO-PA and CoE have many examples of, where according to Sonia Lucarelli (2002: 34) the numbers and levels of workshops and seminars within PfP are almost beyond imagination.
15. This observation was made in conversations with Slovakian members of parliament in the spring of 2002 at a NATO-PA Rose-Roth seminar. At the same occasion the message of the dire consequences of an inclusion of Vladimir Mečiar in the next government were driven home at every opportunity by 'in-group' members.

# Part II

# Promoting Ideas through International Organizations

# 3
# The UN, Democracy and Europe since 1945

*Sally Morphet*

This chapter describes how different groups of UN members worked within the UN system to promote the creation of two universal, democratic, legal sets of norms in regard to self-determination. Secondly, the chapter discusses if and how the different European groupings (and sometimes other groupings) were socialized into accepting these norms, in theory and practice, as well as occasionally acting as socializers themselves.

Two major human rights norms related to democracy within the UN system have been chosen for our discussion. The first human rights norm (cf. White, 2002: 173–96) constitutes the right of 'external' self-determination (the assertion of independence by a potential state and its possible recognition[1] and legitimization by a number of existing states). We shall examine how states came to ensure and accept that the legal right was as expressed in the 1960 General Assembly Declaration on Colonialism – 'applicable not only to peoples under colonial rule, but also to peoples subjected to alien subjugation, domination and exploitation' (Higgins, 1994: 115) – and we shall note that 'any attempt aimed at the partial or total disruption of the national unity and the territorial integrity of a country is incompatible with the purposes and principles of the Charter of the United Nations.' The discussion then continues by considering the legally binding right of self-determination and the way in the 1950s it was put into draft Article 1 of both legally binding human rights Covenants on Civil and Political Rights and Economic, Social and Cultural Rights (the ICCPR and the ICESCR) by Third World countries. These came into legal force in 1976. The Western European group of countries and the United States, under pressure from Third World countries, changed their views on the right of external self-determination in the UN during the 1950s and 1960s. However, their practice has not always agreed with their theory.

The second right, the right of 'internal' self-determination, was given its name at the CSCE (the Conference on Security and Co-operation in Europe) discussions in 1975. 'Internal' self-determination is a process in which individuals become able to determine their political status and pursue their economic, social and cultural development without destroying the territorial integrity of their state. The language used to draft what became Article 25 on democracy in the ICCPR, first agreed by the Human Rights Commission as early as 1953, resembles the 1948 Universal Declaration of Human Rights (UDHR) to a large extent.

The chapter also discusses how certain European states, as well as regional and sub-regional organizations, helped create democratic norms, became socializers of these norms and were socialized by these democratic norms themselves. It considers the 1950 Western European and the UDHR-influenced European Convention for the Protection of Human Rights and Fundamental Freedoms (ECHR), which came into force in 1953, and particularly its First Protocol of 1952, which covered free elections and came into force in 1954. This stated *inter alia* that the High Contracting Parties undertook to hold free elections at reasonable intervals. It continues by discussing the importance of ensuring compatibility between international and regional norms. Other important milestones for the European region were the growing acceptance by Western Europeans of the right of external self-determination as defined in the 1960 Declaration on Colonialism, besides the non-binding 1970 UN General Assembly Friendly Relations Declaration and the non-binding 1975 Helsinki Act (a source for the right of internal self-determination) which set up the CSCE – now the Organization for Security and Co-operation in Europe (OSCE). These had already been basically accepted by Eastern Europeans and initiated by Third World countries.

This provided the background for more *socialization* at the UN of these democratic norms on self-determination, particularly that of internal self-determination by a range of European and other countries just before and after the end of the Cold War, as can be seen in the documents put out by the UN Secretary-General in 1995/6. These were requested by states involved in Conferences on New or Restored Democracies, which had begun with a Conference in Manila in June 1988 (A/43/358, August 1988). Certain European countries were also involved, such as Romania in 1997 (A/52/334, September 1997). Meanwhile Poland, backed by the United States, hosted a meeting on the theme of Towards a Community of Democracies in 2000, which was followed up in South Korea in 2002. The meeting in South Korea was attended by most UN countries including most European countries. It must be noted that certain major Western European countries, such as Germany, have only accepted the right of external self-determination in theory but not, in all circumstances, in practice. As Baros (2001) has stated:

> As the Yugoslav crisis unravelled it became apparent that the *right* to self-determination in a non-colonial context could be brought into being by undemocratic means. Now the invocation of the principle could lead to the disintegration of a state, not to achieving independence from alien regimes, which was its original goal. The function of the principle has been completely reversed and, as a result, a new norm appears to have developed: the *principle of territorial disintegration.*[2] (Baros, 2001: 57)

## The UN Charter

The creation, subsequent legalization (in some cases) and socialization of democratic norms of self-determination can be traced back to the purposes and principles laid down in the UN Charter which came into force in October 1945, and which still remains the legal basis of world order. According to Article 103 of the Charter, the obligations of the Charter shall prevail in the event of a conflict between these obligations and their obligations under any other international agreement. The purposes and principles of the Charter include the adjustment or settlement of international disputes in conformity with the principles of justice and international law; to develop friendly relations among nations based on respect for the principle of equal rights and self-determination of peoples; to achieve international co-operation in solving international problems of an economic, social, cultural or humanitarian character, and in promoting and encouraging respect for human rights and for fundamental freedoms for all without distinction as to race, sex, language or religion. These were recognized under Article 55 as necessary for friendly relations among nations, besides being one of the basic objectives of the trusteeship system under Article 76c. The UN (Article 2.7) was not, however, to intervene in matters essentially within the domestic jurisdiction of any state but this principle should not prejudice the application of enforcement measures under Chapter VII. Furthermore, territorial integrity is upheld under Article 2.4, which states that 'all Members shall refrain in their international relations from the threat or use of force against the territorial integrity or political independence of any state'.

The overall importance of the UN Charter within the European region can be shown by noting the way it has been invoked in the case of three major European legal instruments. Firstly, the 1949 North Atlantic Treaty (NATO) states in its Article 1 that:

> The Parties undertake, as set forth in the Charter of the United Nations, to settle any international dispute in which they may be involved by peaceful means in such a manner that international peace and security and justice are not endangered, and to refrain in their international relations from the threat or use of force in any manner inconsistent with the purposes of the United Nations.

This was followed by the preamble to the 1957 Treaty of Rome establishing the European Economic Community, which states:

> INTENDING to confirm the solidarity which binds Europe and the overseas countries and desiring to ensure the development of their prosperity in accordance with the principles of the United Nations.

Thirdly, the Helsinki Act of 1975, which examined ten principles closely related to the UN Charter stated in its Declaration on Principles Guiding Relations between Participating States:

> *Reaffirming,* in conformity with their membership in the United Nations and in accordance with the purposes and principles of the United Nations, their full and active support for the United Nations and for the enhancement of its role and effectiveness in strengthening international peace and security and justice, and in promoting the solution of international problems, as well as the development of friendly relations and cooperation among States.

And even the UN Secretary-General's 1996 Agenda for Democratization notes in paragraph 8 that 'the founding purposes and principles of the United Nations are the very basis of the present reflection'.

## European groupings at the UN 1946–2004

Since the establishment of the UN in 1946, and particularly throughout the Cold War, inter-European relationships were dominated by divisions flowing from the superpower conflict and, in the context of Third World aspirations, by attitudes to colonialism. These divisions among European states at the UN lessened, but did not completely disappear in either case, as the Cold War ended in the early 1990s. Eastern and Western European negotiators of the UN Charter in 1945[3] included Belarus (then Byelorussia), Czechoslovakia, the Soviet Union, Ukraine and Yugoslavia,[4] Belgium, Denmark, France, Greece, Luxembourg, the Netherlands and Norway. They also included the United Kingdom, which was then part of the Commonwealth grouping and not a member of the Western European group.

Once the United Nations had begun working in 1946 it became necessary to decide which countries should provide the Presidents and Vice-Presidents of the General Assembly and its major committees as well as the non-permanent seats on the Security Council. One UN principle invoked was that of equitable geographical distribution. Countries worked with other countries to help ensure their election when necessary and, often, to pursue their political interests. The European countries in the UN apart from the United Kingdom were divided into Eastern (under the Soviet Union), Western and, occasionally, members of the Third World group. In 1957 the Commonwealth and Western Europe groups were supplanted by the Western European and Other States group (WEOG) and the Asian-African group. WEOG deals mainly with electoral problems: Australia, Canada, New Zealand are the Others and the United States has observer status.

Members of what was then the European Economic Community (EEC) normally take the political lead at the UN for Western Europe in New York though not in the Security Council.[5] EEC members became more powerful in 1973 when West Germany was admitted to the UN and the United Kingdom joined the EEC. The Eastern European group remained extant though less influential than during the Cold War. Belarus, Cyprus and Malta were members of the non-aligned group though both Cyprus and Malta joined the EU in 2004 and left the non-aligned. Serbia and Montenegro remains suspended from the non-aligned group.

## Human rights and democracy

The UN Charter's emphasis on the range of human rights (later defined as civil, political and economic, social and cultural in the two major 1976 Covenants) in its purposes and principles is helpful as certain human rights are closely related to the development of ideas of democracy, and human rights, though often ill-defined, have proved to be a major tool in the socialization of human rights norms for both states and citizens. David Beetham sensibly argues 'that human rights constitute an intrinsic part of democracy, because the guarantee of basic freedoms is a necessary condition for the people's voice to be effective in public affairs, and for popular control over government to be secured' (Beetham, 1999: 93–114). He also suggests that Western governments often overemphasize civil and political rights. He goes on to note that economic and social rights 'stand in a relation of *mutual dependency* with democracy' and that the defence of cultural rights in multicultural societies 'requires a *reevaluated conception* of democracy and its procedures, if equality of citizenship is to be realized and the political nation not to be broken apart' (Beetham, 1999: 114).

As Nigel White states:

> The institutionalization of democratic entitlement from abstract value to concrete individual right has occurred through the practice of UN organs, agencies and bodies set up under UN-sponsored treaties. This has occurred through the principle of self-determination, which has developed into a right belonging to a people, and also through the principle of individual human rights protection. (White, 2002: 177)

The legalization of this right helped ensure that the Covenants became legal instruments. The UN has, as White notes, also been able to promote human rights socialization through UN organs and agencies as well as bodies like the Human Rights Committee, which as a treaty body stands apart from the UN and monitors the reports (in this case on civil and political rights) presented at intervals by states which have ratified the treaty. Both these authors, it should be noted, are more concerned with internal rather than external self-determination.

## The Universal Declaration on Human Rights 1948

The first task of the UN Commission on Human Rights, which was set up in 1946, was to negotiate a bill of rights as called for by the US president in June 1945.[6] The draft Declaration was not a treaty or an international agreement and did not impose any legal obligations. 'It was rather a statement of basic principles of inalienable human rights setting up a common standard of achievements for all peoples and all nations.'[7] Interestingly the representative of Poland criticized the draft as it contained only one mention of the word 'democracy' and made no provision for limiting the application of the rights. The Soviet Union lamented that the Declaration did not include, firstly, a guarantee of basic freedoms for all, within the given constraints of the national sovereignty of states; a guarantee that human rights could be exercised with due regard to the particular economic, social and national circumstances prevailing in each country; or a definition of the duties of citizens to their country, their people and their state.

The Declaration was neither 'the brainchild' nor 'a favoured project of the Western powers' and it did not get unfailing Western support. Third World countries also contributed to the UDHR's drafting.[8] The December 1948 vote in the General Assembly resulted in 48 votes in favour, none against, and 8 abstentions, and was seen as a vote that showed up the differences between Western and Eastern European states. The Eastern Europeans – Belarus, Czechoslovakia, Poland, Ukraine, the Soviet Union plus Yugoslavia – abstained (the other two were Saudi Arabia and South Africa). Interestingly all these countries unanimously adopted both Articles 21 and 28 on separate individual votes, which were all closely related to democratic norms (Verdoodt, 1964: 198–209, 257–61).

Article 21 reads:

1. Everyone has the right to take part in the government of his country, directly or through freely chosen representatives.
2. Everyone has the right of equal access to public service in his country.
3. The will of the people shall be the basis of the authority of government; this will shall be expressed in periodic and genuine elections which shall be by universal and equal suffrage and shall be held by secret vote or by equivalent free voting procedures.

Article 28 states:

> Everyone is entitled to a social and international order in which the rights and freedoms set forth in this Declaration can be fully realized.

## Internal self-determination, 1953

The close interchange between the UDHR and the ECHR was shown in the ECHR'S preamble when it was opened for signature in November 1950. This noted that the UDHR aimed 'at securing the universal and effective recognition and observance of the Rights therein declared' and that 'being resolved as the governments of European countries which are like-minded and have a common heritage of political traditions, ideals, freedom and the rule of law, to take the first steps for the collective enforcement of certain of the rights stated in the Universal Declaration' (Preamble, ECHR).

This thinking was also behind the UN Human Rights Commission's vote to adopt seven new articles for the draft ICCPR in 1953 including one on elections. This, with minor exceptions, was similar to the final ICCPR Article 25. It states:

> Every citizen shall have the right and the opportunity, without any of the distinctions mentioned in article 2 and without unreasonable restrictions:
>
> a. To take part in the conduct of public affairs, directly or through freely chosen representatives
> b. To vote and to be elected at genuine periodic elections which shall be by universal and equal suffrage and shall be held by secret ballot, guaranteeing the free expression of the will of the electors
> c. To have access, on general terms of equality, to public service in his country.

It joined Article 3 of the First Protocol of the ECHR agreed in 1952 of the ECHR. The Protocol's Article 3 states that:

> The High Contracting Parties undertake to hold free elections at reasonable intervals by secret ballot, under conditions which will ensure the free expression of the opinion of the people in the choice of the legislature.

Both these instruments were legally binding once in force and both were influenced by the UDHR. The ICCPR article on democracy was adopted by the General Assembly in 1961 and finally came into force in 1976. These provisions were almost universally acceptable in the context of 'internal' self-determination.

## Negotiation on the right of self-determination

The next task in creating the legal norm of external self-determination was to make the UDHR into two legally binding Covenants, one on civil and political rights and one on economic, social and cultural rights. This involved discussion of the principle and the right of self-determination and what these meant. The UN Charter notes (Article 1.2) that one purpose of the UN is 'to develop friendly relations among nations based on respect for the principle of equal rights and self-determination of peoples'. The principle of self-determination is also mentioned in Article 55 on international economic and social co-operation. The right of self-determination is legally binding: the principle is not.

The major debate[9] between Western countries, the Eastern bloc and the Third World on the incorporation of the articles in the UDHR into a legal framework, began in 1949. This constituted a further step in the process of the creation of the norm and its socialization both within and outside Europe. Third World countries, led by representatives of Afghanistan and Saudi Arabia, took the lead in pressing for a common Article 1 in both the draft Covenants, reading in part:

> All peoples have the right of self-determination. By virtue of that right they freely determine their political status and freely pursue their economic, social and cultural development.

The article on self-determination became the focus of difference. The three groups were eventually able to agree that external self-determination could be considered as 'the right to freedom from hegemony by other states' or the act by which a people determines its future international status and liberates itself from 'alien rule', and that the right of self-determination did not imply the right of secession (Morphet, 1989: 68). The reference to secession is extremely important. Third World countries and others were committed to the territorial integrity of states. As is well known, major problems were set in train in the 1990s with the German recognition of Slovenia and Croatia (Goulding, 2002: 291–321), which were then constituent parts of Yugoslavia. This did not take into account UN Charter Article 2.4 on territorial integrity and avoided invoking the required constitutional procedures. As Crawford (2001: 63) has noted 'there are strong systematic constraints favoring the principle of territorial integrity, which the lessons of the dissolution of the Soviet Union and the former Yugoslavia have powerfully reinforced'.

The Asian-African's Bandung Declaration of April 1955 was also very influential. It marked a major stage in the development and in the socialization of the non-aligned movement after it was set up in 1961. The Declaration 'declared its full support of the fundamental principles of human rights as a common standard of achievement for all peoples and all nations' thus agreeing with the Western Europeans on human rights in general. But the Declaration took a stronger stand on the right of self-determination than most Western Europeans then did stating 'its full support of the principle of self-determination of peoples and nations as set forth in the Charter of the United Nations and took note of the United Nations resolutions on the right of peoples and nations to self-determination, which is a prerequisite of the full enjoyment of all fundamental human rights'.

Bandung clearly showed the Asian-African concern to move the debate on from the question of the *principle* of self-determination to the *right* of self-determination. The Asian-African convenors of the conference were Burma, Ceylon, India, Indonesia and Pakistan.[10] The emotional feelings underlying the debate were well expressed by the Saudi Arabian representative, Mr Baroody, in the General Assembly Third Committee in 1955.

> Regardless of what the constitutional position might be, there remained one fact which could not be ignored: the colonial peoples had awakened to consciousness of their rights, particularly the right of self-determination. They believed as the Universal Declaration of Human Rights entitled them to do, that like all other men they had the right to live in freedom and dignity. The right to decide their own destinies was for them not only a means of putting an end to the subordinate status in which they had been kept, but also the prerequisite for the free development of the personality of each individual member of the population. (Morphet, 1989: 75)

The vote (33 for, 12 against, 13 abstaining) on the final text of Article 1 in the Third Committee of the General Assembly in November 1955, not surprisingly, showed differences between European countries. The Eastern Europeans who voted in favour were Belarus, Czechoslovakia, Poland, the Soviet Union, Ukraine and Yugoslavia. They were joined by the somewhat maverick Greece. Belgium, France, Luxembourg, Netherlands, Norway, Sweden, Turkey and the United Kingdom voted against. Denmark and Iceland abstained. These Western countries were, *inter alia*, concerned that external self-determination could be used outside the colonial context to suggest (both in theory and practice) that minorities could secede or existing and decolonized states should be broken up.

## The theory and practice of decolonization 1956–1960

The UN had, meanwhile, often through the work of the Trusteeship Council, become involved in monitoring aspects of decolonization. This helped embed the norms of external and internal self-determination in colonies, other dependent territories and countries within the UN system. A UN-organized plebiscite, the first ever to be held in a trust territory, was held in British Togoland in 1956 to determine whether the people desired union with the neighbouring Gold Coast, which was about to gain independence. As the UN Secretary-General noted in 1995 in a document entitled 'Support by the United Nations System of the Efforts of Governments to Promote and Consolidate New or Restored Democracies' (A/50/332, August 1995, 3):

> [I]n the course of the past four decades from Togoland in 1956 to Eritrea in 1993 – the United Nations has observed and supervised over 30 plebiscites, referenda, elections and other acts of self-determination, many of them sponsored by the Trusteeship Council.

Third World concern with the creation and sometimes socialization of the norm of external self-determination in order to help bring colonialism to an end was achieved through one seminal General Assembly resolution in 1960. The sponsors succeeded in getting almost complete agreement on their views on the right to external self-determination as a human rights issue, including a condemnation of secession, in the General Assembly from the Eastern bloc as well as WEOG. The 1960 'Declaration on the granting of independence to colonial countries and peoples' was passed by 89 for, 0 against, 9 abstaining, including Belgium, France, Portugal Spain, the United Kingdom and the United States. These countries were slowly being socialized on this topic, as they now abstained rather than voted against the draft resolution.

The main points of the Declaration (GAR 1514(XV)) which embraced a definition of external self-determination and the importance of a state's territorial integrity, were that:

1. The subjection of peoples to alien subjugation, domination and exploitation constitutes a denial of fundamental human rights, is contrary to the Charter of the United Nations and is an impediment to the promotion of world peace and co-operation.
2. All peoples have the right to self-determination; by virtue of that right they freely determine their political status and freely pursue their economic, social and cultural development ...
3. Any attempt aimed at the partial or total disruption of the national unity and the territorial integrity of a country is incompatible with the purposes and principles of the Charter of the United Nations ...

## The Friendly Relations Declaration 1970

Many Western European states finally showed that they could accept the legal norm of the right of external self-determination in the late 1960s when they signed both the human rights covenants (each contains an identical Article 1 which states *inter alia* 'All peoples have the right of self-determination'). Sweden and Italy signed them in 1967; Belgium, Denmark, Germany, Iceland, New Zealand, Norway and the United Kingdom in 1968; and the Netherlands in 1969; and all ratified them later. The Eastern Europeans who signed them in the 1960s were Poland in 1967; Belarus, Bulgaria, Mongolia, Romania, the Soviet Union and the Ukraine in 1968; and Hungary in 1969.

Changing Western attitudes to this norm could also be seen in the debate leading to the adoption without a vote by the General Assembly in 1970 on Principles of International Law concerning Friendly Relations and Co-operation among States. Seven principles were considered including equal rights and self-determination of peoples. This eventually noted in its first paragraph:

> By virtue of the principle of equal rights and self-determination of peoples enshrined in the Charter of the United Nations, all peoples have the right freely to determine, without external interference, their political status and to pursue their economic, social and cultural development, and every State has the duty to respect this right in accordance with the provisions of the Charter.

As the United Kingdom lawyer, Ian Sinclair, noted:

> [T]here can be little doubt that [the Declaration] represents a strenuous effort to find as much common ground as possible between States representing various regional and ideological groups in the United Nations on a whole series of contested issues of international law. That the common ground is limited may be admitted; that it conceals many pitfalls may also be conceded; but that some progress has been made in reconciling differences of approach emerges from a comparison of the final text of the Declaration with the proposals originally tabled. (Sinclair, 1976: 138)

## The Euro-Atlantic partnership and Helsinki 1975

The Final Act of the CSCE was signed by thirty-five delegations in August 1975. All European states, including the Holy See and both

Germanies, were signatories with the exception of Albania and Andorra. Canada and the United States were also represented. Western countries and the European non-aligned often worked together in the negotiations, as did the EC nine, although there were divisions among countries belonging to NATO. However, as one of the British books of documents on this subject noted, 'The EC Nine and the NATO Fifteen were more obviously at one when it came to dealing with the contents of Basket III which dealt with human rights'.[11] A new pan-European spirit had become possible which included a potential Euro-Atlantic partnership.

The Final Act of the Conference looked at ten principles guiding relations between participating states and related to the UN Charter. It dwelt on two in the context of rights: equal rights and self-determination of peoples and respect for human rights and fundamental freedoms, including the freedom of thought, conscience, religion or belief. The first and second paragraphs of the former read as follows:

> The participating States will respect the equal rights of peoples and their right to self-determination, acting at all times in conformity with the purposes and principles of the Charter of the United Nations and with the relevant norms of international law, including those relating to territorial integrity of States. By virtue of the principle of equal rights and self-determination of peoples, all peoples always have the right, in full freedom, to determine when and as they wish, their internal and external political status, without external interference, and to pursue as they wish their political, economic, social and cultural development.

The explicit reference to internal political status was of particular interest. Some non-aligned countries considered that internal self-determination was both an individual and a collective right. But they did not consider that either it or the external right included the right to secession (Morphet, 1989: 78–9; Crawford, 2001).

The British government's account of the Conference and its antecedents stated that drafting of the principle on self-determination 'lasted for some two months, not least because of initial Soviet reluctance to accept that the principle applied to conditions in Europe as well as the rest of the world and that it did not cease to be operative when a particular type of regime had been instituted' (*Selected Documents*, 1977: 21). It points out that the drafting of the other main principle on human rights was 'of major importance to Western, neutral and non-aligned participants' (*Selected Documents*, 1977: 21). The non-aligned participants were the European non-aligned, then Yugoslavia, Cyprus and Malta. The neutrals were Austria, Finland, Liechtenstein, San Marino, Sweden and Switzerland.

The United Kingdom Foreign Secretary, Mr Callaghan, noted in July 1975: 'The Declaration of Principles conforms with the Charter of the United Nations and the United Nations Declaration on Friendly Relations. It amounts to a political code of good behaviour, drafted with an eye to Europe but applicable throughout the world'.[12] He went on to suggest that the emphasis on the rights of the individual throughout the Declaration was the result of hard-fought negotiation. This was useful old-style thinking about the UN. Human rights, including the right of self-determination, however, remained crucial and appealing concepts. There remained a spectrum under which many Western states and many of their citizens took civil and political rights seriously. However, it must be said that it was still the case that many others were more concerned with economic, social and cultural rights. Most European countries were now agreed on the norm of the right of self-determination of states.

## The Human Rights Covenants come into force, 1976

The ability of the CSCE participants to negotiate more successfully on human rights issues in the 1970s was partially due to the fact that both the major human rights covenants (the ICCPR and ICESCR) with their identical Article 1 on the right of external self-determination and Article 25 of the ICCPR relating to internal self-determination were just about to come into force. As already noted, Article 25 of the ICCPR was closely related to the UDHR and Article 3 of the First Protocol (1954) of the ECHR. Both were legally binding unlike the useful 1990 Document of the Copenhagen Meeting of the Conference on the Human Dimension of the CSCE on International Standards of Elections. The states then making up the European Union were normally parties to both the ECHR and the ICCPR. All European states, with the exception of Andorra (not a party to the ICESCR), Belarus (not a party to the ECHR) and the Holy See (not a party to any).

Both the ICCPR and the ICESCR have a monitoring system. The Human Rights Committee, composed of representatives of UN states from all geographical regions, looks after the ICCPR and discusses its implementation with states that have ratified the Covenant. It also puts out General Comments on different articles in the ICCPR. Its 1984

Comment on Article 1 asserts *inter alia* that all peoples have the right of self-determination and notes that:

> The right of self-determination is of particular importance because its realization is an essential condition for the effective guarantee and observance of individual human rights and for the promotion and strengthening of those rights.

It suggested that 'States parties should describe the constitutional and political processes which in practice allow the exercise of this right.'[13]

The Human Rights Committee also put out a Comment on Article 25 in 1996, the same year as the UN Secretary-General, Boutros-Ghali put out his Agenda for Democratization. This stated in part:

1. Article 25 of the Covenant recognizes and protects the right of every citizen to take part in the conduct of public affairs, the right to vote and be elected and the right to have access to public service. Whatever form of constitution or government is in force, the Covenant requires States to adopt such legislative and other measures as may be necessary to ensure that citizens have an effective opportunity to enjoy the rights it protects. Article 25 lies at the core of democratic government based on the consent of the people and in conformity with the principles of the Covenant.
2. The rights under article 25 are related to, but distinct from, the right of peoples to self-determination ... Article 25 deals with the right of individuals to participate in those processes which constitute the conduct of public affairs.

The relationship of the ICCPR with democratic norms is well brought out by this Comment on Article 25.

## Europe and the end of the Cold War

Eleven of the nineteen European countries, which joined the UN from 1990 onwards, came as a consequence of the break-up of the Soviet Union, Yugoslavia and Czechoslovakia. Russia remained a Permanent Member of the Security Council but lost Estonia, Latvia, Lithuania, Armenia, Azerbaijan, Georgia and Moldova (besides Ukraine and Belarus which had been original members of the UN even though completely tied to the Soviet Union). Russia's Asian loss comprised Kazakhstan, Kyrgyzstan, Tajikistan, Turkmenistan and Uzbekistan. The break-up of

Yugoslavia brought Bosnia, Croatia, The Former Yugoslav Republic of Macedonia and Slovenia into the UN to be followed eventually by a shrunken Serbia and Montenegro (formerly Yugoslavia). The status of Kosovo, still under UN transitional administration in January 2004, remains to be determined. Is it to become part of Albania or to remain part of Serbia and Montenegro? The break-up of Czechoslovakia resulted in separate UN membership of two new states, the Czech Republic and Slovakia.

These changes were legally and constitutionally acceptable if the different parties agreed upon them. In former Yugoslavia, however, the right of self-determination was linked by certain Western European states to a right of secession. Others considered that 'Yugoslavia as a whole was dissolving into its constituent entities' (Crawford, 2001: 54).

As Baros has noted:

> [A] regional approach in former Yugoslavia even further complicated the position in current international law regarding the application of the two principles (territorial integrity and the right of self-determination) in a non-colonial context. The way the Macedonian conflict was dealt with diminishes the relevance of Article 51 of the UN Charter because there is no automatic presumption that states have the right to defend themselves and preserve their territorial integrity. (Baros, 2003: 72)

Baros went on to suggest: 'a regional setting allowed Germany to force a premature recognition of the former federal units (Slovenia and Croatia, and then Bosnia and Herzegovina), which exacerbated the situation (in the case of Bosnia and Herzegovina it directly led to the war) …' (Baros, 2003: 78). As such one must conclude that the self-determination norm was not socialized in practice.

Many of the countries which belonged to the UN Eastern European group hoped to join WEOG after the ending of the Cold War. They were surprised to find that many WEOG members did not want this to take place as it would have meant that the electoral chances of WEOG's members within the UN system would be diminished. The Eastern European group still exists. Estonia tried, without success, to join WEOG: it remains in the Eastern European group. The WEOG grouping at the UN is likely to be modified by the enlargement of the European Union in 2004 from 15 to 25, leaving the interesting question of how countries in an enlarged WEOG and/or the EU will work together in New York and Geneva.

## Europe, elections, democracy and the UN

As the Cold War began to ebb away and the UN climate started to change, more space appeared for UN members to think more about electoral norms and democracies. The first Conference on New or Restored Democracies was held in the Philippines as early as June 1988 (A/43/358, August 1988). Its Declaration noted the participants' commitment to human rights, freedom and justice besides trying to eradicate poverty. The European countries present were Greece, Portugal and Spain. Other conferences followed with major European participation such as in Nicaragua in 1994, where the UN Secretary-General was asked to study how the UN system could support the new democracies. The Secretary-General produced two reports in 1995 and 1996 and followed these up with the 1996 Agenda for Democratization (A/50/332 and Corr.1; A/51/512 and A/51/761). As he notes:

> For all States, democratization at the international level has become an indispensable mechanism for global problem-solving in a way that is accountable and acceptable to all and with the participation of all concerned. Dominance by one country or group of countries must over time evolve into a democratic international system in which all countries can participate, along with new non-State actors involved in international affairs. (*An Agenda for Democratization*, 1996: 28)

Democracy of sorts was by then fairly entrenched in a wide range of states after what has been called the 'third wave' of democratization beginning with the overthrow of Salazar in Portugal in 1974. In 1997 researchers found 'only seven countries (out of 212 independent states and related territories) which did not hold direct elections for their legislatures, and of those 98 were classified as "free" on the basis of political rights and civil liberties ...' (Reilly and Reynolds, 1999: 9).

The changing post-Cold War climate meant that certain fears about the use of Article 2(7) of the UN Charter on domestic intervention in the affairs of states were somewhat allayed. This allowed the 'first UN electoral observer mission ever to monitor elections in an *independent country*' (Nicaragua) (Morphet, 1993: 217) in February 1990. These sorts of subjects were now of more interest to European states, especially to those in the Eastern European group, after the end of the Cold War.

A further General Assembly resolution in 1991 (GAR 46/137) designated a focal point for electoral assistance in the Secretary-General's office (Ludwig, 2001). It was passed by 134 votes for, 4 votes against, 13 abstaining. All the European states voted for the resolution as did the non-aligned majority. However, fears about pressure from the international community were reflected in the actions of Cuba – a radical non-aligned state. Cuba's draft resolution was entitled 'Respect for the principles of national sovereignty and non-interference in the internal affairs of States in their electoral processes'. It mentioned both the 1960 Declaration on Colonialism and the Friendly Relations Declaration. It also reaffirmed 'that it is the concern solely of peoples to determine methods and to establish institutions regarding the electoral process, as well as to determine the ways for its implementation according to their constitution and national legislation ...' This was passed by 102 for, 40 against, 13 abstaining, as GAR 46/130. Thirty European states voted against the resolution as did the United States. Furthermore, Poland hosted a meeting on the different theme of 'Towards a Community of Democracies in 2000', which had strong support from the United States. This meeting was attended by around 40 European countries including countries set up from parts of the former Soviet Union, Eastern and Western Europe plus the European non-aligned – Malta and Cyprus – as well as many others. A second conference in this series was held in South Korea in 2002.

## Conclusion

As has been demonstrated in this chapter, Western Europeans have not always been in the forefront of countries taking action over the enshrining of the major democratic norms of external self-determination in the legally binding Covenants, the ICCPR and ICESCR. They moved slowly in the 1940s and 1950s to accept Third World pressure on moving self-determination from a principle to a legal right. Most countries (not including the United States and some Western Europeans) came to accept it (at least partially) by voting for the 1960 Declaration on Colonialism, which stressed the importance of territorial integrity. These countries and some others later showed they were prepared to change their views by their ratification of the two Covenants as well as their subsequent co-operation with their monitoring Committees. Nearly all the Western Europeans at the United Nations have become parties to the ICCPR, which came into force in 1976 and asserts with the ICESCR the legal right of self-determination. The United States finally ratified the ICCPR in 1992 although it is not a party to the ICESCR. This worked in theory. Germany's premature recognition of certain former federal units of Yugoslavia showed that practice could sometimes be ignored.

The Eastern Europeans abstained on the 1948 vote agreeing the UDHR. Nevertheless they were not completely opposed to the Universal Declaration: indeed, they voted with all other states at the UN for its Article 21 setting out democratic norms. These norms, which are related to internal self-determination, have been socialized somewhat easily through the UDHR, the first Protocol of the ECHR and the ICCPR. The different European groups have often voted together on UN resolutions exploring aspects of democratization, which were passed in the General Assembly from 1988 onwards. Furthermore, the Eastern Europeans were more prepared than the Western Europeans to negotiate with Third World countries to put the right of self-determination into both draft Covenants in the 1950s. All Eastern Europeans are now parties to the ICCPR and ICESCR and accept the legal right of self-determination.

Thinking about self-determination norms at the UN did bring more agreement (and socialization) among the different UN groups. All members were able to agree on the 1970 UN Friendly Relations Declaration and, in a related but non-UN arena, on setting up the CSCE in 1975. This was, of course, more Euro-Atlantic, as the United States was a participant. The question that has faced certain European states since the coming into force of both the ICCPR and the ICESCR (1976) has been to find a way of making the norms work well in practice. This has not always been achieved successfully.

## Notes

1. The normal criteria the British government has applied for the recognition of a state is that it should have, and seem likely to continue to have, a clearly defined territory with a population, a government who are able by themselves to exercise effective control of that territory, and independence in their external relations. Written answer, House of Commons, 16 November 1989.
2. The ramifications of the complex right of self-determination in international law including the Canadian Supreme Court's view that the rights of groups within the state do not extend to secession are usefully discussed by Crawford (2001).
3. Poland was not among them although it became the 51st original member state.
4. Yugoslavia was to leave the Eastern bloc politically in 1948.
5. See Morphet (2000).
6. See UN, *Yearbook* (1948/49: 525–37).

7. Opinion of the US Chairman of the Commission, Eleanor Roosevelt, UN *Yearbook* (1948/49: 527).
8. See Waltz (2002).
9. See Morphet (1989). Other useful sources are: Higgins (1994: 111–28); White (2002: 173–96); Beetham (1999) and Crawford (2001). See also Falk (2001) and Joyner (1999).
10. The participants were Afghanistan, Cambodia, China (People's Republic), Egypt, Ethiopia, the Gold Coast, Iran, Iraq, Japan, Jordan, Laos, Lebanon, Liberia, Libya, Nepal, the Philippines, Saudi Arabia, the Sudan, Syria, Thailand, Turkey, the Democratic Republic of (North) Vietnam, the State of Vietnam and Yemen.
11. See Documents on British Policy Overseas, Series III, Volume II, Conference on Security and Cooperation in Europe, 1972, 1975, HMSO (1997: xv).
12. See Documents on British Policy Overseas, Series III, Volume II, Conference on Security and Cooperation in Europe, 1972, 1975, HMSO (1997: xv).
13. Compilation of General Comments and General Recommendations adopted by Human Rights Treaty Bodies, HRI/Gen/1/Rev.3, 15 August 1997.

# 4
# NATO and the European System of Liberal-Democratic Security Communities

*Sonia Lucarelli*

Since 1990, the organizations of the so-called European Security Architecture have paid unprecedented attention to the development of democratic institutions in the neighbouring European area. The Conference on Security and Co-operation in Europe (CSCE later OSCE) was the first to set an explicit link between democracy-building and security, developing innovative security community-building processes and practices according to a new comprehensive concept of security within which the basic principles of liberal democracy apply (Adler, 1997, 1998; Flynn and Farrell, 1999). Other organizations followed and enacted a series of policies aimed at creating security and stability in the neighbouring Central and Eastern European Countries (CEECs) by means of democracy-building practices. In other words, acting as if they were rediscovering the theory of democratic peace of Kantian memory, all institutions of the so-called European Security Architecture responded to the possibly destabilizing effects of the collapse of Communism by adopting *mutandis mutatis*, Immanuel Kant's recipe for 'Perpetual Peace' (Kant, 1795/1991): domestic democracy, international *foedus* of democratic countries and the development of cosmopolitan law.

The North Atlantic Treaty Organization (NATO) followed a similar track and responded to its post-Cold War security concerns by engaging in political implementation of the shared values and norms of liberal-democracy that have always been recognized as crucial for the existence of the transatlantic security community (Deutsch et al., 1957). In particular, it redefined its own role and security concept along the lines of a democratic security community, and then initiated a set of policies with the aim of increasing security through the diffusion of some of the core norms of liberal-democracy in the CEECs. The immediate post-Cold War challenges that NATO was trying to address through this new overall strategy had to do with both a legitimizing discourse for NATO's maintenance after the bipolar structure within which NATO had been conceived and developed, and the actual stabilization of the former Soviet bloc. The instruments used to reach these purposes – such as democracy-building, partnership and, later, enlargement – were by no means obvious choices. As a matter of fact, although the link between democracy and peace seems to be obvious now, it might be useful to recall that from the 1960s to the mid-1980s there was a dominant consensus in the West that security interests could be best guaranteed by authoritarian regimes which could provide political stability and openness to a capitalist-like economy (Zielonka, 2001, and further references therein). In other words NATO has certainly undergone a major change as regards what constitutes the core norms and defining characteristics of its own identity[1] and its basic ideational assumptions regarding best security-building practices.

Besides the basic aims that NATO was trying to satisfy when launching the security-through-democracy discourse and policies, the ultimate effect of its behaviour has been to *de facto* contribute to creating the conditions for an expansion of the so-called transatlantic security community and the development of a 'system of democratic security communities': that is, an environment in which states have developed communities characterized by (1) shared identities, values and meanings provided by liberal-democratic values, (2) many-sided and direct relations amongst themselves, (3) both of which eventually produce diffused reciprocity and dependable expectations of peaceful change.[2] These communities/groups comprise a system in that they share characteristics, but differ in terms of both maturity (degree of consolidation)[3] and tightness (degree of shared we-feeling).[4] There is not just the mature and tightly coupled security community represented by EU member states, but there are also the less mature and tightly coupled security communities represented by the states that in the 1990s were negotiating for NATO membership, those applying for NATO membership but with little possibility of entrance in the medium term and, finally, the larger circle of states including those involved in the Partnership for Peace (PfP) programme but not actually applying for membership such as Russia, Ukraine and Belarus.

Adopting the terminology proposed in this volume, we can claim that the members of the 'in-group' (in our specific case, NATO member states) have pushed both indirectly by virtue of NATO's attractiveness, and directly by virtue of NATO's policies of norms transfer, for the neighbouring countries to develop a shared liberal-democratic norm set. The different ability in absorbing those norms and the specific interactive practice NATO has adopted with the different states has given rise to varying results in the different layers of out-groups in relation to the members of the in-group.

This chapter concentrates on NATO's contribution to the development of such a system of democratic security communities. It starts by presenting an analysis of NATO's immediate reaction to the end of the Cold War and its effort to respond to the challenges represented by this international breaking point, which in social constructivist terms might be seen as a critical juncture or destabilizing shock, leading to an ideational vacuum both in relation to the organization's own *raison d'être* but certainly also in relation to its future relations with its former opponents. The organization's new-found attention to democracy and its promotion is here regarded as a response to such an ideational crisis and identity/legitimization problem. The chapter then presents a review of the main policies and practices undertaken by NATO that have contributed to the development of the conditions for the development of a system of democratic security communities in a much larger part of Europe than that covered during the Cold War. It is claimed that NATO has contributed to creating the conditions for democratic security communities in Europe both for *what it is* (its international identity as it is perceived by itself and by external actors) and for *what it does* (policies and communicative practices). The two roles have coexisted since the early 1990s, but the first one was predominant in the immediate aftermath of the Cold War. Finally, the chapter summarizes the instruments, targets and style of NATO's attempt at norms transfer in CEECs, and ends by concluding on NATO's successes and failures in democratic norms transfer in Central and Eastern Europe.

## A narrative reconstruction of NATO's post-Cold War identity

Since 1990, NATO documents such as the London Declaration on East–West Co-operation (July 1990), the Rome Declaration on Peace and Co-operation, those concerning the definition of a New Alliance's Strategic Concept (November 1991 and then April 1999), as well as those launching the North Atlantic Co-operation Council (NACC, December 1991), and the Partnership for Peace initiative (December 1994) have identified new security threats and the possible responses that NATO could offer.[5] These documents include in the definition of both security threats and security strategies a direct reference to the concept of democracy, to related concepts such as 'transparency' or 'respect of rules', and to concepts related to '*liberal* democracy' such as 'respect of human rights'.

NATO's security concepts before 1991 were not made public and so a comparison between those concepts developed before and after 1991 is not possible. However, rather than containing specific references to democratic principles, documents signed before this date, and in particular the Washington Treaty, reveal a rather general claim to common democratic values among the Allies:

> The Parties to this Treaty ... reaffirm their faith in the purposes and principles of the Charter of the United Nations and their desire to live in peace with all peoples and all governments.
>
> They are *determined to safeguard the freedom, common heritage and civilization of their peoples, founded on the principles of democracy, individual liberty and the rule of law.* They seek to promote stability and well-being in the North Atlantic area. (North Atlantic Treaty, 1949, Preamble. Emphasis added)

However, it must be said that, despite the formulations in the North Atlantic Treaty, NATO's actual record of democracy-defence was very low, if not non-existent, during its first fifty years. In contrast, post-Cold War security documents and practice expose a growing link between security and the development of democracy.

The New Strategic Concept of 1991 defined the new threats to security in Europe and NATO's role in it. The document presents a wide concept of security and a renewed role for the organization in the changed scenario, with the reaffirmation of Article V collective security tasks but also with a broader role in the construction of security in Europe:

> In contrast with the predominant threat of the past, the risks to Allied security that remain are multi-faceted in nature and multi-directional ... [and they are most] likely to result from ... the adverse consequences of instabilities that may arise from the serious economic, social and political difficulties, including ethnic rivalries and territorial disputes, which are faced by many countries in Central and Eastern Europe ... To achieve its essential purpose [to provide security in Europe], the Alliance performs the following fundamental security tasks: (i) to provide one of the indispensable foundations for a *stable security environment in Europe, based on the growth of democratic*

*institutions and commitment to the peaceful resolution of disputes* ... (The Alliance's New Strategic Concept, 1991. Emphasis added)

Attention to the respect for human rights and to democratic national institutions was restated with the establishment of the North Atlantic Co-operation Council (NACC) in December 1991. This was the culmination of a process of increased co-operation with the former Soviet bloc of Europe.[6] A further step was represented by the launch of the Partnership for Peace in 1994, in which participating partners started to be engaged in concrete co-operation activities, in order to increase transparency, ensuring democratic control of the armed forces, maintaining a capability to contribute to UN or CSCE operations, strengthening the capability of the participants for undertaking peacekeeping and humanitarian operations and enhancing the compatibility of the partners' and the allies' military forces (*PfP Invitation*, NAC, 10–11/1/1994, Brussels). The subscribing state would sign a Framework Document in which it accepts to commit itself to the preservation of a democratic society; to respect obligations undertaken in the field of arms control; to respect the principles of international law, of the UN Charter, the Universal Declaration on Human Rights and all CSCE/ OSCE documents. In many ways PfP invited partner countries to engage in self-categorization, as it asked applicants to submit a Presentation Document in which they should state their desired scope and level of participation in co-operation activities with NATO, as well as the necessary steps to achieve the political goals of the partnership.

Building upon the success of NACC and PfP, the Foreign Ministers of the Allied and Co-operation countries, meeting in Sintra, Portugal in May 1997, inaugurated the Euro-Atlantic Partnership Council (EAPC). The aim was to raise political and military co-operation among the participant countries to a new qualitative level. In the EAPC Basic Document NATO members, in close co-operation with partner states, reaffirmed their joint commitment to strengthening and extending peace and stability in the Euro-Atlantic area and to co-operating to this end on the basis of shared values and principles, notably those set out in the PfP Framework Document. Furthermore, in view of the enlargement of the organization, the NATO Participation Action Plan of 1994 stated that 'participants in the Partnership for peace should be invited to become full NATO members if they ... remain committed to protecting the rights of all their citizens ...' because – as clarified by the NATO Enlargement Facilitation Act of 1996 – 'protection and promotion of human rights is an integral part of genuine security'. As is clearly evident in the NATO Enlargement Facilitation Act, conditionality became an integral part of NATO enlargement. The document stated that:

> [I]n evaluating requests for membership in NATO, the human rights record of the emerging democracies in Central and Eastern Europe should be evaluated according to their commitment to fulfil in good faith the human rights obligations of the Charter of the United Nations, the principles of the Universal Declaration on Human Rights, and the Helsinki Final Act. (NATO Enlargement Facilitation Act, 1996)

Finally, in 1999 the Alliance's Security Concept implicitly reserved the possibility of entering the Alliance only to *democratic* states.[7] The Membership Action Plan (MAP), adopted at the same Washington Summit on April 1999, further clarified that:

> Future members must conform to basic principles ... such as democracy, individual liberty ... [and] would also be expected: (a) to settle their international disputes by peaceful means; [and] (b) to demonstrate commitment to the rule of law and human rights. (Membership Action Plan, 1999)

Meanwhile, in the same years of NATO's transformation, it is interesting to observe that the Clinton Administration also seemed to rediscover the Wilsonian tradition. Clinton put 'democracy-export' high up on the foreign policy agenda of the post-Cold War United States (Cox, 2000) and founded the legacy of NATO's enlargement on extending Western European liberal-democratic ties. In October 1995, he declared:

> NATO's success has involved promoting security interests, advancing values, supporting democracy and economic opportunity. We have literally created a community of shared values and interests, as well as an alliance for common defense. Now, the new democracies of Central and Eastern Europe and the former Soviet Union want to be part of enlarging the circle of common purpose, and in doing so, increasing our own security. (Remarks by the President at the Harry S. Truman Library Institute 'Legacy of Leadership Dinner', 25 October 1995)

It appears clear from the brief reconstruction above that drawing a direct link between security and liberal-democratic institutions and norms was a fundamental part of NATO's transformation in the 1990s. The organization clearly responded with this formula to the two major threats it faced in the aftermath of the post-Cold War: the possible end of its *raison d'être* after the collapse of its historical enemy, and instability, if not violent conflicts, in the neighbouring former Eastern bloc.

The core values already recognized by Karl Deutsch in the 1950s as a basic glue of the transatlantic community provided the conceptual framework within which security, and NATO's role in it, could be redefined in the changed international circumstances. The choice among the possible alternative solutions provided was smoothed by the core values of the community of reference which made alternative solutions (dissolution and return to an *ex ante* situation; construction of a new enemy – as it was suggested in the early 1990s) unacceptable or dysfunctional with respect to the core problem of redefining the international identity of the organization so as to maintain international legitimacy.

Following the New Security Concept of 1991 and its generic calls for the development of democracy as a means towards security in the early 1990s, were concrete steps towards the progressive definition of a new role for NATO that not only reiterated the importance of democracy and human rights in public documents, but made actual and direct demands for proven transition towards democracy for the states applying for a closer partnership with the organization. Furthermore, and most of all, NATO progressively defined itself as a security provider far beyond Article V tasks (collective defence) (Yost, 1998). The progressive definition of a role for NATO in the enforcement of UN resolutions in the Balkan conflicts is part of the same evolving role for NATO. The same applies to the organization's tasks in the implementation of the Dayton peace agreement in Bosnia-Herzegovina and peace-enforcement in Kosovo. The Partnership for Peace machine, however, represented the core of NATO's response to new challenges and *the* major step towards a new type of organization that is now going to face a new significant shift with the decisions taken at the Prague Atlantic Council in November 2002 to proceed with the second post-Cold War enlargement.[8]

The narrative reconstruction of NATO's identity in the post-Cold War period along the lines of a 'democratic security community' rather than a collective defence club affected not just what NATO stated in its documents, but also what was demanded for the new partners. Most of all, it contributed to defining the *boundaries of appropriateness*, understood as the boundaries of what could be considered appropriate and acceptable behaviour and identity, both for NATO and for applicant and partner countries. As Michael Williams and Iver Neumann have demonstrated, the 'narrative reconstruction of NATO's identity played a powerful role in the debates taking place simultaneously within Russia regarding its post-Cold War identity' (2000: 361) by rendering a powerful political option (anti-Western identity) 'inappropriate' given the transformed nature of NATO.

More specifically, the creation of frameworks for co-operation and exchange such as the NACC, the PfP and the MAP, have progressively impacted more and more on the process of self–other categorization of the participants. In the NACC, NATO had not developed a specific policy for individual countries, but treated all the NACC non-NATO members as belonging to the same out-group. Participants were generically requested to reject an anti-Western identity. The launch of the Partnership for Peace signified the beginning of a categorization process where the partner countries were asked to engage in a self-differentiation process leading to the identification of different out-groups with different interactive practices with NATO itself. The Individual Partnership Programme presented by the partner country to a large extent defines its perception of its distance from the in-group. The MAP adopted at the same Washington Summit in April 1999, and setting the precise roadmap for membership of the organization, signified a further step in the process of self- and other-categorization. As a matter of fact, the signature of MAP is possible only if an applicant country has reached an out-group situated close to the in-group in terms of domestic democracy and respect for human rights.

## Activities for social learning: NATO at work

The story of how in the early stages of the post-Cold War period NATO's response and efforts to adapt shaped and constrained the response of other state actors in the surrounding area is a story of structural power of a peculiar type. *Power* is recognized to be one of the fundamental structural conditions for the development of mutual trust and collective identity (Adler and Barnett, 1998: 38–41). In the very early stages of post-Cold War transition NATO exercised both a *power of attraction* and the less conventional *power to set the boundaries of appropriateness* for subsequent behaviour and self-definition efforts of the applicant and partner countries. I argue that the effectiveness of this power had to do not just with the threat of punishment, but with the fact that the boundaries of appropriateness were set implicitly by providing a tangible example of an international identity built within such boundaries and according to clearly defined norms and rules that provided shared meanings and understandings. In the terminology of Social Identity Theory (Flockhart, this volume), the in-group's efforts to redefine its norms not only reshaped the identity of the in-group and the normative ground for its subsequent behaviour, but it also influenced the process of self-identification of external actors that attached a positive value to the in-group (if anything else, NATO was regarded as a gateway to Europe). This process of self-identification and self-categorization has eventually produced various layers of out-groups, hierarchically ordered on the basis of their distance from the in-group's values and norms.

In a further stage of transition, NATO continued to exercise a similar type of power, which became even stronger due to the leverage represented by the prospect of future membership for either security or economic reasons (Paquette, 2001; Drulak, Königová, this volume: 153). To this structural power NATO added specific policies that in fact are recognized to be conducive for the development of mutual trust and collective identity. The effect was increased transactions and social learning. The quantity and quality of transactions, *bounded communication* in Adler and Barnett's definition (1998: 41), between Western Europe and CEECs and within the latter group have dramatically increased also due to the policies of NATO. NATO has contributed to the creation of multiple channels of communication through which socialization can take place both at the level of institutions and at the level of domestic societies by having set up permanent forums for discussion and regular high-level meetings and by virtue of running workshops, seminars and more informal gatherings as well as by giving very substantial financial support to transboundary scientific programmes. This could not but contribute to the establishment of the many-sided and direct relations amongst states and societies indispensable for the development of a security community.

At the same time, NATO contributed to elite and/or mass social learning around social practices, decision-making styles, basic values and norms. This created the conditions for deep social learning through persuasion (Flockhart, this volume: 16) that has sometimes led to an actual reinterpretation of national beliefs and identities. The degree to which this process has taken place varies considerably, however, in the different Central and Eastern European countries, mainly due to domestic circumstances (Cottey et al., 2002; Forster et al., 2002; Part III, this volume), but the conditions created by the international actors were such that room for social learning was created. In particular, the more or less formal gatherings of national and international elites organized by

NATO resulted in real communicative frameworks within which different meanings and understandings could be compared, but most frequently where Western meanings and understandings were powerfully put forward. These gatherings ranged from more formal meetings in the NACC, to the far less politically stringent participation of local parliamentarians in the meetings of the NATO Parliamentary Assembly. Finally, NATO, together with other organizations, has contributed to the promotion of democratic *institutional structures* by means of (1) 'hard conditionality' by issuing set conditions that should be met according to specific procedures and specified ends; (2) 'soft conditionality' by defining a generally set aim that could be reached in a variety of ways; (3) technical advice and actual teaching; and (4) by providing models to emulate. In this case social learning has led to institutional adaptation, particularly in the field of democratic control of the armed forces, foreign policy and defence policy.

## NATO's instruments of norms transfer

The main vehicle for NATO's contribution to the development of a security community in Central and Eastern Europe has been represented by the various activities and forms of institutionalized co-operation with former adversaries that I here put under the label 'PfP & Co.', which have all been geared towards the development of partnerships in some cases leading to membership. A similar process is taking place vis-à-vis South-eastern Europe through the South-east Europe Initiative, which includes a series of programmes aimed at promoting regional co-operation and long-term stability in the Balkans.[9]

The NACC, then EAPC, is an important part of the 'PfP & Co.'. The EAPC still brings twenty-seven partners[10] and nineteen allies together for regular consultations on issues encompassing and concerning security in the broad sense of the word. Meetings take place regularly at the level of ambassadors, foreign and defence ministers, and chiefs of defence and occasionally heads of state or government. Work on areas of particular interest is done at the level of working groups, where states participate according to their specific security concerns. The effectiveness of co-operation is facilitated by participation in the working groups, the various levels of regular meetings and the diplomatic missions of non-NATO EAPC members at NATO headquarters in Brussels. In this framework there is some room for both social influence, exercised through social rewards and punishment, and persuasion, exercised though the practice of best argument.

*Table 4.1* NATO's contribution to the development of an enlarged European liberal-democratic security community

| **Phase 0** | **Phase 1** | **Phase 2** |
|---|---|---|
| Precipitating condition: structural change at the international level (end of the Cold War). | NATO power of attraction and power to set the boundaries of appropriateness for<br>• behaviour and collective identities in post-Communist states and<br>• the organizations' behaviour in the area. | (a) NATO and power of attraction and power to set boundaries of appropriateness;<br>(b) NATO policies aimed at (or with the involuntary effect of):<br>• increasing transactions and allowing social learning<br>• constructing institutions embodying the norms and values which the organization wishes to embody and to export. |

Actual PfP, however, still represents by far the largest and probably most influential programme of bilateral co-operation between NATO and individual partner countries with its effects going well beyond the enhanced communication and co-operation between NATO and the individual country, as a range of activities require the individual countries to communicate and co-operate also among themselves. The basic aims of the PfP are to promote transparency in national defence planning and military budgeting, ensure democratic control of national armed forces, and develop the capacity for joint action. These aims are pursued though an Individual Partnership Programme drawn up between NATO and the partner country from a wide menu of activities listed in the PfP Work Programme for the coming year. The flexibility of the system, already visible in the EAPC, is evident in the case of PfP where the partner countries themselves shape their programme within boundaries defined by NATO and with tailor-made technical advice from NATO's international staff.

How has the PfP & Co. contributed to the expansion of the 'democratic security community'; specifically how have the participants been socialized around democratic and related norms through the PfP initiative? The PfP includes some of the worst autocratic regimes in Central Asia and in its relationship with Russia a serious screening of the democratic progress of this country has never been on the agenda. Furthermore, NATO's record of military intervention in support of violated democracy and/or human rights is not exactly excellent although it has 'improved' over time with its interventions in Bosnia, Kosovo and Macedonia (FYROM). So, can it be claimed here that NATO has contributed to the expansion of the liberal-democratic security community in Central and Eastern Europe, and that democratic norms are being exported simply because it has created forms of technical co-operation? NATO has done a very good job through the creation of communicative frameworks where the only acceptable shared meaning was provided by a liberal-democratic conception of defence and an institutional relationship between civilians and the military. This despite having used reference to democracy more as a 'rhetorical' tool than an actual 'condition' for military co-operation. As a matter of fact, the various initiatives described above allowed NATO to develop high-intensity communication between the allies and partner countries. These arenas for communication have been used by NATO to engage in social influence, as well as providing arenas for persuasion to convince the participating individuals of the validity of the proposed norms. Indeed, the opportunities for persuasion, as we will see below, had mainly to do with the communicative style adopted by NATO participants.

An important feature of NATO's communication with the partners is the *intensity* of communication. The number of meetings at various levels, involving both civilians and military personnel, is impressive as is the number of workshops, seminars and other types of international gatherings organized within the PfP. The biennial PfP Work Programme contains more than 2000 activities, which can vary considerably in type (seminar, lecture, workshop, conference, course, military exercise), length (from a few days to far longer periods), and areas of concern (from the purely military to defence-related co-operation in fields such as crisis management, peacekeeping, civil emergency planning, air traffic management and armaments co-operation). The activities involve very different numbers and types/levels of people and are performed in various parts of the world. The intensity of gatherings at various levels creates a framework in which norms transfer is facilitated. However, as the actual socialization is directed towards 'individuals' rather than 'states', it is important that these individuals come from the political and administrative apparatus of a partner country, and have the ability to communicate the outcome of the socialization back to domestic political actors hence leading to political action.

In the example of countries that have signed a Membership Action Plan, the intensity of consultations between the country and the allies at various levels is very clear. MAP requires that each year the candidate country submit an updated Annual National Programme (ANP). The programme is first subject to consultation between the allies and each candidate in the autumn; then in the spring this preliminary dialogue is followed by in-depth discussions in the candidate's capital with a NATO team of experts (both military and civilian). NATO then issues a report on the progress made in individual countries, which provides the basis for further consultation between NATO ambassadors and a delegation of the aspirant country usually led by foreign and defence ministers, hence ensuring the link to the domestic political structures. Finally, NATO issues a general report on MAP for the following spring NATO ministerial meetings (Boland, 2002). This process can be seen as an almost textbook example of combined social influence and persuasion techniques (Flockhart, this volume), as the setting up of individual goals is achieved through persuasion and dialogue in a private setting, but the evaluation contained in the general report will amount to either reward or a degree of shaming if goals have not been achieved. As such, MAP countries are under a significant degree of pressure to achieve the targets set in the ANP. This dense area of communication is not only functional to the adaptation of the national Eastern European structure to Western standards, but also provides the framework within which values, norms and ideas are transferred. This takes place in five different ways:

1. PfP & Co. activities provide an arena in which communication takes place within normatively set boundaries that define what is *appropriate* and what is not.
2. The PfP & Co. provides a communicative framework in which the *construction of a common interpretation of the same norm* is developed *though a process of communication* (arguing).[11]
3. By reinforcing control on compliance with respect to the *conditionality* adopted, although in reality, the type of conditionality that NATO sets is rather soft if we compare it with the EU conditionality policy. NATO's conditions are not only more limited in scope (as they focus on NATO's primary area of concerns) but also different in strictness. Usually NATO sets boundaries within which transitions should take place and then sets certain objectives leaving the countries fairly free in the way they want to achieve them. Then it sets procedures whereby the interaction between NATO and the country on that particular objective is frequent and at various levels, including procedures of control and evaluation that always come after exchanges of opinion and NATO advice have taken place. This implies that although there is conditionality and a verification of the extent to which the country has matched the conditions, there is also the possibility of influencing the transition of the country by intervening with softer communicative instruments that include arguing and persuading rather than dictating.
4. NATO's position is frequently reintroduced in the bilateral debate through an apparently neutral tool: *technical advice*. Technical advice is usually very welcome and does not take the form of a teaching activity on NATO's part. Technical advice is also the basis of state-to-state military co-operation between individual NATO member states and individual partners.
5. Explicit *teaching* activities do take place in the context of courses and seminars that have the further advantage to provide forums of interaction among people (frequently young military men and women) from different countries.

Of course the question that is begged in all this is to what extent the result of this extensive socialization process remains confined to the individuals that attend the meetings, courses and other venues for socialization. In other words, in relation to the model presented in

Chapter 2, does the norm transfer reach any further than to the intermediate agents, or are the norms also successfully transferred to the domestic level? Very frequently in the CEEC, there has been a gap between government and society regarding NATO (Part III, this volume). Has NATO been able to bridge the gap? There is some evidence that norms are indeed transferred to the domestic political environment. Firstly, the effects of the entire process have already been translated into documents and institutions in the partner country in line with Western norms of liberal-democracy. In some cases it has been demonstrated that the institutions for civilian control of the military have been the result of a shift in the political culture of the elites. For instance, in the Polish context, as Paul Latawski explains, 'the laws and institutions have tended to reflect the evolution of thinking of political society on civil–military relations rather than the other way round' (Latawski, 2002: 39). In institutional terms, the civilian control of the military has proved to be quite successful in the countries applying for NATO membership. In particular, the informative work on democratic control on the military directed by Andrew Cottey et al. (2002) shows that in these countries the implementation of institutional forms of democratic control of the armed forces was relatively easy. Progress was made also as far as the democratic control of foreign policy is concerned, with the establishment of clear constitutional and political procedures for the deployment of the armed forces. Less developed in institutional terms remains the third form of civilian control of the military: the democratic control of defence policy. However, although with some difficulties, since the early 1990s various mechanisms to ensure the civilian control of defence policy have been activated and have profited from participation in the PfP (Cottey et al., 2002: 257–60), which 'required them to adopt detailed defence planning standards and practices operating within NATO'. Far more backward in all aspects of democratic control of the armed forces are former Yugoslav republics (with the exception of Slovenia) and Albania, not to mention Russia, Ukraine and other former socialist republics.

It is equally interesting to look at the evolution of the basic national documents developed in the PfP & Co. framework by individual partner countries. In the first documents the countries were underlining their effort to construct the type of democratic institutions that the PfP and other basic NATO documents requested. In the ANP for 2000–2001 however, this reference was no longer explicit as the affection of the country for liberal-democratic norms is now taken for granted. In other words, it seems that the overall democratic norm set is well on the way to having become institutionalized to such an extent that it is no longer in doubt.

Secondly, the vocabulary and principles which individuals find and use on the NATO level tend to be transferred by the same individuals in the public domestic debate. This is particularly clear in the case of members of national parliaments attending the meetings of the NATO Parliamentary Assembly (NATO-PA). Frequently, through participation in the Parliamentary Assembly, local MPs and parliamentary staff develop personal channels of communication with their counterparts in other countries, play an international game within the rules of the framework of reference, gain knowledge about security issues and gain sufficient domestic legitimization so as to be able to import into the agenda of their own parliament certain items and terms of discussion developed in the international framework. Furthermore, this international experience gives the MP in question a stronger voice in security issues in his or her own parliament and country, and enables the individual MP to ask relevant questions in defence and security-related parliamentary debates, hence adding another dimension to the democratic control of defence policies.[12]

Thirdly, although the bulk of NATO's activities have targeted the political and military elites in the partner countries, NATO has also developed some other ways to influence the state concerned. One is represented by the media campaigns (co-ordinated with the applicant countries) to gain popular support for the new 1997 members. The second, and even more interesting, activity is connected to NATO's Science Programme that offers grants for collaboration in civil science between scientists in partner countries and NATO countries. In fact, the programme contributes to the development of further strong transnational links between the societies of Western and Central and Eastern European countries. In 2001 over 10 000 scientists from NATO and partner countries collaborated together through joint research projects, as well as participation in conferences or workshops.

## NATO as an effective norm promoter

What has made NATO, and perhaps particularly PfP, such a promising socializing agent? As put forward in this chapter part of NATO's success may stem from its different forms of power – power of attraction and power to define the borders of appropriateness. Secondly, as pointed out earlier, NATO has been able to create communicative frameworks where these powers could be used. Both types of power contributed to set the initial conditions for the transition of Central and Eastern Europe towards Western norms and rules, setting what was (and was not) acceptable and what could be the implications of falling outside the boundaries of appropriateness. Immediately afterwards, NATO was able to use both its powers to get the most out of the communicative interaction it started with neighbour countries without giving the impression of 'dictating' policy change, but rather presenting its contribution to policy change more in the form of technical advice and support.

The fact that countries willing to become members of NATO were more successful in making institutional reforms could demonstrate that material incentives mattered more, but it could simply mean that those that could aim at membership (the better off) were better equipped to meet the conditions for it. The very fact that they were in the first wave of entrants would indicate that their ideational distance from the in-group was short, placing them in out-group 1, which, as suggested by Trine Flockhart, in many cases can be seen to be almost self-socializing. However, it cannot be denied that the prospect of NATO's enlargement was an important incentive for strategic adaptation in all applicant countries.

Next to this, however, there are mechanisms of social learning that go beyond strategic adaptation and that are made possible by intensive communication, especially in a framework where apparent conditions of equal level partnership are created. In these conditions, there seems to be more space for the *logic of argumentative rationality* and for actual persuasion. As I have shown elsewhere (Lucarelli, 2002), this differentiates NATO's approach from that of the EU quite substantially. As a matter of fact, contrary to what can be said about the EU (Schimmelfennig 2001a; and this volume), NATO has not adopted conditionality with a very clear hierarchical relationship between norms-deliverer and norms-receiver as the main form of norms transfer. The reasons for this difference could be found in the huge *acquis communautaire* of the EU compared with the small one of NATO. What counts more in the case of NATO is mutual trust and effective inter-operability that can be achieved by learning though performing rather than through plans on paper. Furthermore, the EU is a normatively dense organization and shows a faith in regulatory systems in a way that NATO does not. The two organizations do not differ only in terms of degree of integration and tightness of the relative security communities, but also in the cultural value attributed to regulation in the two institutional frameworks. One of the explanations is the influence of US political culture in NATO, which calls for more pragmatism, flexibility and horizontal social relations.

Whatever the reasons for the two organizations' style and choice of tools, it is here claimed that NATO's style has shown itself to have more chances to lead to *persuasion* rather than simply to institutional changes as a result of strategic adaptation. NATO's communicative style seems to be more conducive to socialization of the elites through a process of communicative interaction that leads to behaviour on the basis of the best argument.

## Conclusion

It has been argued here that NATO has contributed to the creation of the conditions for the expansion of the Western European democratic security community through:

1. The development of shared identities and meanings around liberal-democratic values
2. The establishment of many-sided and direct relations amongst the states and their societies
3. The establishment of democratic institutions of government.

Starting from the latter condition for a democratic security community, NATO probably did not have the role that other actors have had either domestically or internationally, but it nevertheless contributed to the way in which certain institutions were developed in CEECs. NATO's military co-operation, for example, has already shown concrete results in the area of democratic control of the armed forces. However, the most important condition for the formation of a security community based on liberal-democratic norms is not procedural democracy but the diffusion of liberal-democratic norms that give full sense to the institutional machinery and provide the basis for an arena of democratic peace. The diffusion of norms can occur in different ways and actual change in beliefs can take place or not according to the way in which norm-compliance occurs. In this respect, the first, fundamental, contribution of NATO was an indirect effect of its own role redefinition in the post-Cold War system. Had this organization not existed or had it reinterpreted its international identity in a different way after bipolarity, Central and Eastern Europe might have missed a strong point of reference and incentive for democratization of the military defence sector. The second, relevant contribution to the spread of liberal-democratic norms was a result of NATO's policies and practices in the area. NATO has explicitly adopted policies and practices formally aimed at enhancing compliance with liberal-democratic norms, but what might have contributed most to the good results obtained is the interactive style adopted. Contrary to expectations, the horizontal and flexible style adopted by NATO has sometimes induced social learning and persuasion amongst the local elites, which *then* produced institutional adaptation.

If social learning by the elites has been more effective in the case of NATO than in other cases, it might also be claimed that this organization has been less effective than others in targeting civil society of the norm-adopting states. However, the actual impact at the nation/people level may be more robust than usually assumed, as recent studies on the transformation of the relations between soldiers and societies in Central and Eastern Europe demonstrate that national militaries have regained their legitimacy vis-à-vis their societies through their participation in NATO operations as partner nations (Forster et al., 2002).

As far as the categorization of the out-group states is concerned, NATO has gradually included new countries to an out-group, which is closer to the in-group. An EAPC member which signs the MAP and is then invited to join the Alliance is a country which has shifted from a more remote out-group to an out-group closer to the in-group. It has also shifted from a group (NACC/EAPC), which did not distinguish between actual and self-perceived differences among its members, to one (PfP and MAP) where differentiation among the members is recognized and self-categorization encouraged. In moving from NACC/EAPC to PfP/MAP the socialization strategies of the Alliance also change with respect to the socializee in the different out-groups. As a matter of fact, the different circles comprising full members (NACC/EAPC, PfP, MAP and invitees) vary on the intensity of communication, the preciseness of the action plan for a country's transformation, and the planning and review process.

Finally, a great deal of emphasis has been put here on the flexible, horizontal, seemingly non-dictating communicative style used by NATO and opportunities for persuasion that this opened up, with some evidence of actual persuasion induced by NATO's efforts. What should be added in these concluding remarks is that NATO's flexible approach has not been immune to criticism. As a matter of fact, such an approach has been regarded as a negative element, in that it created confusion among the recipient countries. According to some analysts, the fact that NATO did not present just *one* solution to the problem of, for example, democratization of military–civilian relations, compromised what could have been better results (Donnelly, 2001).[13] Concluding on such a pessimistic stance is not to deny the overall optimism of this chapter but recalling that norms transfer and social learning is indeed a complex enterprise which cannot rest exclusively on the adoption of good tools but needs the capacity to adapt those tools to domestic circumstances and domestic categorization and interpretation. It shows that NATO's socialization can only be the outcome of a two-way process rather than merely an imposition 'from above' as other chapters in this volume testify.

## Notes

1. As suggested by Bill Park in this volume, Turkey today would have difficulty in living up to NATO's present criteria, as would other current members such as Spain, Portugal and Greece in their not too distant past.
2. The concept draws from Karl Deutsch's concept of a 'security community' (1957) as redefined by Adler and Barnett (1998), and from the theory of democratic peace reintroduced in the contemporary debate by Michael Doyle (1983, 1986. See also Russett, 1993; Russett and Zeev, 1993; Russett et al., 1995).
3. According to Adler and Barnett (1998), mature security communities have accomplished all three phases of the creation of a security community: a *nascent phase*, where governments start considering how they might co-ordinate their relations with others to increase security; an *ascendant phase*, in which new institutions are created and a network of transnational communication is developed that facilitates mutual trust and the emergence of collective identities; and a *mature phase* in which there is a high degree of mutual trust, shared identities, common sense of 'we-ness' with respect to others outside the community, leading to low or no probability of war (Adler and Barnett, 1998: 56–7).
4. Adler and Barnett (1998) distinguish between 'loosely-coupled' and 'tightly-coupled' security communities. The former is 'a transnational region comprised of sovereign states whose people maintain dependable expectations of peaceful change ... [by virtue of] their shared structure of meanings and identity' (Adler and Barnett, 1998: 30). Tightly-coupled security communities go beyond the minimal definitional properties of a security community in that they (1) have a 'mutual aid' society and (2) 'possess a system of rule that lies somewhere between a sovereign state and a regional, centralized government' (Adler and Barnett, 1998: 30).
5. http://www.nato.int/docu/basics.htm; http://www.nato.int/issues/pfp/index.htm.
6. At the July 1990 Summit in London, the allies invited the governments of the USSR, Czechoslovakia, Hungary, Poland, Bulgaria and Romania to establish regular diplomatic liaisons with NATO. In November, the allies and their new partners signed a Joint Declaration stating that they would not regard each other as adversaries any more. The relationship between the allies and the new partners went further with the June 1991 meeting of NATO Foreign Ministers in Copenhagen. On this occasion, contacts and exchanges of views between the allies and the partners took place at various levels. Eventually, when the NATO heads of state and government met in Rome in November 1991, the process of consultation with the 'former enemies' called for a decisive step.

7. The document stated that 'No European democratic country whose admission would fulfil the objectives of the Treaty will be excluded from consideration'. It might be worth clarifying that, contrary to a large literature, this chapter intends to go beyond specific attention to enlargement and claim that the basic problem of international identity-legitimization has always guided the role of the Alliance beyond the areas of possible future membership. For alternative explanations of NATO enlargements, see, amongst many works, Fierke and Wiener (1999); McGwire (1998); Menotti (1999); Schimmelfennig (1998/9); Gaddis (1998); Solomon (1998). For a comparison between NATO and EU enlargements, see Fierke and Wiener (1999); Sperling (1999). On NATO's transformation in the post-Cold War era, see, among many others, Brenner (1998); Drew (1995); McCalla (1996); Yost (1998).
8. At the Prague North Atlantic Council (November 2002), NATO invited Bulgaria, Estonia, Latvia, Lithuania, Romania, Slovakia and Slovenia to join the Alliance. A series of meetings between NATO and the individual invitees confirmed their willingness and ability to meet the political, legal and military commitments.
9. The Initiative included countries that did not belong to the PfP or the EAPC – Bosnia-Herzegovina and (at the time) Croatia – and foresaw the eventual extension to the Federal Republic of Yugoslavia (http://www.nato.int/docu/facts/2001/seei.htm).
10. Albania, Armenia, Austria, Azerbaijan, Belarus, Bulgaria, Croatia, Estonia, Finland, Georgia, Ireland, Kazakhstan, Kyrghyz Republic, Latvia, Lithuania, Moldova, Romania, Russia, Slovakia, Slovenia, Sweden, Switzerland, the former Yugoslav Republic of Macedonia, Tadjikistan, Turkmenistan, Ukraine, Uzbekistan.
11. For example, both existing literature and research interviews provide evidence of the fact that at the beginning of NATO's partnership the allies and the partners had a completely different interpretation of what 'civilian control of the armed forces' meant (Cottey et al., 2002; Gheciu, 2002). By presenting itself as a Western institution embodying a set of values opposite to those represented by the former Soviet bloc, NATO was able to use the PfP communicative frameworks to change the partners' conception of civil–military relations Interviews with parliamentarians and defence advisers of CEECs, May 2002.
12. Interview with Gediminas Kirkilas (Lithuaninan MP, Chairman of Foreign Affairs Committee and Committee on European Affairs), May 2002. For an original study on socialization though NATO-PA see Flockhart (2004a).
13. According to Chris Donnelly, '[a] lot of our [European] well-meant efforts have been wasted because it was inappropriate, inapplicable or just plain wrong. We overestimated the competences of Central and Eastern European governments to draw up and implement plans in this sphere' (2001: 8).

# 5
# The EU: Promoting Liberal-Democracy through Membership Conditionality

*Frank Schimmelfennig*

The European Union (EU) primarily uses a strategy of political conditionality to promote liberal-democracy in Central and Eastern Europe. In the theoretical terminology of this volume, this is a strategy based on social influence or reinforcement rather than persuasion. In this chapter, I will describe the EU socialization policy more precisely as intergovernmental reinforcement by material rewards. EU socialization efforts are primarily directed at governments; the EU offers them material rewards such as assistance and the benefits from EU membership on the condition that they comply with the norms of liberal-democracy. If they do not, the EU simply withholds the reward; it neither inflicts extra punishment on the non-compliant countries, nor does it support them with extra assistance to change their cost–benefit relationships. I attribute this low-cost, material socialization strategy to the predominantly economic capabilities of the EU and its low vulnerability vis-à-vis the Central and Eastern European countries (CEECs).

I will argue, further, that the international conditions for effective reinforcement by material rewards are favourable in EU–CEEC relations. The determinacy of EU conditions, the size of the rewards, and the credibility of conditionality are generally high. Under these circumstances, the effectiveness of EU socialization will mainly depend on domestic factors in the target countries: domestic adoption costs for governments and societal strength.

In the first section of this chapter, I provide a typology of reinforcement strategies and discuss the conditions of their effectiveness. In the second section, I describe and explain the EU strategy of reinforcement by reward. In section three, I assess the general conditions of effectiveness of this strategy in EU–CEEC relations.

## Reinforcement strategies of international norm promotion

In this section, I provide a typology of reinforcement strategies of international norm promotion and discuss the conditions of their success. First, I distinguish between three different uses of incentives in reinforcement: reinforcement by reward, punishment and support. Second, these reinforcement strategies may emphasize different kinds of incentives, material or non-material. Third, socialization may work through different channels or pathways, intergovernmental or transnational. In the remainder of this theoretical section, I discuss the conditions under which these reinforcement strategies are expected to be effective.

### A typology of reinforcement strategies

In applying conditionality, a social actor uses the mechanism of *reinforcement* to change the behaviour of another actor. Reinforcement is a form of social control by which pro-social behaviour is rewarded and anti-social behaviour is punished. It is based on the expectation that, after a certain time, the actors subjected to reinforcement will stick to pro-social behaviour in order to avoid punishment and continue to be rewarded. Reinforcement differs from 'persuasion' in two ways. First, it is not based on 'arguing'. The socialization agency does not put forward arguments to justify the norms it disseminates and to convince the target actors of their validity. Rather, it belongs to a 'bargaining mode' of negotiations, the use of incentives and disincentives or threats and promises to motivate the target actors to adopt the norms. Second, it does not aim at the internalization of norms by the target actors resulting in their intrinsic motivation to follow the norms. Rather, reinforcement produces stable behavioural compliance. Over time, successful reinforcement will increasingly discourage deviant behaviour and lead the socializees to follow the community norms and rules in a routine manner.

I distinguish three types of reinforcement, which can be modelled as a decision tree (see Figure 5.1). First, international organization IO offers state S a reward and specifies the conditions under which S will receive it. S then has the choice of either accepting and fulfilling the conditions or rejecting them. Generally, this decision results from cost–benefit

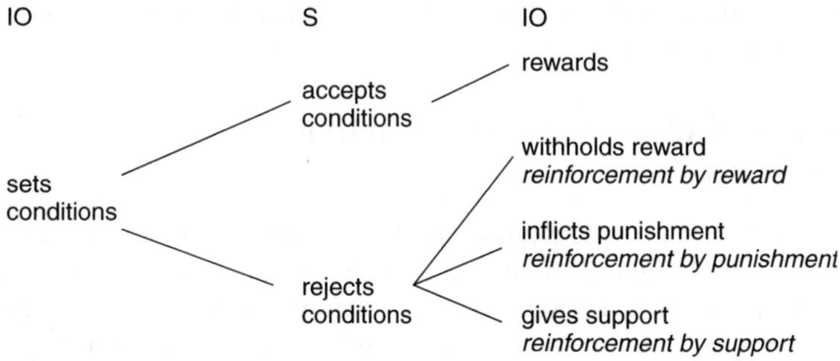


*Figure 5.1* Strategies of conditionality

calculations. If S values IO's reward more highly than the costs of fulfilling IO's conditions, S accepts the conditions and receives the reward. If costs exceed benefits, S rejects the conditions. In this case, IO can react in three different ways, which represent different strategies of conditionality.

(a) *Reinforcement by reward*: IO does not intervene beyond withholding the reward. If the reward remains constant, S will only comply if the domestic costs of compliance decrease below the benefits of the reward.
(b) *Reinforcement by punishment*: IO not only withholds the reward but inflicts extra punishment on the non-compliant state in order to increase the costs of non-compliance beyond the costs of compliance. If punishment is sufficiently severe, S will comply.
(c) *Reinforcement by support*: IO withholds the reward but gives extra support to the non-compliant state in order to decrease the costs of compliance or to enable S to fulfil the conditions. If support is sufficiently high to close the gap between the rewards and the costs of compliance, S will comply and obtain the reward.

Reinforcement strategies can be further classified according to the kind and the channel of incentives. The basic classification is dichotomous in each case.

First, the incentives used may be material or social. Accordingly, I distinguish *material* and *social reinforcement*. In *material reinforcement* by reward, the target countries are offered material or other tangible political rewards in return for compliance – such as financial assistance, market access, technical expertise, and participation in international decision-making. In material reinforcement by punishment, the socialization agency inflicts material sanctions to increase the costs of non-compliance. These may range from economic sanctions such as an embargo or the freezing of bank accounts to the (threat of the) use of violence to impose a norm on a non-compliant actor. In material reinforcement by support, the socialization agency offers, for instance, technical aid to enhance the target state's capacity to comply with international norms or financial compensation to dampen domestic opposition.

By contrast, *social reinforcement* uses socio-psychological rewards, punishment, and support. Social reinforcement by reward consists, for instance, of international recognition and public praise by the socialization agency for a state that has adopted international norms. Correspondingly, social punishment comes in the form of shaming and shunning. States are publicly named and blamed for their non-compliance; their leaders are not invited to international conferences or banned from entering the countries of the community. The lowest and most isolated status is that of a pariah state. Finally, social support can be thought of as a class of instruments through which a non-compliant target state receives extra attention and encouragement. These may consist of additional meetings with the socialization agency, the sending of expert and support teams and assurances of respect for the efforts undertaken.

Finally, reinforcement can use an *intergovernmental* or a *transnational channel*. Through the intergovernmental channel, the international organization targets governments directly and seeks to influence their material and social cost–benefit calculations. By contrast, in transnational socialization, the international organization interacts with non-governmental actors in the target countries such as social movement organizations, interest groups, parties or business actors. It is through these actors that the international organizations attempt to create social demand for norm acceptance and adoption and to have an indirect impact on the target state government. A combination of these classifications yields the typology shown in Table 5.1.

### Conditions of effectiveness

Under which conditions are these strategies effective? Most basically, for any reinforcement strategy to be effective, the benefits of compliance must balance its costs. Theoretically, four variables influence the effectiveness of reinforcement in general: the determinacy of conditions; the size of rewards, punishments or support; their credibility; and the size of domestic

*Table 5.1* A typology of reinforcement strategies of international norm promotion

| | Reinforcement | | | | | |
|---|---|---|---|---|---|---|
| | By reward | | By punishment | | By support | |
| | Material | Social | Material | Social | Material | Social |
| Intergovernmental | | | | | | |
| Transnational | | | | | | |

compliance costs (see Schimmelfennig and Sedelmeier, 2005). Two further conditions concern the effectiveness of social reinforcement and transnational socialization in particular: the degree of identification between socializee and socialization agency and the strength of society.

*Determinacy of conditions*

Determinacy refers both to the clarity and formality of a rule. The clearer the behavioural implications of a rule, and the more 'legalized' and binding its status, the higher its determinacy.[1] Determinacy matters in two respects. First, it has an informational value. It helps the target actors to know exactly what they have to do to receive the rewards or to avoid punishment. Second, determinacy enhances the credibility of conditionality. It is a signal to the target countries that they cannot manipulate the rule to their advantage or avoid adopting it at all. At the same time, however, it binds the organization. If a condition is determinate, it becomes more difficult for the organization to claim unjustly that it has not been fulfilled and to withhold the reward.

*Size of rewards, punishment and support*

All else being equal, the size of the promised rewards, the threatened punishment and the expected support determine the impact of an incentives-based socialization strategy. Accordingly, the promise of membership should be more powerful than the promise of association or assistance; the threat of military intervention is usually more efficient than the threat of an embargo; and the amount and quality of support will have an impact on the ability of the target government to meet international conditions.

*Credibility of conditionality*

Size alone, however, is not effective if it is not credible, too. A third set of factors, therefore, has to do with the credibility of the rewards, punishments and support from the socialization agency. In reinforcement by reward, the threat to withhold rewards in case of non-compliance and, conversely, the promise to deliver the reward in case of rule adoption must be credible. Correspondingly, a strategy of reinforcement by punishment requires that the threat to inflict punishment and the promise to refrain from sanctions in case of compliance be equally credible. By contrast, reinforcement by support does not require credible threats. Instead, support must be reliable.

Credibility depends on several factors. The first issue is *capabilities and costs* of the socialization agency. The agency must be capable of monitoring the target actors' compliance. It must also be capable of paying the rewards, inflicting the punishment, or giving the necessary support, and these promises and threats are the more credible, the lower their costs are to the agency. The same is true, of course, for the agency's capability and costs of withholding the reward and stopping the punishment. Second, credibility depends on the *consistency* of an organization's policies of norm promotion. If the socialization agency were perceived to subordinate conditionality to other political, strategic, or economic considerations, the target state might either hope to receive the benefits or avoid punishment without fulfilling the conditions, or it might conclude that it will not receive the rewards or support, or be spared the punishment, in any case. The same goes for consistency across international organizations. If one organization offers the same reward for less compliance, effectiveness will be impaired.

### *Size of domestic adoption costs*

If conditions are determinate, and rewards, punishment and support are credible, the effectiveness of reinforcement will depend on how the size of domestic adoption costs compares with the size of international rewards, punishment and support. In the case of the international promotion of liberal democracy, international norms generally enhance the autonomy and freedom of individuals and societal associations while they limit the autonomy of governments and prohibit the use of certain instruments to preserve their power (such as closing down opposition newspapers, manipulating elections, or abolishing an independent judiciary). Therefore, the most relevant domestic adoption costs are the government's costs of power preservation.

### *Identification*

The conditions of effectiveness discussed above are relevant for both material bargaining and social influence. Just like material rewards and punishments, social rewards and punishments need to be sizeable, credible and based on determinate conditions to have an impact. However, whereas tangible material or physical rewards and punishments can be assumed to affect any political actor, social influence only works inside the actor's in-group or aspiration group. Thus its effectiveness will mainly depend on the degree to which target actors identify themselves with the community of the socialization agency. Otherwise, they will not appreciate the recognition and respect of the community and will not find it painful to be shamed and shunned. According to the complex socialization model (Flockhart, this volume), intergovernmental social reinforcement will only be effective vis-à-vis out-groups 1 and 2, whereas transnational social reinforcement will be likely to work in out-group 3, provided that societal strength is high (see below). With regard to out-group 4, the socialization agency must rely on material reinforcement.

*Societal strength*

If neither material nor social rewards, punishments or support are sufficient to induce *governments* to comply, conditionality can still be effective via the transnational channel, that is, via societal actors. Basically, societal actors will be responsive to reinforcement under the same conditions as state actors, that is, if their material cost-benefit balance is positive (transnational material reinforcement) or if they aspire to belong to the international community in question (transnational social influence). To have an impact on an unresponsive government's policy, however, societal responsiveness must be combined with societal strength. The targeted societal actors must be strong enough to force the government to comply with the rules, for instance as a result of their institutional or coalition-building power in the political system, their ability to mobilize the electorate, or their capacity to stage anti-government revolts.

In sum, then, the effectiveness of a reinforcement strategy of norm promotion depends on the determinacy of conditions, the size and credibility of the socialization agency's rewards, punishments and support, and the domestic adoption costs of the target actors. In addition, social reinforcement requires that the target actor identify with the international community of the socialization agency, and transnational reinforcement requires strong societal actors in order to be effective.

## The predominant EU strategy: intergovernmental reinforcement by material rewards

On the basis of the typology developed above, I will argue, in this section, that the EU has predominantly used a strategy of *intergovernmental reinforcement by material rewards*. More concretely, it has sought to induce European non-member countries to comply with international norms of human rights and democracy by setting the fulfilment of these norms as conditions for membership and other material rewards. Although the EU has also used social rewards – and possibly persuasion in some cases – it is the high material incentive of membership that distinguishes the socialization activity of the EU from that of other European organizations such as the OSCE or the Council of Europe. Moreover, in comparison with intergovernmental reinforcement by reward, the EU has used transnational instruments as well as punishment and support only in a few exceptional circumstances. In this section, I will focus on the general features of the EU's strategy of democratic norm promotion and explain why the EU has chosen this particular strategy.

The EU offers two kinds of rewards to non-member states: assistance and institutional ties. The most important programmes of external assistance for European non-members in the post-Cold War era are *Tacis* (for the thirteen member countries of the Community of Independent States including Mongolia) and *Phare* (for the other CEECs – Central and Eastern European Countries). They offer technical and financial assistance in the transition of these countries to market economies. Institutional ties range from trade and co-operation agreements via association agreements to full membership. In addition to assistance, they provide increasing inclusion in the EU market with the prospect of gains from trade and investment and increasing participation in EU decision-making.

Yet the EU makes these offers conditional upon the prior compliance with basic liberal democratic norms. Generally, the stronger the institutional ties, the more demanding the political conditions. Already in January 1989, the European Parliament demanded that 'reference to human rights should figure' in the Trade and Co-operation Agreements the EC was beginning to negotiate with the CEECs and should be mentioned specifically in the negotiating mandates given to the Commission.[2] In April, the Council made resumption of the negotiations with Romania conditional upon this country's compliance with its human rights commitments in the CSCE framework.[3] And in November, the Paris summit established that 'initiatives aimed at the countries of Eastern Europe as a whole are applicable only to those which re-establish freedom and democracy'.[4]

After the dissolution of the Soviet Union, the Commission confirmed that 'negotiating ... new types of agreements has to be subject to political conditions (respect of human rights and democratic freedoms, guarantees for minorities, etc.)'.[5] In May 1992, the Council underscored that 'respect for democratic principles and human rights ... as well as the principles of a market economy, constitute essential elements of co-operation and association agreements between the Community and its CSCE partners'.[6] Henceforth, the EU added a clause to the agreements, which stipulated a suspension of the agreements if CEECs fail to comply with these principles. In November of the same year, the Council approved Phare guidelines, which made aid conditional upon the 'state of advance of the reforms in each of the beneficiary countries'.[7] In July 1993, the new Tacis regulations strengthened conditionality, too: 'The level and intensity of the assistance will take into account the extent and progress of reform efforts in the beneficiary country.'[8]

At its Copenhagen summit in June 1993, the European Council established the 'stability of institutions guaranteeing democracy, the rule of law, human rights and respect for and protection of minorities' as the *sine qua non* political condition of accession to the EU. The importance of minority rights was underscored by the 'Pact on Stability in Europe' launched in May 1994 at the initiative of French prime minister Edouard Balladur, which called upon all EU membership candidates to settle their border and minority conflicts and provide for minority protection in a series of bilateral negotiations and treaties. The concrete terms of the treaties were left to the negotiating parties but it was understood that without such a settlement, the road to accession would be blocked.

In its 1997 Opinion on the applications for membership and in subsequent annual progress reports, the Commission has regularly evaluated the political conditions in all candidate countries. Based on these opinions and reports, the Commission made recommendations on the beginning of accession negotiations and later pointed out reforms that needed to be undertaken before the conclusion of accession negotiations.

Because of the ethno-political wars on the territory of former Yugoslavia, the so-called Western Balkans has long been sidelined in this conditional integration process. After the Dayton Peace Agreements, however, the EU developed a special approach to the five countries of this region – Albania, Bosnia-Herzegovina, Croatia, Macedonia and Serbia. As with the earlier candidates for membership, however, the core strategy of this approach was conditionality. In April 1997, the EU adopted the Regional Approach, which made the intensification of bilateral relations dependent on 'respect for democratic principles, human rights, the rule of law, protection of minorities, market economy reforms and regional co-operation'.[9] After the war in Kosovo, the Stabilization and Association Process superseded the Regional Approach in 2000, based on 'a recognition that the main motivator for reform – including the establishment of a dependable rule of law, democratic and stable institutions and a free economy – in these countries is a relationship with the EU that is based on a credible prospect of membership once the relevant conditions have been met'.[10] Again, the Commission evaluates the progress of the five countries in Stabilization and Association Reports and makes recommendations on whether or not the conditions are met to negotiate Stabilization and Association Agreements.

By contrast, the East European member states of the Community of Independent States – Belarus, Ukraine, Moldova and Russia – have not been offered a concrete prospect of membership. For these and other neighbouring countries of the enlarged Union, the European Commission proposed, in 2003, the Wider Europe framework 'to develop a zone of prosperity and a friendly neighborhood'. However, conditionality is at the core of this framework, too: 'In return for concrete progress demonstrating shared values and effective implementation of political, economic and institutional reforms ... the EU's neighbourhood should benefit from the prospect of closer economic integration with the EU'.[11]

EU political conditionality comes under 'reinforcement by reward' because countries that fail to meet the criteria are simply denied assistance, association or membership and left behind in the competition for EU funds and the 'regatta' for accession. Only in a few early and minor cases did the EU suspend existing agreements (Romania, 1989; Yugoslavia, 1991), and it has never invoked the 1992 'human rights clause' in Central and Eastern Europe to terminate agreements that had already been in force. The EU generally thus does not inflict extra punishment (in addition to withholding the conditional reward) on non-compliant governments. Although EU members have participated in UN sanctions and NATO military interventions against Yugoslavia, the EU as an organization has not been prominently involved in these coercive measures.

On the other hand, the EU does not give extra support to those who fail to meet the conditions either. Rather, the EU regularly exhorts the CEEC governments that it is their own responsibility to create the conditions to be rewarded. To be sure, the EU does provide funding for projects designed to promote democracy and human rights in Central and Eastern Europe directly. In 1992, both a Phare Democracy and a Tacis Democracy Programme were launched; both were merged in 1997 as the Phare and Tacis Democracy Programme (PTDP). Since 1999, the European Initiative for Democracy and Human Rights (EIDHR) has been the most important EU programme to promote liberal democracy in third countries.

In comparison with the rewards-based technical and financial assistance under the main Phare and Tacis programmes, however, direct support was rather marginal. According to Karen Smith (2001: 49), only 1 per cent of the EU's total aid budget was dedicated to the direct support of democratization in the CEECs. The typical biennial budget for PDTP in the 1990s was in the range of €40 million, and according to the Programming Document of EIDHR for the years 2002–4, Bosnia-Herzegovina, Serbia-Montenegro, Russia, Turkey and Ukraine have been allotted a total of €12.8 million.[12] Yet the 1997–8 Phare budget alone was €1.6 billion. Finally, to give a concrete, country-specific example, Belarus received ECU 54 million between 1991 and 1996 in Tacis aid. In 1996, when President Lukashenka abolished the democratic constitution of Belarus, the EU decided to discontinue this aid and to replace it with a 'democratization and development programme for civil society in Belarus'.[13] However, it only approved ECU 5 million for this programme in 1997 and another 5 million in 2000.

It is clear from the description above that the EU primarily pursues an *intergovernmental* strategy of reinforcement by reward. Governments are the recipients of financial and technical assistance, and agreements and treaties are also negotiated and concluded with governments. By contrast, the EU uses the transnational channel for its secondary and complementary strategy of reinforcement by support. In addition, however, the EU also counts on indirect, transnational effects of its intergovernmental rewards. By offering rewards that are popular and attractive with the target country's society, the EU hopes to generate sufficient demand 'from below' to bring about norm compliance. If a government still does not comply with EU conditions, and the EU reward is withheld, the electorate is expected to replace the non-compliant government (see Vachudova, 2001).

Finally, the rewards offered by the EU are predominantly *material*. This is obvious in the case of financial and technical assistance. Although any material reward always carries with it an element of social recognition, it is the material utility that dominates. Institutional ties such as 'partnership', 'association' and 'membership' already indicate by their names that they imply a certain social relationship with the international community and a gradual shift from out-group to in-group. The socializee is regarded as a partner, then as an associate, and finally as a member. However, in the case of the EU, each of these steps involves material benefits as well, and it is these benefits that dominate the cost-benefit calculations of the actors and the negotiations. Conversely, whenever the EU used social incentives and disincentives – that is, appealed to the legitimate aspirations of a country to join the community of democratic European nations or shamed a government for violating the basic values and norms of this community and its obligations under international law – they were directly tied to material incentives (the promise of assistance and membership) and disincentives (the threat to withhold assistance and exclude a country from membership).

At any rate, institutional ties with the EU differ strongly in this respect from those with the OSCE or the Council of Europe, which cannot offer any sizeable material benefits. Whereas the EU does not distinguish itself from these other organizations by the conditions it sets and the democratic and human rights changes it demands – it has generally followed and taken up the demands of the OSCE or the Council of Europe – its distinctive 'function' as a socialization agency has been to put the weight of its material power and attractiveness behind these demands.

In sum, although we can find examples of other types of socialization strategies in EU policies of international norm promotion, intergovernmental reinforcement by material rewards constitutes the hallmark of EU socialization policy. But how can we explain the choice of this strategy? Why did the EU focus on reinforcement by material rewards? I suggest that this choice has to do with the specific capabilities and cost-benefit calculations of the EU and its member states.

First of all, the focus on *material, economic* rewards has to do with the specific capabilities of the EU. On the one hand, economic power is the EU's main asset. It is what distinguishes the EU from the other European organizations. On the other hand, its military power is too limited to intervene militarily against massive human rights violations or to try to overthrow autocratic governments.

Most importantly, reinforcement by reward is generally a low-cost strategy. First, the cost of rewarding is usually lower than the cost of punishing and supporting. If target states do not comply, reinforcement by punishment requires inflicting extra costs and reinforcement by support requires the transfer of extra assistance. Both are costly. Second, in reinforcement by reward, the rewards are paid only after the successful adoption of norms, whereas reinforcement by punishment or support require costly coercive and supportive engagements the success of which is uncertain. Third, a strategy of reinforcement by reward avoids the 'moral hazard' problems of reinforcement by support: governments cannot count on receiving EU assistance by just remaining 'needy' and not adapting to EU rules. For these reasons, a socialization agency prefers, *ceteris paribus*, rewarding to punishing or supporting. It will only engage in the more costly strategies if it is vulnerable to negative externalities from developments and policies in the target states and if reinforcement by reward is not sufficiently effective to control these negative externalities. In addition, I assume socialization agencies to prefer, *ceteris paribus*, intergovernmental to transnational reinforcement because intergovernmental reinforcement is the more direct channel and gives the socialization agency better control over the socialization process.

On the basis of these theoretical considerations, the predominance of reinforcement by reward can be explained by the fact that EU vulnerability is low. First, the EU's economic stakes in the CEECs are low in general; the CEECs pose no military or economic threat. CEECs do not possess strategic resources and their share of foreign trade has remained below 5 per cent for the EU as a whole throughout the 1990s. The material effects of war as well as political and economic deterioration in Central and Eastern Europe on the West have been small and manageable. Western countries have been able to protect themselves effectively against a massive inflow of refugees or migrants (see Lavenex, 1998). Second, the international socialization of the CEECs is generally regarded as a low-priority issue in EU societies. No Western government had to fear domestic pressure if it was miserly with support to the CEECs and if it opposed or sought to put off the Eastern enlargement.[14] Even if rewards are ineffective, this low vulnerability will discourage EU member states from engaging themselves in costly coercive or supportive policies. This explains the comparatively minor funding for civil society development in autocratic countries such as Belarus and Yugoslavia under Milošević.

In sum, the predominance of intergovernmental reinforcement by material rewards in EU policy of democratic socialization can be explained by the specific capabilities of the EU (economic power) and its low vulnerability vis-à-vis the CEECs. It is therefore the conditions of effectiveness for this particular strategy that I will turn to in the next section.

## Conditions of effectiveness in EU–CEEC relations

In the section on 'strategies of international promotion', I discussed several conditions that influence the effectiveness of reinforcement strategies of socialization. In this section, I will discuss to what extent they were present in the EU relationship with Central and Eastern Europe and which expectations on the effectiveness of intergovernmental reinforcement by material rewards follow from this assessment. The analysis suggests that the determinacy, size and credibility of EU material rewards were generally high. It follows, then, that the effectiveness of EU political conditionality will depend on domestic factors in the target countries: domestic adoption costs for governments and societal strength.

Many observers point to the *lack of determinacy* in EU political conditionality. First, the EU has set political conditions that are not part of the *acquis* and are not even shared and met by some of its members (Grabbe, 1999: 8). This is particularly true for minority protection (De Witte, 2000: 3; Schwellnus, 2005). Second, the concrete EU demands for minority rights and protection varied significantly between candidate countries (Schimmelfennig et al., 2005; Schwellnus, 2005). For instance, the EU generally accepted a situation in Estonia and Latvia, where a large part of the resident population will be deprived of citizenship for a long time to come, while it heavily criticized the Slovak government under Mečiar for its treatment of the Hungarian minority, which enjoyed the full rights of Slovak citizens. Third, as Mineshima (2002) showed for the rule of law principle, the political conditions are so vaguely and broadly defined that target governments might not know precisely which changes are required of them and which measures will satisfy EU conditions. Whereas respect for democracy, human rights and the rule of law are listed in the EU treaties as the core norms of state purpose and conduct in the European international community, these norms are not clearly defined and specified there. The EU partly referred to the more specific rules of other organizations such as those of the Council of Europe for human rights and minority rights. Partly, it developed the criteria in the process, in an ad hoc fashion. Under these circumstances, the effectiveness of political conditionality might have suffered.

Whereas these shortcomings are correctly observed in principle, they were less grave in practice and did not matter for compliance (Schimmelfennig et al., 2005; Schwellnus, 2005). The general lack of determinacy was offset by concrete demands for changes in state rules and behaviour in all kinds of EU communications including, above all, the Commission's opinions and annual progress reports. The continuous stream of EU evaluations of the political situation in the candidate countries provided them with sufficiently clear feedback to know whether they met the necessary conditions and which further steps were required of them. Thus, determinacy – although not a quality of the rules as such – has been high, indeed.

The *size of the rewards* offered to the CEECs has grown over time as the EU moved from the conclusion of trade and co-operation agreements to association agreement and finally to the negotiation of membership. EU membership is probably the highest reward that any European organization has on offer in return for compliance with liberal democratic norms. It not only gives the CEECs access to the EU's internal market and its subsidies for agriculture and regional development but also accords them full participation and decision-making rights in Europe's most powerful international organization. Thus, ever since the EU had made the principled decision to enlarge to the East at the Copenhagen European Council in June 1993, the size of the reward has been high.

To have a strong impact, however, conditionality has to have *credibility*, too. In the case of reinforcement by rewards, both the threat to withhold the reward and the promise to pay the reward after compliance need to fulfil this condition. For the *threat* to be credible, the EU must be able to withhold the rewards at no or low costs to itself, and it has to be less interested in giving the reward than the target government is in getting it. This condition has generally been present in EU–CEEC relations. Interdependence is highly asymmetrical in favour of the EU. Whereas the CEECs are only of marginal importance to the EU economy, the CEECs are heavily dependent on the EU market and will benefit much more strongly from accession than the EU member states (Baldwin et al., 1997; Moravcsik and Vachudova, 2003: 46–52). Moreover, transparency is high across Europe because international organizations as well as NGOs monitor democratic and human rights practices extensively. Information asymmetries undermining the threat of withholding the reward in case of non-compliance are therefore not an issue.

On the other hand, however, the EU must be capable of paying the rewards (at a low cost to itself). *Promises* are not credible if they go beyond capabilities. The higher the costs of the rewards to the EU are, the more doubtful their eventual payment to the target countries will be. On the basis of this reasoning, the credibility of the promise of membership could be doubted at the beginning. Eastern enlargement involves substantial costs to the organization, which, although far from being prohibitive, are likely to exceed the marginal benefits of most member states (Schimmelfennig, 2003: 52–62).

However, one also has to take into account the 'sunk costs' of rewarding. Enlargement involves costly, long-term negotiations and preparations and a restructuring of EU institutions and policies. The more the pre-accession process advances, the higher are the costs of withholding the reward, that is, the investments that would be lost if the process was broken off or postponed to sanction a candidate state. The credibility of conditional rewards therefore increases considerably with the opening of accession negotiations, since in the words of Commission officials they 'require a large input of political and human resources [and] because opening them implies a willingness to conclude them' (Avery and Cameron, 1998: 27). Even for countries not yet involved in accession negotiations, the opening of accession negotiations with, and the subsequent accession of, a first group of candidate countries increased the credibility of rewards for the remaining candidates, as it demonstrated that the EU was serious about enlargement.

In sum, then, the overall credibility of EU promises and threats peaked in the second half of the 1990s, when the EU made its decisions to open negotiations with the CEECs. Whereas the start of accession negotiations with the democratic front-runners of the region in 1998 signalled to the remaining countries that the EU would reward successful socialization with membership, the exclusion of other CEECs from the first round, above all Slovakia, made it clear that membership would not be granted in the absence of norm compliance. Turkey is a key case for demonstrating the relevance of credibility. As long as the EU's longest-standing associate did not have a credible promise of membership, EU political conditionality did not produce strong results in Turkey. When, however, Turkey was accorded official candidate status on the same footing as the CEECs in 1999, the credible promise of membership triggered a series of thorough reforms and improvements in the human rights situation that were not deemed possible before.

*High consistency* added to the credibility of EU political conditionality. First, despite the fact that some of the political conditions were understood and applied inconsistently among the member states, they were not contested as conditions of membership and thus could not be manipulated by the candidate countries. Most conspicuously, France, probably the most sceptical EU member state with regard to minority protection on its own territory, has been at the same time most active in demanding the settlement of minority conflicts in the East as a precondition of membership (see, above all, the Balladur plan for a Pact on Stability in Europe).

Second, parallel and additive conditionality have generally been high. The basic reason was that all relevant socialization agencies in the region were part of the Western community and therefore shared the liberal democratic norms. In addition, the lack of determinacy of EU conditions helped. The EU's need to 'borrow' concrete criteria from other organizations made sure that political conditions have been in line with recommendations and demands of the OSCE and the Council of Europe, that is, those European organizations most directly concerned with the human and minority rights situation in the CEECs. Moreover, EU conditionality was reinforced by the fact that NATO had made accession subject to the same conditions as the EU and, finally, the benefits of EU membership could not be replaced by those offered by any other organization.

It is sometimes suggested, however, that the EU applied its conditionality inconsistently to the CEECs, that is, it rewarded countries despite norm violations and did not reward others, even though they complied with the norms. Such inconsistent behaviour is attributed to strategic or economic motives. For instance, because of its strategic relevance, Russia was rewarded with aid and institutional ties despite severe human rights violations in Chechnya (see Smith, 2001: 39). In addition, whereas the EU stopped the ratification of the Partnership and Co-operation Agreement with Belarus, the no less dictatorial regimes of Central Asia have not been sanctioned in this way.

When it comes to the prospect of association and membership for the European post-Communist countries, however, the political criteria have been applied rigidly. First, no country has been invited to membership negotiations if it has not passed a certain threshold of democratic consolidation and respect for civil and political rights. Second, the ranking of CEECs with regard to their democratic consolidation closely corresponds to their ranking with regard to the intensity of their institutional ties with the EU.

Table 5.2 provides evidence for this high degree of consistency on the basis of Freedom House ratings of the civil and political rights situation in the CEECs.[15] The table lists the Freedom House ratings of the CEECs in 1997, 1999 and 2004. In 1997, the EU decided to open accession negotiations with the first group of five Central and Eastern European candidates; in 1999, it invited the second group of five CEECs. The columns for 2004 reflect the most recent assessment; moreover, the EU is expected to invite Croatia to begin accession talks in the summer. For each of the selected years, the countries are ordered according to their institutional status ranging from 'membership' as the highest

*Table 5.2* Selection of CEECs for EU association and accession

| **Status** | **Country** | **1997** | | **1999** | | **2004** | |
|---|---|---|---|---|---|---|---|
| | | **PR/CL[1]** | **Freedom Index** | **PR/CL** | **Freedom Index** | **PR/CL** | **Freedom Index** |
| **EU membership** | Czech Rep. | 1/2 | Free | 1/2 | Free | 1/2 | Free |
| | Estonia | 1/2 | Free | 1/2 | Free | 1/2 | Free |
| | Hungary | 1/2 | Free | 1/2 | Free | 1/2 | Free |
| | Poland | 1/2 | Free | 1/2 | Free | 1/2 | Free |
| | Slovenia | 1/2 | Free | 1/2 | Free | 1/1 | Free |
| **EU accession talks** | Latvia | 2/2 | Free | 1/2 | Free | 1/2 | Free |
| | Lithuania | 1/2 | Free | 1/2 | Free | 1/2 | Free |
| | Slovakia | 2/4 | Partly free | 2/2 | Free | 1/2 | Free |
| **EU association** | Bulgaria | 2/3 | Free | 2/3 | Free | 1/2 | Free |
| | Romania | 2/3 | Free | 2/2 | Free | 2/2 | Free |
| **No association** | Croatia | 4/4 | Partly free | 4/4 | Partly free | 2/2 | Free |
| | Macedonia | 4/3 | Partly free | 3/3 | Partly free | 3/3 | Partly free |
| | Albania | 4/4 | Partly free | 4/5 | Partly free | 3/3 | Partly free |
| | Belarus | 6/6 | Not free | 6/6 | Not free | 6/6 | Not free |
| | Bosnia-H. | 5/5 | Partly free | 5/5 | Partly free | 4/4 | Partly free |
| | Moldova | 3/4 | Partly free | 2/4 | Partly free | 3/4 | Partly free |
| | Russia | 3/4 | Partly free | 4/4 | Partly free | 5/5 | Partly free |
| | Ukraine | 3/4 | Partly free | 3/4 | Partly free | 4/4 | Partly free |
| | Yugoslavia | 6/6 | Not free | 6/6 | Not free | 3/2 | Partly free |

*Note*: [1] PR stands for 'political rights', CL for 'civil liberties'.

status via 'accession talks' and 'association' to 'no association' as the lowest status.

First, the most conspicuous cleavage is that between 'free' countries, on the one hand, and countries rated 'partly free' or 'not free', on the other. Countries rated 'free' have always had a status of 'association' or higher, whereas, in general, 'partly free' and 'not free' countries have not achieved this status. The only exceptions in the table are Slovakia in 1997 and Macedonia in 2004. Moreover, the EU has not invited any country not rated 'free' to accession talks. Thus, the intensity of institutional relationships between the EU and the CEECs generally corresponds to the level of compliance with liberal norms in the CEECs. More precisely, being a 'free' European country appears to be a sufficient condition for EU association and a necessary condition for an invitation to accession negotiations.

Second, the more detailed figures for political rights and civil liberties reveal a distinction between the five CEECs that were invited, in 1997, to formal accession talks and the other associated countries: all countries of the top group received the best rating for political rights (1) and the second-best rating (2) for civil liberties, whereas Bulgaria, Latvia, Romania and Slovakia scored only 2 for political rights and 2 or worse for civil liberties. Moreover, these ratings for the invited countries match the ratings for current EU members. EU members are generally rated 1 for political rights and 1 or 2 for civil liberties.

As in the case of EU association of two only 'partly free' countries, there are a few marginal inconsistencies. First, Lithuania was not invited to formal accession talks in 1997 even though its record was as good as that of the first-rate candidates. Second, the EU appears to have lowered its standards slightly after 1997, when it invited Bulgaria, Romania and Slovakia in 1999, and Croatia in 2004.

In sum, the international conditions for an effective intergovernmental reinforcement by material reward have generally been extremely favourable since 1997. EU membership is the highest material reward offered by any of the European organizations. Beginning with the Commission's Opinions on the applicants for EU membership, and even more so with the follow-up Progress Reports, EU rules and conditions have become more and more determinate. The start of accession negotiations increased the credibility of the promise of membership and demonstrated that the EU was serious about excluding non-compliant governments at the same time. Finally, consistency was high. Given that international conditions were generally favourable, variation in the effectiveness of EU political conditionality must be explained by domestic factors – variation in governments' domestic power costs of adopting liberal democratic norms and/or variation in societal interest in membership and societal strength vis-à-vis the state.[16]

## Conclusions

In conclusion, then, I will briefly explore the possibilities and conditions for the dominant EU strategy of reinforcement by material rewards to create winning coalitions in the target states – an issue that will be taken up in more detail in the country chapters. First, I submit that a distinct impact of EU political conditionality on compliance with democratic norms was limited to countries with unfavourable conditions for effective social reinforcement or persuasion, that is, governments with a low identification with the European international community and its constitutive values and norms and/or high domestic power costs of compliance. All other governments should already have consolidated liberal democracy autonomously or responded positively to the early socialization efforts of the OSCE or the Council of Europe, leaving the more problematic cases to be influenced by the prospect of EU membership.

In this group of reluctant democratizers, the EU's intergovernmental reinforcement by reward is effective if the benefits that CEEC governments reap from EU membership are higher than the domestic adaptation costs. Generally, however, if that means giving up authoritarian and illiberal practices of power preservation, governments will not respond positively to EU political conditionality. In other words, the prospects for creating intergovernmental winning coalitions with authoritarian or autocratic governments in the region are bleak – and the lack of a positive EU impact on Belarus under Lukashenka, Slovakia under Mečiar, or Serbia under Milošević confirms this expectation.

In these cases, the EU must hope to mobilize domestic society against the non-compliant governments or wait for domestic dissatisfaction with the incumbent government to result in a change in government and in the coming to power of liberal democratic, reform and EU-oriented political forces who regard the power costs of implementing democratic reforms as low in comparison to the benefits of EU membership.

## Notes

1. For discussions of 'determinacy' or 'specificity' of rules and norms, see Franck (1990: 52–83); Legro (1997: 34). For an explication of the concept of 'legalization', see Abbott et al. (2000).
2. Agence Europe, 20 January 1989.
3. Agence Europe, 24/25 April 1989.
4. Agence Europe, 22 November 1989.
5. Agence Europe, 27 February 1992.
6. Agence Europe, 14 May 1992.
7. Agence Europe, 16/17 November 1992.
8. Agence Europe, 24 July 1993.
9. http://www.europa.eu.int/comm/external_relations/see/region/europe_integration.pdf.
10. http://www.europa.eu.int/comm/external_relations/see/actions/sap.htm.
11. Commission, 'Wider Europe – Neighborhood: A New Framework for Relations with our Eastern and Southern Neighbours', COM (2003) 104 final, 11 March 2003.
12. http://europa.eu.int/comm/external_relations/human_rights/doc/eidhr02_04.pdf.
13. Agence Europe, 24 December 1997.
14. See Harris (2002); Schimmelfennig (2001b: 64); Sedelmeier and Wallace (2000: 457) as well as Eurobarometer polls cited there.

15. 'Freedom House' is a US-based non-governmental organization publishing annual reports on 'Freedom in the World' (www.freedomhouse.org). Its central indicators are ratings for 'Political Rights' and 'Civil Liberties' ranging from 1 (best) to 7 (worst). On their basis, Freedom House constructs a 'Freedom Index' classifying countries as 'free', 'partly free' or 'not free'.
16. For a comparative assessment of the impact of EU conditionality in the candidate countries emphasizing these factors, see Schimmelfennig et al., 2003, 2005.

# 6
# The OSCE: the Somewhat Different Socializing Agency

*Michael Merlingen and Rasa Ostrauskaitė**

The Organization for Security and Co-operation (OSCE) is a generally underrated institution. For instance, in a symptomatic statement, a well-known student of European affairs describes it in denigrating manner as a 'talking shop' (van Ham, 2001: 404). Yet such a perspective overlooks the power of norms. A talking shop may be a social environment well suited for international socialization. In this chapter, we shall argue that, firstly, the OSCE is an important niche player in the spread of Euro-Atlantic community norms and, secondly, it differs in important ways from other socializing agencies.

We proceed as follows. To begin with, we briefly describe the transformation of the former Cold War security regime into an agency for the promotion of norms centred on human security. Next, we turn to the OSCE's socialization toolkit. From the organizational attributes of the institution, we deduce the relative weight it attaches to different socializing strategies, and we predict the relative effectiveness of each strategy depending on whether the OSCE or one of the other major Euro-Atlantic community organizations uses it. We move on to explore how the OSCE assembles its own very specific categorization of out-groups, whose post-Socialist members are imagined to need assistance in their induction into the organization's ways of behaviour. Linking this discussion to research on the scope conditions for socialization, we predict variation in the OSCE's deployment of socialization strategies across out-groups. In the penultimate section, we draw on micro-level

* The views expressed in this chapter are the views of the authors and do not represent the official position of the Policy Planning and Early Warning Unit of the General Secretariat of the Council of the EU.

evidence, based partly on field research and partly on the analysis of OSCE documents, to show how the interaction of the organization's attributes with its definition of out-groups and the situation on the ground in the countries to be socialized gives rise to particular patterns of norm promotion. We end by bringing into focus the distinct socialization ethos characterizing the OSCE.

## The making of a socializing agency

The forerunner of the OSCE – the Conference on Security and Co-operation in Europe (CSCE) – was created in 1975 as a pan-European security institution designed to stabilize Europe's Cold War order while at the same time making it more humane.[1] Initially, the Soviet leadership thought that it had achieved the legitimization of the geopolitical status quo in Europe and gained greater access to Western goods and technology while signing up to yet another negligible human rights document. Western governments, too, believed that Helsinki represented 'a defeat for the West': the Final Act would do nothing to improve the human rights situation in the East. Yet, contra widespread expectations, the Helsinki norms, in particular Principle VII of the Decalogue – respect for human rights and fundamental freedoms – and Basket III concerning co-operation in humanitarian issues, played an important role in the demise of Communism (cf. Thomas, 2001; also Chilton, 1995; Ghebali, 1989; and Schlotter, 1999). Yet these normative consequences of the Helsinki Final Act were, by and large, unexpected effects. The CSCE was not intended by those who created it to be a socializing agent.

After the collapse of the Eastern bloc, the C/OSCE gradually refocused its activities on conflict prevention, conflict management and post-conflict rehabilitation, based notably on its proliferating human-dimension commitments.[2] The objective of this incremental adaptation to the post-Cold War environment was to transform the institution into one of the principal players in the dissemination of Western norms in post-Socialist space.

We argue that the very large majority of the norms diffused by the OSCE aim at promoting human security. The term denotes the belief that the proper reference point for politics is a concern with human life and dignity, including meaningful participation in the life of the community (cf. UNDP, 1994: 22). Human security, in this view, is about emancipation from oppressive power structures and the promotion of institutions and practices that embody respect for human rights and fundamental freedoms, democracy and the rule of law.[3] The OSCE elaborated a host of regulatory norms through which the notion of human security is concretized in the form of specific prescriptions and proscriptions for action in a wide range of policy areas covering, among others, human rights, elections, inter-ethnic relations, gender equality and criminal justice. To promote its norms, the organization created new organs, especially the High Commissioner on National Minorities (HCNM), the Office for Democratic Institutions and Human Rights (ODIHR) and long-term field missions (LTMs).

## The OSCE's socialization toolkit

International organizations vary in terms of their socialization toolkit. In this section, we bring together an analysis of the OSCE's institutional structure with research on the scope conditions of socialization that identifies the attributes and conduct that make an actor an effective socializer. From this discussion, we deduce the limits and strengths of the organization's socialization toolkit and contrast it with that of other players active in the promulgation of Euro-Atlantic norms.

Following the theoretical reference point established by the editor of this volume, we argue that international organizations that operate in a normatively institutionalized environment can make use of two basic social psychological strategies to socialize countries into their norms: social influence and persuasion. However, we believe that for the purpose of this chapter, it is useful to subdivide the persuasion category into normative intermediation and training. As we shall see further below, this move allows for a more fine-grained empirical analysis of the socializing activities of the OSCE than would otherwise be possible.

Beginning with social influence, it seeks to 'elicit pro-norm behavior through the distribution of social rewards and punishments' (Johnston, 2001: 499). By allocating social rewards, say through praising, a socializing agency provides in-group normative support for norm-consistent behaviour. By carrying out social punishment, say through shaming, a socializing agency exerts social pressure on those at the receiving end to alter their behaviour, without requiring them to modify their beliefs or attitudes. As is the case with all socialization strategies, the *conditio sine qua non* for social influence is that the socializees identify with the in-group. Beyond this prerequisite, research suggests that among the factors influencing the ability of socializers to make use of the strategy are their prominence and the availability of mechanisms linking social rewards and punishments to material consequences (cf. Finnemore and Sikkink, 1998: 906; Ikenberry and Kupchan, 1990; Schimmelfennig,

2000: 125–6). From these scope conditions, we deduce that the strategy plays a secondary role in the socializing activities of the OSCE.

In contrast to the European Union (EU) and NATO, the OSCE has only a very limited capacity to articulate social influence to material rewards and punishments. For instance, the EU can back up its use of shaming by withholding substantial pre-accession technical and financial support to countries wishing to join the club or hoping to benefit from support available under the European Neighbourhood Policy (ENP). The OSCE, on the other hand, has few funds of its own to allocate to socializees and acts more as a lobbyist that asks 'partner organizations' such as the United Nations to support assistance projects in post-Socialist countries. Moreover, compared to the other major Euro-Atlantic community organizations, including the Council of Europe (CoE), the OSCE is the least prominent, that is, its social approval is valued less by post-Socialist countries. The reason for its relatively low status seems to be its lack of a legal foundation. While the other international socializing agencies are all based on a constitutive treaty, the OSCE was created by a political accord and, consequently, its norms lack the prestige of law. Thus, even though the CoE's material capabilities are as limited as those of the OSCE, 'states squeak louder when reprimanded by the CoE' than when shamed by the OSCE.[4]

Yet, despite these weaknesses, which are inscribed in its institutional structure, we hypothesize that the OSCE, under certain conditions, is able to exert some social influence over post-Socialist countries. Firstly, policy-makers, as individuals who value and aspire to join the in-group, are sensitive to the organization's social opprobrium and the dissonance that comes from conduct that is inconsistent with their self-professed norms. And even if they may not be overly concerned with social punishment administered by the OSCE, they may wish to avoid being shamed by powerful members of the in-group who follow up on statements by the OSCE in their bilateral contacts with the state in question. Secondly, and more importantly, governments want to avoid the material disadvantages that are, indirectly, linked to social punishment by the OSCE. The material costs of being shamed by the organization are the result of the interlocking nature of international institutions in Europe. In deciding which countries to accept into their fold, the EU and NATO take on board the view of the OSCE as expressed, among other things, in its statements and reports on the compliance of post-Socialist states with international norms. Hence, we argue that, lacking its own sticks and carrots, the OSCE's ability to mobilize social influence depends at least partly on the willingness of Europe's most powerful political and military institutions to let the OSCE play a gatekeeper role with regard to countries aspiring to join them or to establish closer relations with them.

Turning to training, this socializing strategy seeks to promote pro-social behaviour through the inculcation of norms and skills on the basis of well-defined lesson plans (Finnemore, 1996). Going beyond social influence, training does not operate just through external pressures but has recourse to processes by which individuals act upon their 'attitude systems'. These processes are based on subject positions defined in terms of competences, that is, work identities and skills deemed to underpin professional conduct in a specific issue area. Through pedagogical work, the 'pupils' are hailed into these positions, that is, their abilities, values and desires are shaped by the socializing agency in the name of best international practice. They are incited to engage in practices of self-monitoring and self-improvement in search of excellence. Socialization through training, then, aims at a deeper level of norm internalization than the strategy of social influence by instilling certain competences in socializees and by cultivating their self-regulating capacities. Research on persuasion and learning suggests that one of the conditions under which this socializing strategy can be expected to work best is the use of a co-operative teaching methodology by the socializing agency (cf. Adler, 1998; Checkel, 2000). This leads us to hypothesize that, other things being equal, the OSCE is a more effective 'trainer' than the EU and the CoE. We shall briefly elaborate on our argument.

One of the key features of the organization's pedagogical work, which mostly consists of small-scale training projects aimed at grassroots actors as well as junior- and mid-level state officials, is the distinct philosophy on which it is based. It embodies a paradigm of knowledge creation and transfer according to which teaching best avoids being overly prescriptive. The OSCE thus values experiential learning, which incorporates local values and knowledge and aims at nurturing the latent aptitudes of trainees. This training philosophy sets the organization apart from the EU and the CoE, which primarily target elites and operate with a unilateral paradigm of knowledge production and dissemination in which the 'pupils' figure principally as uncritical recipients of established Western 'truths'. For instance, the CoE organizes numerous seminars and workshops, in which it teaches post-Socialist decision-makers clearly defined elements of a standardized model of European statehood. The key elements of this model are non-negotiable, that is, the CoE does not enter into any argument about their normative rightness or applicability to particular countries (cf. Merlingen and Ostrauskaitė, 2003).

The explanation for the distinct training philosophy of the OSCE lies in its organizational attributes. To begin with, without exception the socializees are members of the organization rather than countries aspiring to join it. Moreover, the organization is the least institutionalized Euro-Atlantic community institution and thus more dependent on, and sensitive to, the interests of participating states. Finally, the norms embedded in the OSCE's training projects are soft law provisions which do not create the same 'hard' obligations as for instance the legal conventions of the CoE or the treaty-based commitments of the EU. Together these features constrain the OSCE to adopt a pronounced co-operative approach to the transfer of its norms to the East. The same attributes also predispose the organization to make extensive use of yet another socializing strategy.

Normative intermediation aims at bringing about pro-social behaviour through the give and take of argumentation (cf. Ratner, 2000; Risse, 2000). Just like training, normative intermediation thus seeks to change the deeply held beliefs, norms and values of the socializees. However, unlike the former, socialization based on argumentation is mostly centred on governmental decision-makers and elites. Moreover, in contrast to training it is premised not on a teacher–pupil relationship but on a relationship among equals in which no one claims a monopoly on correct interpretations. Hence, intermediation is an open-ended, dialogical process based on a reciprocal perspective rather than a mimetic process, however diluted by a co-operative teaching philosophy, through which Western norms are distributed to Eastern countries. The strategy aims at persuading the socializees of the validity of normative claims through argumentative reasoning. Moreover, normative intermediation implies that the socializing agency itself is willing to be persuaded by good arguments as to why its norms have to be adapted to the cultural and political contexts of the countries to be socialized.

As to the attributes that enable an actor to engage in normative intermediation, research suggests that institutional features that facilitate confidential exchanges among small groups outside the limelight of the media are an important asset (cf. Checkel, 1999: 549). In politicized public settings, the constituencies of the (sub-)national dialogue partners are likely to find it socially unacceptable that their representatives yield to international persuasive influence. The ensuing constraints on the freedom of action of the interlocutors undermine the very notion of an open-ended policy dialogue aimed at transcending existing standpoints. From this condition we deduce that the OSCE is Europe's most potent international normative intermediary. Our reasoning is as follows.

The OSCE uses a number of institutional venues such as seminars or conferences for normative intermediation. Among its main institutional organs, the HCNM – a political body mandated to intervene as an independent third party within states in situations having the potential to create inter-ethnic conflicts – is especially well suited for this socializing strategy. The HCNM's principal conflict prevention tools are 'communicative devices', especially recommendations and the organization of roundtables. Through trial and error, the first Commissioner Max van der Stoel developed a particular strategy for utilizing these tools, a strategy which has by now become institutionalized in the office. Among the main elements of this strategy are confidentiality and a focus on a restricted number of interlocutors. The strategy reflects the experience of the Commissioner that any attempt to conduct 'public diplomacy' is likely to undermine his credibility and good working relations with his counterparts, thus impeding his ability to engage in normative intermediation aimed at the resolution of ethnic tensions (van der Stoel, 1998; Vasilev, 1999).

Normative intermediation, just like its distinct form of training, is a hallmark of the OSCE, which sets it apart from the other Euro-Atlantic community organizations. While, for instance, NATO too uses normative intermediation to transfer its norms to post-Socialist countries, the dialogical quality of this process is more restricted than in the case of the OSCE because at least those countries that wish to join NATO are expected to adapt unilaterally to its ways of behaviour. Moreover, as mentioned earlier, the OSCE has only a very limited material capability to structure the preferences of post-Socialist countries. Thus, the context in which the organization seeks to socialize its interlocutors is marked by the absence of materially based power differentials. Conversely, in the case of NATO the socializer and the socializees are generally bound together in a highly asymmetrical relationship, even if power is allowed to recede into the background and the participants in the policy dialogue pretend, or genuinely try, to interact as equals.

Finally, we want to briefly draw attention to yet another strategy used by the OSCE in its efforts to disseminate its norms to post-Socialist countries: awareness raising. Technically speaking, this is not a socialization strategy because its use does not presuppose prior identification of the socializees with the norms of the socializing agency. Nominally, of course, all participating states do subscribe to the OSCE's normative *acquis*, to which they have politically committed themselves by joining the organization. But as we shall see in the next section, as the Euro-Atlantic community organization whose norm diffusion activities reach furthest into post-Soviet space, the OSCE has member states with political traditions far removed from the liberal democratic values at the core of the OSCE. Before these countries can be expected to internalize OSCE norms, they have to be, firstly, familiarized with them and, secondly, incited to reconceptualize their identity in relation to the new norms. Only once the awareness-raising strategies have succeeded in this task, can socialization proper begin.

Having identified the distinctiveness of the OSCE's socialization toolkit, we turn next to another feature of the organization that makes it a somewhat different socializing agency.

## Categorizing OSCE states

One of the principal propositions of this volume is that the categorization of the socializees into a set of differentiated out-groups by the socializer affects the latter's choice of socializing strategy. Extending this line of thinking, we submit that the system of out-groups can be expected to vary across socializing agencies. Our claim is informed by social identity theories, which suggest that definitions of self and others are context-specific rather than objective (cf. Oakes et al., 1999). In the case of the Euro-Atlantic community organizations, the context within which they assemble their categorizations of socializees varies from one organization to the other because of differences in their membership and institutional contexts such as norms and discursive structures.

In what follows, we first sketch out how the OSCE informally orders its post-Socialist member states before linking this discussion to research on the attributes that make socializer–socializee relations conducive to the transmission of norms and actors receptive to being socialized. Thus, we bring into focus the conceptual links between the different out-groups imagined by the organization, the absence or presence in these groups, and between them and the OSCE, of the scope conditions for effective socialization and the strategies deployed by the organization to transfer its norms to these out-groups. To highlight the specificity of the out-group categorization deployed by the OSCE and to avoid confusion with the definition of out-groups used in the editor's model of complex socialization, we shall speak of 'OSCE out-groups'.

One of the institutional attributes of the OSCE is its inclusiveness. Consequently, it does not engage in official self- and other-categorization processes, unlike NATO, the CoE and the EU. Thus, the OSCE space is not formally differentiated into a hierarchical system of social groups. There are two principal manifestations of this undifferentiated inclusiveness. First, the OSCE has never used a policy of conditionality that would require of countries to take certain clearly defined policy actions before they are allowed to become members. For instance, the OSCE did not make accession of the successor states of the Soviet Union conditional on their acting in accordance with the principles laid down in the 1990 Charter of Paris for a New Europe and other C/OSCE documents. Second, while the OSCE has the power to suspend the membership of countries that are in flagrant violation of its principles, it is very reluctant to do so.

International institutions constitute the world around them as fictive spaces marked out and differentiated by a grid of institutional norms (cf. Merlingen, 2003). The OSCE is no exception. Without such categorical differentiations, and the knowledge of local politics, economics, peoples, customs and so forth on which they are based, it could not contemplate, calculate, plan and carry out its governance activities, including the socialization of the East. However, in the case of the OSCE, the assemblage of a country-based system of categorical differences is an informal process.

The OSCE's ordering of post-Socialist space has become more nuanced over the years, corresponding to the growing differentiation of its norm catalogue, the unequal political development of the different countries in transition and the different categorizations of other international socializing agencies, notably the EU. In the early 1990s, 'the East' was imagined by the OSCE in-group – the Western democracies – as one big, more or less undifferentiated landmass characterized by instability and human insecurity.

> Economic decline, social tension, aggressive nationalism, intolerance, xenophobia and ethnic conflicts threaten stability in the CSCE area. Gross violations of CSCE commitments in the field of human rights and fundamental freedoms, including those related to national minorities, pose a special threat to the peaceful development of society, in particular in new democracies.[5]

However, by the second half of the 1990s, this hinterland had been re-envisaged by the OSCE as consisting *de facto* of three distinct out-groups.

The first category was made up of countries that aspired to democratic government centred on human security but that were believed to lack a fully developed organizational and attitudinal infrastructure to implement it. The second category was composed of countries that were seen as having the long-term potential for such government but that were not yet (fully) convinced of its desirability. The only member of the third category was the former Yugoslavia, whose conduct was judged in 1992 to deviate so far from the standard of civilization that it had become a pariah to be suspended from the organization. However, after the downfall of Slobodan Milošević in 2000, the country was readmitted to the organization. Since then no member state has been ordered into this particular OSCE out-group. To these three groupings, the OSCE added a fourth category at the beginning of the new millennium: countries that were recognized as having established, though not yet sufficiently solidified, the institutions and practices of democratic governance.

The fourfold categorization by the OSCE of post-Socialist member states persists to this day, although the membership of most of the OSCE out-groups has changed. This differentiated vision of post-Socialist space influences how the organization relates to individual countries. Current OSCE out-group 1 members such as the Visegrad countries and the Baltics are imagined by the organization not, say, as fresh democracies reinvigorating the stale liberal ethos of the Euro-Atlantic in-group but as 'upstarts' whose political systems lack maturity and which displayed 'growing pains' in the recent past resulting, notably, in ethnic tensions. While there is nothing inevitable about this imagining, it does have powerful effects: the countries in question, unlike the in-group members, remain, for the time being, under close surveillance by the OSCE. However, because they do comply with the norms of the Euro-Atlantic community – arguably their norm compliance is no worse than that of the in-group – the OSCE has significantly scaled down its socializing activities on the ground. It limits itself mostly to providing expert assistance and to using a modest dose of social influence.

A recent example of the use of social influence by the OSCE in relation to an out-group 1 member is the HCNM's involvement in Hungary. In 2001, the country passed the Status Law, which provides Hungarians living in neighbouring countries with special rights and benefits. The HCNM, believing just like the EU that the law fell short of minimum international standards, intervened by issuing, over the following years, a series of recommendations to the government on how to make the law consistent with international norms. To encourage this amendment process and to ensure appropriate secondary legislation, the Commissioner engaged in confidential dialogue with the authorities. However, he also used social influence, expressing his appreciation when the government took on board his recommendations and criticizing it for paying insufficient attention early on to the compatibility of the Status Law with the country's international normative obligations and good neighbourly relations.[6]

Turning to OSCE out-group 2, it currently comprises, among others, the states of the Western Balkans. Both the governments and the citizens of the concerned countries have a (more or less pronounced) pro-Western orientation, but significant attitude-behaviour inconsistencies remain. While out-group 2 members are seen by the OSCE to consist of novices eager to adopt the norms and behaviour preferred by the Western in-group, they are also believed to be incapable of accomplishing their objective by themselves. In the organization's imagining, decades of Communism and the pre-Communist legacies feature as serious obstacles to 'self-socialization'. Consequently, the OSCE imagines a major role for itself in assisting them in their induction into its ways of behaviour.

Particularly in the more Westernized countries of this group, social psychological and institutional factors combine to enable the OSCE to make comprehensive and intensive use of its socialization toolkit, both at the elite and the grassroots level. The governments and important elements of the civil societies look to the Euro-Atlantic community for upward social comparison and self-evaluation. The resulting perception on their part of similarity and equivalence between themselves and that community makes them open to its social pressure, pedagogical work and normative intermediation. Furthermore, the dense institutional network linking countries such as Croatia or the former Yugoslav Republic of Macedonia (FYROM) to the OSCE and other international socializing agents provides multiple channels of communication through which norms can be transferred as well as mechanisms through which shame and praise can be publicly administered.

Last but not least, the reasonably well-developed democratic political structures and processes in these countries enable the OSCE to make good use of its bottom-up approach to socialization to enrol and empower civil society actors as allies in the diffusion of its norms. The countries' relatively independent civil societies hedge numerous, albeit often disorganized and under-resourced pro-democracy grassroots actors and non-governmental organizations. They are a ready-made OSCE constituency, which, once their mobilization potential has been upgraded, generate bottom-up pressure for norm compliance on governmental decision-makers (cf. Alderson, 2001: 419; Checkel, 2001: 557). In those OSCE out-group 2 countries in which the Western orientation of either the government or the mass public is less pronounced, or in which the density of institutional links with Western organizations is lower, such as in Moldova, Armenia or Azerbaijan, the OSCE has to do with fewer points of access and less propitious conditions for its socializing activities.

As to OSCE out-group 3 – the Central Asian republics and Belarus – their governments subscribe to more or less illiberal ideologies and the Western orientation in the societies is weak. Hence, the countries tend to emphasize the between-group contrast between themselves and the Euro-Atlantic in-group, positively valuing their own distinct social identities. Moreover, there are few institutional ties between this out-group and the OSCE and other Euro-Atlantic community organizations. While the scope conditions for the diffusion of Western norms to these countries are thus largely absent, just as they were in the former Yugoslavia under Milošević, the OSCE does not order them into its out-group 4. Hence, rather than treating a human rights 'black hole' such as Turkmenistan as a pariah with at best very uncertain long-term prospects (cf. Stoudmann, 2003), it imagines that the country does have the potential to become a fully-fledged member of the OSCE family of values. Furthermore, it believes that by engaging it constructively, it can prompt it to re-evaluate its own positively perceived 'distinguishedness' and induct it into its ways of behaviour (cf. Flockhart, 2004c: 14).

The main strategies deployed by the organization to promote its norms in out-group 3 members are awareness-raising activities and technical assistance projects, including limited forms of training. A typical feature of these activities is that they are low profile and small-scale, targeting a limited number of mostly junior- and mid-level state officials and/or grassroots actors. In the case of Belarus the OSCE, in addition, uses its limited access to segments of the political opposition with a pro-Western leaning in an effort to diffuse its norms into society at large. However, the weakness of the opposition and independent non-governmental organizations provides difficult conditions for these attempts to induct new recruits into the community of values embodied by the OSCE.

To conclude this section, the OSCE *de facto* orders its post-Socialist member states into four broad categories. The imagined social distances created by this ordering matter because, together with the scope conditions for socialization, they shape how the OSCE relates to its post-Socialist member states. Next, we look in more detail at the organization's socializing activities on the ground to illustrate our claim.

## Socialization in action

Throughout most of the 1990s, the C/OSCE was actively involved in the socialization of post-Socialist countries in all sub-regions of the OSCE space. By 2004, the organization had significantly reduced its activities in the post-Socialist EU members and candidate countries, focusing its attention squarely on the remaining parts of Eastern Europe, South-eastern Europe, the Caucasus and Central Asia. In what follows, we draw on our field research and textual analysis to present fine-grained empirical evidence that documents how the OSCE's socializing strategies differ across out-groups 2 and 3.

### OSCE out-group 2

In its out-group 2, the OSCE finds good-to-excellent scope conditions for its socializing activities. In the latter case, the organization's distinctiveness as a socializing agency comes to the fore. To bring this distinctiveness into focus, we concentrate our attention on the most Western-leaning countries of the out-group.

We begin with social influence. While the organization's social influence is low in OSCE out-group 2 members, such as Russia or Ukraine, the situation is different in countries such as Croatia and the FYROM. Here, the OSCE is in a position to articulate the reputation effects of shaming and praising to significant material costs and benefits.

There are a number of factors that in this case enhance the organization's otherwise low ability to produce normative pressure. The desire of these countries to remake themselves in the image of the Euro-Atlantic in-group makes them susceptible to the social psychological effects of being publicly shamed and praised by those actors such as the OSCE that embody the norms and values of the in-group. In addition, two politico-legal factors reinforce the social influence of the OSCE in the concerned countries by explicitly linking compliance with OSCE norms to integration into the EU or a European perspective and thus to access to large material benefits.[7]

First, the Europe Agreements establishing an association between the EU and candidate countries contain a statement in the preamble reaffirming the commitment of the signatories to the full implementation of all provisions and principles in the OSCE documents. Similar provisions are included in the EU's Stabilization and Association Agreements, the Partnership and Co-operation Agreements and, finally, the ENP, too, requires countries to show commitment to international norms, including those of the OSCE. Clearly, the link in these agreements and initiatives between access to EU funds and compliance with OSCE norms enhances the 'persuasiveness' of the normative pressure exerted by the OSCE. Second, the Copenhagen European Council in 1993 spelled out, among other things, respect for minorities as one of the conditions for accession. This gives the HCNM, who is the only institutional actor exclusively tasked to deal with inter-ethnic relations, a significant informal voice in the assessment by the EU of whether a country meets this membership criterion (Kemp, 2001: 27, 99; Packer, 2000: 718–19; Zellner and Lange, 2001: 8). The point to be made here is that the combination of a psychological predisposition on the part of the most Western-leaning out-group 2 members to let themselves be influenced by the OSCE and the explicit link between the organization's evaluation of their conformity with international norms and their relationship with the EU enables the OSCE to punch above its weight and to use social influence to promote pro-norm behaviour.

Moving from social influence to training, in particular in those OSCE out-group 2 countries that have advanced most to close the gap between themselves and the Euro-Atlantic community, the OSCE finds very good institutional and attitudinal conditions on the ground for its activities. Thus, while generally the OSCE designs and implements small-scale training projects, it operates large-scale schemes in some of these countries. Moreover, because the gap between the norms at the core of these pedagogical activities and the beliefs of the trainees is relatively small, the organization can more fully than elsewhere enact its co-operative training philosophy. In short, in out-group 2 the organization's distinctive strengths as a training agency come to the fore. This is clearly visible in a large-scale professionalization project in the FYROM, which targets police officers.

In the wake of the Ohrid Framework Agreement in 2001, which ended the ethnic hostilities and fighting in the country, the Macedonian government approached the OSCE to ask for assistance in the implementation of the accord. The OSCE agreed. It significantly reinforced its already existing LTM on the ground with a view to assisting the authorities in reforming the police. A principal pillar of these efforts is training.

The Training and Educational Support Divisions of the Police Development Unit (PDU), which was set up by the mission to organize its police-related socializing activities, design and deliver training to Macedonian police cadets and officers. Besides providing technical skills training such as drug identification and firearms instruction, the curriculum is designed to socialize police officers into core OSCE norms. It thus emphasizes subjects such as human rights training, police ethics, policing in a multiethnic society, community policing and domestic violence awareness. These subjects aim at bringing about a shift in ethos in the police organization from being a regime police to a human-rights-oriented service provider, from top-down law enforcement to bottom-up community orientation and from policing alone to democratic policing in partnership with citizens and non-governmental organizations.[8]

As to the teaching philosophy underpinning this training regime, it is co-operative in orientation, emphasizing the importance of mutual movement and development among trainers and trainees rather than a hierarchical teacher–pupil relationship (Merlingen and Ostrauskaitė, 2004). Moreover, in its efforts to instil certain professional competences, including norms, into Macedonian police officers, the OSCE takes account of local cultural and political contexts. This distinctive approach is based on the presupposition that universal(izing) notions of democratic policing have to be adapted to particular(izing) preferences and practices on the ground (cf. Marenin, 1998: 165).

An important supplement to these training activities is the empowerment by the PDU of ordinary citizens and non-governmental organizations in policing matters, notably through its assistance in creating and strengthening Citizen Advisory Groups. Through its community development activities (seminars, conferences, town hall meetings, and so on), the PDU seeks to incite ordinary people to recategorize themselves in relation to the police and to become involved, in partnership with the police, in addressing deep-seated community problems of which crime and disorder are merely the symptoms. The point we want to make here is that the OSCE's pedagogical work in the FYROM brings out the organization's distinct profile as a teacher of norms: the police training is markedly co-operative and embedded in broader reforms aimed at strengthening the capacity of citizens to play an active role in the provision of public security.

Finally, we turn to normative intermediation. We argued earlier that its organizational attributes predispose the OSCE towards the use of this socialization strategy. In OSCE out-group 2, it encounters the scope conditions under which it can develop this potential. The identification of the more democratic and open countries with the Euro-Atlantic community and the densely institutionalized environment linking them together combine to constitute a 'community of communication' in which the moral rightness of norms can be openly discussed and a reasoned consensus on the issues under debate can be established (cf. Risse, 2000: 10).

A case in which one can say with some confidence that normative intermediation was a significant, albeit not necessarily the only factor in bringing about norm-consistent behaviour in a (former) OSCE out-group 2 country is Hungary. In 1993 the HCNM was faced with complaints from Slovakia about Hungary's treatment of its Slovak minority.[9]

The then Commissioner van der Stoel dispatched a team of minority rights specialists to assist Budapest in revising its minority policy (Kemp, 2001: 245–8). Between 1993 and 1996, when its mission was terminated, the team of three experts visited the country twice each year to hear first-hand accounts of the problems and to meet in person with governmental officials, Members of Parliament, the representatives of the Slovak minority and concerned non-governmental organizations. While technically speaking these visits were fact-finding missions, they inevitably also served the purpose of involving the parties in dialogue, encouraging patterns of co-operation and modifying perceptions and feelings of suspicion.

After each visit, the experts submitted their findings to the HCNM who, on a number of occasions, decided to issue recommendations to the government based on these findings. The recommendations, which took the form of letters to the foreign minister, drew on normative arguments, highlighting, for instance, the 'repeatedly expressed commitments of the Government to grant the minorities in Hungary a wide range of possibilities' before pointing out a number of specific policy implications of this stance.[10] The foreign minister, in turn, responded to these recommendations in writing too. In the ensuing exchange of letters, the government was drawn into a process that displayed typical features of argumentative discourse. For instance, in his response to the first letter sent by the Commissioner, the then foreign minister Jeszenszky engaged in a reasoned argument more reminiscent of a scholarly paper than a political communication. To strengthen his case, he even enclosed a study on nationalism, which he had written himself 'back in the early 1980s and whose publication was prevented by the censorship of the time, so that it eventually appeared only at the end of the 1980s in a small-circulation university publication'.[11]

Overall, the involvement of the HCNM in Hungary between 1993 and 1996 displays clear signs of normative intermediation. The work on the ground carried out by the experts and the recommendations of the Commissioner were by and large insulated from public exposure and political pressure. The recommendations carried weight because they were based on expert advice and put forward in a non-partisan manner. Finally, the exchange of letters between the Commissioner and the foreign minister was based on reasoned arguments. As to the policy implications of this dialogue, the Hungarian government acted on the principal recommendations of the HCNM, establishing *inter alia* an office for national and ethnic minorities, an ombudsman institution and a parliamentary commissioner for minority rights. This suggests that normative intermediation contributed to the emergence of an argumentative consensus on how best to implement the commitment of the government to politically empower the minorities in Hungary.

**OSCE out-group 3**

In our analysis of the socialization of OSCE out-group 3, we focus on the countries of Central Asia as they present the most interesting case given that they are the furthest removed from the norms and values embodied by the OSCE. The region has in recent years been declared a focal point for OSCE activities as the organization attempts 'to bring it into the fold'. Yet, if one turns one's gaze from the corridors of high diplomacy to the mundane world of field operations, the hurdles facing the OSCE become apparent.

The significant social distance between the predominant authoritarian and patriarchal political cultures of the region and the civic culture that is at the heart of the OSCE norm catalogue makes the promotion of norm cascades in Central Asia very difficult. The task of the OSCE is not made easier by the fact that the available resources are very limited. Declarations notwithstanding, the funds channelled by the OSCE to projects in the region are dwarfed by those allocated to the Balkans. Moreover, the political context since 9/11 has not always been conducive to the OSCE's norm-promoting activities as, under the cover of fighting terrorism, some countries reverted to more authoritarian policies and the 'social transformation that began after the collapse of the Soviet Union [has begun] to stagnate'.[12] What, then, does the OSCE do on the ground to promote its norms? It mostly implements small-scale awareness-raising and empowerment campaigns targeting grassroots actors, especially women, and technical assistance projects aimed, on the one hand, at providing expertise on particular issue-areas to decision-makers and, on the other, at upgrading the competence of state officials (cf. Ghebali, 2004: 4–6). In what follows, we shall limit our discussion to technical assistance programmes.

It may at first sight seem odd that we cover such projects under the heading of norm-promoting activities. Yet, by providing technical expertise, say, to help lawmakers revise domestic laws in line with international treaty obligations, the OSCE is clearly involved in encouraging pro-norm behaviour. More interesting from the point of view of socialization, by disseminating technical knowledge and skills with a view to enhancing the professional competence of public servants in host countries, the OSCE seeks to foster certain fundamental norms that can be summarized in the Weberian notion of the 'ethos of office'.

The goal is to inscribe a particular kind of ethical subjectivity in the participants so that they see themselves as vocationally responsible and accountable to the public rather than solely to their superiors or a clientage network. For instance, one OSCE project aimed at the professionalization of border guards describes its objectives as instilling in participants 'generosity, dedication and senses of professional bonds and care for the authority of performed duties' (OSCE, 2002a: 14). Clearly, these goals are not simply about technical knowledge and skills but also about the ethical sort of person the OSCE wants border guards to be.

In Central Asia such an ethical stylization of the state, however, is difficult to achieve because the post-Socialist states in the region are highly personalized and characterized by the capricious use of power and coercion in as much as they are not, or only to a limited extent, compatible with the rational-legal ethos promoted by the OSCE (cf. MacFarlane, 2003). Also, compared to the scope and depth of the institutionalization of the relationship between OSCE out-group 1 and the Euro-Atlantic community, the institutionalization of relations between the latter and Central Asia is thin. Given these external constraints as well as its lack of internal resources, the OSCE training projects in Central Asia typically are of short duration and modest in their aims. They are mostly designed to familiarize a delimited group of lower officials with how core OSCE norms relate to particular issue areas such as prison management in the expectation that this will positively affect their attitudes and conduct and generate multiplier effects in the bureaucratic structures within which they serve. However, in the absence of a significant identification with OSCE norms on the part of the Central Asian republics and the inability of the organization to mobilize social influence in the region, it has to package its socialization projects in such a way that they become interesting for those in power. To this end, the OSCE 'sells' its projects to the local authorities by linking them to their policy objectives such as the fight against terrorism or border security. The upshot is that technical skills transfer takes clear priority over norm diffusion in training projects in Central Asia.

For instance, in 2002 the OSCE organized a training course in Almaty for border service officials from Kazakhstan, Kyrgyzstan and Tajikistan (OSCE, 2002b). The project was billed as technical assistance to upgrade the level of professionalism of serving border guards with a view to enhancing their capacity to secure borders and combat terrorism, illegal migration and smuggling, all of which are objectives high on the agenda of the governments of the region. The course (lectures and practical training) covered basic technical subjects such as 'border control procedures for people, transport and goods at checkpoints'; 'special technical means of border control'; 'rules regarding the reading of foreign passports'; and 'places of possible concealment of narcotics and smuggled items in transport and goods'. Most of the training schedule was devoted to these topics. Only towards the end of the course were some hours devoted to familiarizing trainees with normative issues such as the rights of migrants and the protection of the rights of refugees.

While this project illustrates the limits of promoting a 'Weberian ethos' in Central Asia, it also highlights that, as the only transatlantic organization that incorporates the countries as members, the OSCE is well positioned to engage in this slow and difficult process. This is what one senior diplomat interviewed by us seemed to have in mind when he remarked that the OSCE 'makes these states not only known, but also to some extent controllable' by the Euro-Atlantic community.[13]

## Conclusion

In this chapter, we argued that the OSCE is a potent, albeit somewhat different socializing agency. Its will to socialize traverses all of post-Socialist space, though its socializing strategies differ across its identified out-groups. In contrast to NATO, the EU and the CoE, it pays great attention to the socialization of grassroots actors. While it has less ability than these institutions to mobilize social influence, it has succeeded in developing the expertise and organizational capacity to engage in genuine communicative action. Its manifold pedagogical activities are based on a teaching philosophy that, unlike that of the CoE and the EU, aims at empowering local knowledge and values insofar as they do not violate fundamental OSCE beliefs. To conclude, the organization has a unique profile among the major Euro-Atlantic socializing agencies. It is underpinned by a socialization ethos that is marked by the value it places on co-operation. The OSCE works primarily through enrolment, empowerment and dialogue rather than through social pressure and lecturing. In short, the OSCE approach is more egalitarian and less paternalistic than that of Europe's other socializing agencies.

### Notes

1. For the standard history of the negotiations leading to the 1975 Helsinki Final Act, see Maresca (1987). For useful discussions of the evolution of the C/OSCE in the 1990s, see Ghebali (1996) and Heraclides (1993).

2. The OSCE's comprehensive concept of security comprises three dimensions, which evolved out of the three baskets of the Helsinki Accord: the human, politico-military and economic and environmental dimensions.
3. Cf. *inter alia* the Document of the Copenhagen Meeting of the Conference on the Human Dimension of the CSCE and the Charter of Paris for a New Europe, in Bloed (1993).
4. Interview with a senior diplomat from an Eastern European state, 21 March 2003.
5. CSCE Helsinki Document 1992: 'The Challenges of Change', in Bloed (1993: 703–4).
6. Cf. HCNM.GAL/8/02, 31 October 2002; http://www.osce.org/news/show_news.php?id=3372. Other actors, notably the CoE, were also active in this case.
7. This link was well captured by a senior Croatian diplomat who told us, when asked about the role of the OSCE in his country, that 'the road to Brussels goes via Vienna', where the OSCE has its headquarters. Interview with a senior diplomat of the Croatian Foreign Ministry, 7 June 2002.
8. Cf. Superindentent Roy Fleming, contribution to the Supplementary Human Dimension Meeting on 'The Role of Community Policing in Building Confidence in Minority Communities', Vienna, 28–29 October 2002, CIO.GAL/104/02, 12 December 2002, p. 25.
9. Similar concerns were voiced by Hungary with regard to the treatment of ethnic Hungarians in Slovakia.
10. Letter of Commissioner van der Stoel to Hungarian foreign minister Géza Jeszenszky, CSCE Communication No. 307, Rome, 29 November 1993.
11. Letter of foreign minister Jeszenszky to van der Stoel, ibid.
12. Address by the OSCE Chairman-in-Office, Jaap de Hoop Scheffer, at a hearing by the Helsinki Commission of the United States Congress, Washington, 3 September 2003.
13. Interview with a senior diplomat of an Eastern European state, 3 March 2003.

# Part III

# Receiving and Internalizing Ideas in Transforming Societies

# 7
# The Czech Republic: from Socialist Past to Socialized Future

*Petr Drulák and Lucie Königová*

This chapter deals with the socialization of the Czech Republic into the West European normative order after the democratic revolution of 1989. We use the 'complex socialization' framework (Flockhart, this volume) to address this process. We focus therefore on the domestic structure as a key variable of complex socialization, distinguishing between the government and society or the state/elite and nation/people level within that structure. In this respect, the Czech Republic represents a country whose governmental ideology has consistently been based on Western democratic principles and whose society has been West-oriented. These features make it a representative member of out-group 1 within our framework (Flockhart, this volume) whose socialization should be smoother than in other groups and in which a high degree of self-socialization is to be expected.

Our analysis proceeds in several steps. Firstly, we address a revolutionary change in the self/other distinction and in the relationship between the post-1989 governing elites and society. Contrary to most other post-Communist countries, the new political elite recruited mainly from society, instead of relying on the former Communist elite. Hence, for some time, there was no clear sociological distinction between the government and society, which greatly enhanced the socialization by making the second filter between state and nation (Flockhart, this volume) highly permeable. Even though the government–society distinction has subsequently become more pronounced, it has never become too sharp. Two societal groups were of special importance: Havel-led 'dissidents' and Klaus-led 'neo-liberal economists'. We will show that despite numerous differences the two groups shared an unambiguous liberal democratic orientation calling for the 'return to

Europe' and laid the grounds for the creation of decisive democratic forces within the newly established political system.

Secondly, we analyse the milestones of socialization as linked to the Czech(oslovak) accession to the key international institutions – the Council of Europe (CoE), OECD, NATO and the EU. We argue that self-socialization played a seminal role in each instance as the membership obligations coincided to a large extent with domestic priorities. Hence, in each case a variety of influential 'intermediate agents' can be seen who identified themselves with the norms of the given organization. This contributed to the permeability of the 'international/domestic elite filter' (Flockhart, this volume). However, we also observe that the self-socialization had to be supported by active norm-promotion efforts by the international organizations. These efforts were especially important when tackling some long-term issues recognized by the domestic policy-makers as vital but difficult to address because of their long-term nature such as in the cases of building up a modern civil service or modernizing the armed forces. Also, activities of international organizations were essential in ensuring the actual fulfilment of the commitments undertaken.

Each accession and socialization process had its own specificities. The Council of Europe and the OECD are two early milestones on the Czech(oslovak) journey back to Europe. Each can be seen as a pet project of one of the two mentioned societal groups: the former promoted by 'dissidents', the latter championed by 'neo-liberal economists'. NATO accession hinted at a gap between the governing elite and society and, contrary to membership in the previous two institutions was widely discussed in the public. Also, the NATO post-accession socialization process was somewhat more controversial and more politically sensitive than the accession process itself. The EU, however, represents the most complex case of socialization: EU membership obligations cover most of the CoE and OECD duties while adding many other commitments. Pre-accession interactions with the EU were by far the longest and the most intensive of all, involving both the elected political elites and a great part of the civil service. It is especially the EU socialization of Czech civil servants that provides an interesting example of socialization of a group located at the state/elite level but with extensive links to society at large. A very strong element of the 'social influence' method of socialization (Flockhart, this volume) guided these three accession processes. Still, persuasion played an important role in the socialization of Czech civil servants and during the NATO accession period. The transfer of adopted norms and values from the state/elite level to the nation/people level, however, has been more problematic.

## Reversal of identities and the emergence of two thought communities

The Velvet Revolution in December 1989 brought about a radical reversal of the self/other and government/society relationships in Czechoslovakia. The hierarchies of these relationships were turned upside down, where actors of the government and actors of society exchanged roles. On the one hand, the Communists left the government although they remained on the political scene as a significant social force. On the other hand, societal actors such as dissidents and informal groups took up government positions. Hence, the previous sharp separation between government and society loosened up, and remained so for some time. Secondly, this exchange of roles linked up with the reversal in the self/other relationship through which the state identity was constructed. The identity of the Communist state was based on a positive identification with the Soviet Union and its model of society and on a negative delimitation against the capitalist other, the Western countries. The identity of post-1989 Czechoslovakia undergoing democratization, on the contrary, was based on a positive identification with Western democracies and on a negative profiling against the concept of Communism and against the Soviet oppressor.

The positive identification with the West was symbolized by the idea of a 'return to Europe', which was one of the most important slogans both during the Velvet Revolution and in official speeches of the new leaders. This Western orientation could draw on a variety of well-internalized structures by which modern Czech identity was constructed (Drulák, 2000, 2004). Moreover, the success of the Western market economy contrasted with the failure of central planning, thus further enhancing the legitimacy of a Western orientation.

The 'return to Europe' was understood in terms of a transition to a model of society and political economy known from Western Europe and from the USA. In this respect, the accession to the multilateral organizations of Western liberal democracies was pursued with great effort. These organizations were seen as facilitators of domestic transition and, more importantly, as the 'significant we' providing the new democracies with recognition of their return. Hence, they were perceived by the new leaders and by the bulk of Czech society as guarantors of their newly established Western/European, democratic, liberal and market-oriented identities. However, ideas about what path exactly Czechoslovakia should take on its journey back to Europe have changed over time, shaped by a gradual learning process, and influenced by the kind of leaders formulating them. Czech foreign policy elites were very narrow indeed back then: these new leaders were recruited from informal groups and networks, which existed in the late Communist society. These two groups of key actors have striven for the authoritative interpretation of the 'European homecoming'.

Focusing on the Czech side, two Prague-based networks of norm entrepreneurs can be distinguished: 'dissidents' and 'liberal economists'. Despite the internal heterogeneity within each group and the important differences between them, they share several common features. Both have their intellectual roots in the reform process in the late 1960s, which ended with the 1968 Soviet invasion. Each network had its own intellectual leader capable of transforming the network into a politically relevant 'thought community' during the Velvet Revolution. These thought communities came up with different visions of society.

## Dissidents

Dissidents openly voiced their criticism of the Communist regime for which they were harshly persecuted. It was an extremely heterogeneous group including former reformist Communists, who lost their positions after the Soviet invasion in 1968, Catholics, liberals, artists or Trotskyites *inter alia*. What they had in common was their peaceful and civic resistance against the renewed totalitarization of the post-1968 society. They often lived apart from the greater society, mostly in secluded settings or abroad (Stroehlein, 1999a; Havel, 1990a; Pithart, 1990; Šafaříková et al., 1996). In 1977, dissidents, artists and intellectuals headed by Václav Havel issued a manifesto known as 'Charter 77', demanding that the Czechoslovak government should respect the fundamental human rights of its people. Charter 77 became the most important dissident organization, aiming to monitor the CSCE human rights commitments made by the Czechoslovak Communist government, and Havel became the uncontested central figure of this network.

Havel's intellectual leadership of dissidents turned into the political leadership of the country when he became the Czechoslovak president in December 1989. Together with Havel, other high-profile dissidents occupied key political and administrative posts, including in the foreign, interior and defence ministries. But it was the powerful office of the president where dissidents clearly dominated. Foreign policy was shaped by President Havel and foreign minister Jiří Dienstbier, a leading dissident and a close friend of Havel. Their foreign policy drew on their 1980s debates about and reflections on Europe.

The community of dissidents was shaped by close ties between politics and morality. Havel's formulation of 'Europeanness' rested on a search for a unity of European entities through culture and cultivation of individuals (Havel, 1978). Besides morality and humanism, security of the undivided continent was a prime concern to dissidents (cf. Dienstbier, 1992). They called for an undivided European continent without nationalism. Both Havel (1990a, 1990b, 1991) and Dienstbier (1990) were quite critical of the West. Criticizing the 'West', however, they retained a positive attitude to 'Europe'. Both were therefore in favour of an integrated Europe but found faults with the *Western* European EC as 'economically restrictive and politically without much perspective' (Dienstbier, 1990: 117). Both identified with Milan Kundera's depiction of Central Europe as a 'kidnapped Europe' (Kundera, 1984). After 1989, this intellectual concept changed into an explicitly political one to draw a line between the 'stable' Central Europe and the unstable 'Wild East' (Neumann, 2000: 209). This explains why dissidents in Central Europe set up the Visegrad Co-operation initiative and invested many hopes in its working.

Given the heterogeneity of their community, dissidents did not have any articulated vision of an alternative order. Their idea was to work for change from below through independent civil activities such as Charter 77. Dissent was rather an intellectual trend emphasizing morality and human rights (Stroehlein, 1999b), calling for a promotion of 'civil society'. That is why they sought membership in the CoE and CSCE with so much commitment. In general, however, they were lacking any other political programme. Their 'noble' (Stroehlein, 1999b) views met with little public support. Dissidents failed to retain public support, as they were mostly unable to deliver any *substantive* policies for economic and political transition. The broader public perceived the former dissidents as mostly 'impractical, overly intellectual and out-of-touch' (Stroehlein, 1999b). After the 1992 election and Klaus' rise to power their influence and significance in practical politics – with the specific exception of Václav Havel – dwindled over time. Dissidents could be seen as a 'transitional elite' bridging two political systems.

### Liberal economists

Unlike dissidents, liberal economists lived in conformity with the Communist system, usually having positions of research fellows with official institutes of economic research. Václav Klaus was the central figure of this network (Husák, 1997). In the 1980s, Klaus organized seminars on contemporary economic theories and edited volumes in which these theories were applied proposing *perestroika* reforms of the command economy (Klaus, 1991). A list of participants at his seminars and co-authors of his volumes in the 1980s turned into a list of key economic policy-makers in the 1990s (Klaus, 1991: 9).

What ideas shaped this thought community? All seemed to agree on the existence of one economic science represented by Paul Samuelson's *Economics* among others. In spite of some important internal differences within the community, where, for example, Václav Klaus was particularly inspired by the macroeconomic theories of Milton Friedman while Tomáš Ježek, a future minister of privatization, was more influenced by F. A. Hayek and the Austrian School – all of them shared an epistemological belief in the universal applicability of neo-classical economic theories. As Ježek observes, Klaus was able to sell Friedmanian macroeconomics even to the Communist central bank, which made it, in Ježek's view, 'one of the best working bank institutions in the Eastern bloc' (Husák, 1997: 48). In that sense one could say that the 'hard core' of the community was represented by 'young economists' (Klaus, 1991: 215–19). This self-identification came from the late 1960s when the then young economists, such as Klaus, were involved in the planning of a reform of the centrally planned economy by economist Ota Šik, who was one of the pillars of both the Czechoslovak and the Communist-led, political reform process. These 'young economists' criticized both the official economic reform for not being radical enough, as well as the Marxist political economy in general. Later on, they embraced standard American economics as an alternative framework for their economic thinking.

This intellectual background had important implications for the political practice of the thought community of liberal economists in the 1990s, especially after Klaus became the Czech prime minister in 1992. At the domestic level, they were able to design and implement a plan for a radically liberal economic reform, which, however, did not take into account institutional questions and other issues not addressed by the Friedmanian macroeconomics. They also sharply rejected attempts at a revival of the 1960s economic reforms, arguing that their goal was not a third way between market and planning but a free market economy, as they said, 'without any adjectives', alluding implicitly to adjectives such as 'social' or 'environmental' (Klaus, 1994: 49). At the international level, they easily established good contacts with governments and international institutions whose policies came from the same intellectual background such as Great Britain's Tory governments, US Republican administrations, the IMF or OECD. Similarly, they supported free trade initiatives such as the Central European Free Trade Area

(CEFTA) or an association with the European Communities (EC). Liberal economists, however, neglected such international organizations and initiatives such as the CSCE, the CoE or the Visegrad co-operation which did not fit into the neo-liberal framework, and which were often promoted by the previous dissident-led foreign policy. The attitude towards the EU was ambiguous. On the one hand, it was appreciated because of its negative, liberalizing integration; on the other hand, its political dimension was heavily criticized as leftist social engineering.

How did the thought communities influence and shape the political landscape after 1989? During the Velvet Revolution both communities joined in a single political force: the Civic Forum (OF), representing society and opposing the Communist elite. Soon after, the OF turned into a decisive political force winning the first free election in 1990. Later on, however, it split into three political parties along the fault lines between the two thought communities. A Klaus-led Civic Democratic Party (ODS) and a small Civic Democratic Alliance (ODA) of liberal conservatives built on the neo-liberal thought community. A Civic Movement (OH) led by Jiří Dienstbier, on the other hand, sought to develop the dissident legacy. ODS dominated the Czech political landscape from 1992 to 1997, staying on as one of the two decisive political forces in Czech politics to this day.

The main challenge to ODS did not come from the OH, which slowly disappeared after 1992. It was the Czech Social Democratic Party (ČSSD) which grew into its strongest opponent, unseating the ODS in 1998 and becoming a senior coalition party in the government up to now. Unlike most social democratic parties in the region, ČSSD is not a successor of the totalitarian Communist Party (a typical post-Communist party) though relying heavily on the rank-and-file Communists. ČSSD was built from scratch, referring to the legacy of the pre-war Social Democratic Party and having Western European social democratic parties as its role models in striving for a social market economy and society based on solidarity. This orientation made it open to EU socialization while explaining its ambiguity about NATO. The Communist Party, in the meantime, did not disappear. It has been the third strongest party since the early 1990s, keeping the adjective 'Communist' in its name and still praising the totalitarian past. Yet, this makes it a pariah with whom no other party is ready to form a coalition. Also, the Communist Party has resisted all socialization efforts, opposing Czech membership in both NATO and the EU.

To sum up, after the Velvet Revolution the new government elite was primarily recruited from societal networks of neo-liberals and dissidents which blurred the distinction between the government and nation for years to come. These thought communities shaped the Czechoslovak policies immediately after November 1989. Later, they transformed into political parties out of which only the neo-liberal ODS survived and dominated Czech politics until the late 1990s to be replaced by a non-Communist Social Democratic Party while the Communist Party remained a significant force despite its isolation by other political forces.

## CoE and OECD: two thought communities, two separate projects

Membership of the Council of Europe (1991) and the OECD (1995) were the first milestones on the journey back to Europe. Agendas and membership obligations of each of these fitted into the agendas of the two thought communities acting as intermediate agents who greatly facilitated the Czech(oslovak) accession to these organizations. Moreover, the accessions took place when the distinction between government and society was still blurred, and this contributed to the popular internalization of the norms. So, while dissidents shared their concern about human rights and democratic norms with the CoE, neo-liberals in the ODS and ODA could easily relate to the neo-liberal OECD. In this connection, the abolition of the death penalty and the radical liberalization of the economy were important aspects of the self-socialization process.

The CoE was closest to a common organization of all Europeans, and was regarded as a symbol of 'Europeanness' (cf. Ort, 1993: 18), particularly European civilization and its cultural and humanistic heritage. Due to its Convention for the Protection of Human Rights and Fundamental Freedoms, the CoE became a symbol of acceptance into a community of European democratic states after 1989, a policy issue of prime concern to dissidents. Moreover, admission into the CoE – unlike the membership of the EC – was possible within a relatively short time frame (Bugge, 2000: 3). Czechoslovakia became an active CoE member in February 1991.[1]

The CoE was a 'prime mover' (Leff, 1998: 245) in post-1989 external political influences on the domestic structure in terms of the political system, governance, courts and, vicariously, public access to voice opportunities. It had the clearest mandate for promoting political and social tolerance and democratic governance, becoming thus the principal target of affiliation for all CEE countries. Both the Czech and Slovak Republics sought CoE advice when drafting their constitutions in 1992. The admission process itself was a feedback cycle of sustained and detailed consultation between the CoE and Czechoslovakia, followed by a 'probation period' (Leff, 1998: 246), a subsequent evaluation of the CoE membership conditions. These included compliance with the CoE's conventions but focused mainly on the domestic system, that is, the existence of competitive elections, good public governance, protection of (ethnic and other) minority interests and opinions. Signing the CoE's Convention on the European Court of Human Rights (ECHR) has effectively extended the international monitoring process into the future (Leff, 1998: 246).

Importantly, any violation of the right to a due process of law is widely covered by both domestic and international media when appeals or grievances are taken to the ECHR by individual citizens. There have been several appeals already by Czech citizens and more complaints are expected, due to protracted, decade-long legal proceedings. A Strasburg Committee, an NGO for Czech claimants, was thus set up in Prague in 2003 to make the public aware of their rights, thus 'filtering' down the democratic norms and values of the CoE.[2] Finally, since 1994, the CoE's Congress of Local and Regional Authorities of Europe (CLRAE) has helped new CoE members with the practical aspects of establishing effective local and regional self-government to cover yet another layer of governance. The newly formed Czech regions report positively on this co-operative initiative (Drulák et al., 2004).

Introducing a pluralist democracy and seeking to join the CoE, post-Communist countries decided to abolish the death penalty. The disagreement between the government (abolishing it) and society (in favour of retaining the death penalty) was huge, chiefly due to soaring crime in the early 1990s. Over time, however, this norm of the democratic Western community of states has filtered down from the government to the nation level, with the supporters of capital punishment's reintroduction in a steady decline, dropping from 76 per cent in 1992 to 56 per cent in 2002 (České veřejné mínění v evropských souvislostech 3/2002). In other words it would appear that 'state' culture has been translated into a 'nation' culture.

The accession to the OECD was a pet project of the Czech neo-liberal thought community. Three forces attracted the Czech government to the OECD. Firstly, the government and the OECD belonged to the same transnational, neo-liberal epistemic community based on a shared understanding of economics and economic policy. Secondly, the OECD was more exclusive than the previous Western organizations acceded to, so the perceived value of the membership was much higher (Provazník, 1995: 37). Thirdly, the recognition in the area of the OECD activities was the recognition of the Czech radical economic reform, the political project of the Czech neo-liberal thought community.

The Czech OECD accession policy was very active. In January 1994 it was the first post-Communist country applying for OECD membership (Fajkusová, 1999: 82). Also, during the accession period the Czech Republic delivered the requested analyses ahead of schedule. The accession process concentrated on two areas: free movement of capital and environmental protection. It was especially in the former where a detailed schedule of the complete liberalization was agreed as a condition for accession. Although liberalization was a proclaimed goal of the government which fitted into its neo-liberal perspective, the original government draft of the schedule was still considered too protectionist by the OECD and had to be redrafted (Provazník, 1995). A raft of laws and economic policy decisions, including the full convertibility of the Czech currency, had to be approved prior to accession. All the same, in December 1995, the Czech Republic became the first post-Communist country to enter the OECD.

The foreign minister compared the OECD membership with 'becoming part of the West' (Zieleniec, 1995), although the country subsequently often struggled to fulfil its membership commitments. Hence, the Czech Republic was repeatedly criticized for falling behind the liberalization schedule or taking measures which discriminated against foreign entities in the Czech capital market (Trajlinková, 2001). Still, in OECD reviews the country achieved the highest degree of liberalization among the CEE countries. This process may have been strengthened as an important part of the OECD agenda is shared with the EU from which probably the main socialization pressure has been exercised since the late 1990s.

## NATO: dissidents and neo-liberals agree, society hesitates

The NATO socialization could also rely on intermediate agents: the ruling coalition government (ODS, ODA, Christian Democrats), President Havel and military officers. These were enablers of a strong self-socialization based on a shared Czech–NATO interest in modernizing the Czech armed forces. However, the issue of NATO accession opened a gap between the nation/people level and the state/elite level. Public opinion was almost equally divided, which may have been because of the low esteem attached by the Czechs to military issues. On the other hand, NATO acted in a non-intrusive manner during accession, allowing Czechs to co-define their membership obligations and targets. It also helped to focus on long-term issues. NATO's pressure increased in some respects after the accession when the Czech leaders experienced some difficulty in presenting a clear position on air-strikes against Yugoslavia and when the reform of the armed forces slowed down. However, in all stages the pressure was based on persuasion within the shared Czech–NATO interest.

As a political successor to the neo-liberal thought community, ODS based its support of NATO on Klaus' discursive connection between NATO accession and a radical economic reform, the defining project of ODS. Each is based on the rejection of a 'third way', which is associated with dissident and reformist Communist projects (Drulák, 2004). The radical economic reform rejects the third way attempts to reconcile Communism and market/democracy (Klaus, 1993). The NATO accession rejects the third way in the shape of 'useless experiments' such as the CSCE or the Visegrad co-operation, opting for a 'direct way into the West European structures' (Václav Klaus, Salzburg, 7 January 1993). This support of NATO as a US led organization was also linked to the liberal economists' inspiration by the USA in terms of both economic theories and practical policies.

However, Klaus' association of dissidents with alternatives to NATO is misleading. Even though Havel and like-minded policy-makers were rather sceptical about NATO before 1991, favouring Europe without military blocks based on the CSCE architecture, they changed their opinion following such events as the failed coup attempt in Moscow and the growing tension in Yugoslavia. Moreover, like liberal economists, dissidents were Americaphiles, seeing the USA as their major ally in their struggle against the Communist regime and as the main guarantor of their shared values of democracy and human rights (Havel, 1990b). This construction of the USA as a major ally and guarantor was extended to include NATO, too. Hence, the Czech NATO accession process enjoyed a high degree of support from both thought communities, which shaped Czech politics after the collapse of Communism. Both President Havel and Prime Minister Klaus agreed on the issue and ODS became its chief promoter. On the other hand, Communists were against while Social Democrats were ambiguous. The support was based on the argument that NATO was a value community capable of protecting the values of the Euro-Atlantic civilization (Šedivý, 1995: 10). Indeed, opinion polls identify the Czech 'joining of the West' as the most important and the least controversial feature of the membership (Gabal et al., 2002).

Moreover, the picture of NATO as a gateway to Europe helped to counter criticism of the Czech NATO accession. Unlike the previous socialization steps, NATO accession revealed a significant gap between the government and society. While being one of the government's chief policy goals, the accession had public opinion almost equally divided between supporters and opponents for quite a long time (Výběr z výzkumů veřejného mínění v České republice, MZV, 20, 1997). The gap can be explained by the traditionally low reputation of the military in Czech society and by a widespread belief that the country does not face any real security threat. Compared to the EU accession, therefore, the NATO accession kept a low public profile. Even though this profile altered before the actual accession when support for NATO increased to a clear majority, it returned to its low profile after the accession again.[3]

On the other hand, the NATO accession was supported by a clear majority of military officers (Sarvaš, 1997). This may seem surprising as most of them had close ties with the Communist regime and were educated in the belief that NATO was their mortal enemy. Yet officers were also badly hit by the transformation of the armed forces with its financial cuts and accompanying chaos and confusion (Simon, 2004). Interestingly, they associated NATO with exclusively positive values only while evaluating their own armed forces in wholly negative terms (Sarvaš, 1997). Hence, they expected NATO membership to bring stability and funds to the armed forces. The attitude of officers was exceptional in how they linked NATO membership with specific benefits whereas other supporters considered the accession in broad terms of the Czech return to Europe. Still, even the nuts and bolts of the accession did not represent a major challenge which would force the Czech Republic to take steps it would otherwise prefer avoiding. Sets of priorities of the Czech(oslovak) governments coincided with the NATO enlargement principles (Šedivý, 2001: 43).[4]

However, despite the high expectations on behalf of the armed forces the government was not always able to put these priorities into effect. The modernization of troops and development of a working system of their civilian control were launched when the first civilian minister of defence came to office in the autumn of 1990. However, leaders responsible for the defence ministry often lacked the funds and know-how needed for this task. For example, the share of defence in the country's GDP decreased from 2.6 per cent in 1993 to 1.7 per cent in 1997 when Prime Minister Klaus admitted that 'from 1989 until recent times we have always balanced the budget by cutting a few billion crowns from the military budget' (Simon, 2004: 55).

Institutional aspects were even more important than financial ones. In total, the Czech Republic and NATO jointly identified eleven areas where changes were needed, including *inter alia* the inter-operability of capabilities, military service legislation, crisis management, financial planning, or protection of classified information. The inter-operability issue proved difficult whenever the Czech Republic tried to put into effect its repeated desire to actively contribute to international security, whether in joint international exercises or with Czech missions of multinational troops abroad (Simon, 2004). Obsolete legislation was another problem, often detrimental to both inter-operability and overall modernizing efforts. This was especially the case of military service law and the protection of classified information (Informace o výsledcích analýz a srovnání provedených podle usnesení Vlády České Republiky ze dne 25. června 1997 č. 383, MZV, září 1997). Even the traditionally neglected crisis management (Fučík, 1999: 41) proved a big problem when the government failed to act efficiently during the enormous floods of 1997.

Hence, the financial and institutional problems were recognized for some time by the government. NATO itself lowered its profile down to pointing these issues out and reminding the government of its own commitments, which were set after a period of 'intensified dialogue' between NATO and the Czech Republic. Given the general agreement that the Czech Republic and NATO shared the same goal of creating a modern and well-functioning armed force and given the various intermediate agents, the dialogue could be based on persuasion rather than on social influence using the unequal power relationship. On the basis of these commitments, Czech governments made significant investments and created a variety of institutions and procedures in the identified areas during the accession and post-accession period. They also stuck to their commitment to increase the GDP share of military expenditure to 2 per cent in 2000. Indeed, the ratio has steadily grown from its low point reached in 1997 (Simon, 2004).

Yet the post-accession period was not completely without problems. While NATO appreciated the performance of the Czech troops in foreign operations (Simon, 2004: 120), there was a growing frustration with the management of the defence ministry. 'Non-conceptual defence planning' was a particular point of NATO's criticisms (Simon, 2004: 120). This critique points to the most difficult part of the NATO socialization efforts. Whereas the acquisition of modern equipment and legislative changes represent a relatively easy task, attitudes and administrative practices are much more difficult to change. Not only did the mismanagement of the defence ministry give rise to a mounting criticism by the opposition, armed forces and ministry insiders (Simon, 2004), but it also made NATO's Secretary-General voice his concerns during his visit to Prague in February 2001. Soon after that, the defence minister resigned and an ambitious raft of reforms was launched.

A problem of even greater political sensitivity appeared when the Czech loyalty to the Alliance became an issue. The Czech Republic joined NATO in March 1999 in the midst of the Kosovo crisis. The NATO air strikes against Yugoslavia were resented by the public and divided the Czech political elites: ODS and President Havel supported the air strikes while the leftist political forces, including the Social Democratic government, were against them (Simon, 2004: 80). For some time, it was not clear what the official position was. The perceived NATO pressure on the Czech compliance with the NATO strategy peaked when the Czech ambassador to NATO made a public statement about NATO observing the views of some Czech leaders with misunderstanding and embarrassment (Simon, 2004: 81). Also, the Czech Republic, together with Greece, came up with a peace plan, which was more lenient to Yugoslavia than was the NATO strategy. In spite of that, both the government and Parliament eventually complied with all NATO requirements (use of airspace, landing rights for NATO aircraft, transit of ground troops and assistance to the Albanian refugees and even commitment of troops). One may argue that this was a result of the moral pressure stemming from an assumption that the Czech Republic, as a fresh member, should be loyal to the USA and to NATO, especially as the pressure by the domestic opposition and by the president meant that the time had come for really showing how deep the commitment ran.

## European Union: 'interactive' elites, tired society

In the case of EU accession, self-socialization, once again, played a crucial role. The EU represents the most complex case of socialization: EU membership obligations cover most of the CoE and OECD duties while adding many other commitments. The membership coincided with the domestic priorities of the Social Democratic governments and Czech society more than in any of the above cases. Accession interactions with the EU were the longest and the most intensive, involving both members of the elected political elites and a substantial part of the civil service. It is especially the EU socialization of Czech civil servants that provides an interesting example of socialization of a group located at the state/elite level but with strong ties to the nation/people level.

Socialization at the level of 'public administration elites' has been very complex and relatively effective. The transfer of adopted norms and values from the state/elite level to the nation/people level, however, has been more problematic. Moreover, this socialization has left largely unaffected a number of anti-system forces.

Since 1995, the EU influence and impact has increased, with direct institutional and policy implications. These influences were two-fold, depending on the approaches and mechanisms used. On the one hand, a clear conditionality was guiding the process of *acquis communautaire* adoption. On the other hand, institutional changes in the Czech public administration depended largely on the socialization of Czech civil servants and their interactions with the EU. The *acquis* provided a key framework of reference for legal self-approximation (Bugge, 2000: 9) and the European Commission was carefully watching and commenting on compliance with this mutually agreed commitment. Following the 1995 White Paper, candidate countries started receiving specific support from the Commission to accelerate and enhance their pre-accession preparations. A Government Committee for European Integration headed by the prime minister was established in the Czech Republic, aided by over twenty working groups. Later on, the ČSSD government introduced the post of 'European minister', which was basically a deputy prime minister responsible for the country's pre-accession preparation. While the Social Democrats were happy to 'use' the EU as a facilitator of and justification for further transformation, two major political forces, the ODS and the Communist Party, expressed their doubts and suspicion about the accession process. In spite of their liberal economic criticism based on the rejection of the European social model and the current EU functioning, the ODS elites still advised their electorate to say 'yes' in the referendum since the ODS electorate has always shown the strongest support for the EU. Only the Communist Party, the major anti-system force in the country, remained consistently opposed to EU accession.

In 1998, the European Commission introduced a powerful instrument of active norm promotion: a regular assessment of the candidates published each autumn. Each publication of the Regular Report on the Czech Republic's Progress Towards Accession was followed by an extensive media debate featuring politicians and, increasingly, experts.[5] Each autumn, new measures were designed and some put into practice by the government and/or the Parliament. Then the whole issue slowly faded out from the dominant public discourse again. Except for this short period of heavy media coverage, the media reflection was limited to accession technicalities, mostly negotiations of the membership conditions and the related successes or failures, chiefly in terms of transitional periods. Only few truly political issues cut through these technicalities: the Benes decrees and the Temelin nuclear plant as the major sources of controversies between the Czech Republic and its German-speaking neighbours (and EU members). Most of the EU-level discourse and agenda, including the planned institutional reform, passed unnoticed by the public. It was only in late 2002 and then in 2003 that the EU accession emerged as a political issue out of the 'undercurrent' of technicalities again: the accession referendum was drawing near and the campaign brought the EU accession into the limelight. Fundamental freedoms of the EU as well as some key principles of integration were discussed again at the nation level. However, the people seemed to experience 'EU accession fatigue'. The process of joining had been so long and become so self-evident that public support, which started out at a high standing at 84 per cent in February 1993 (Leff, 1998: 255), subsequently dropped and remained around 57 per cent, until 1998 when it rose slightly after the drop in 1996 attributable to extensive media coverage of the economic and social hardship to be endured on the way to the EU.[6]

The impact these regular reviews had on Czech institutions and state structures, however, was immense. Not only was the Minister for European Affairs forced to step down following the publication of a very critical Regular Report in 1999 but the agenda and institutional structure of ministries and state agencies were influenced by the content and implications of the Regular Reports, taken very seriously by the subsequent governments. This was because the reports included an assessment of the country's performance in terms of many long-term issues considered vital but proving hard to tackle for domestic policy-making elites.

### The role and socialization of Czech civil servants

Besides the governing Social Democratic elites, Czech civil servants were the principal 'intermediate agents' of this top-down socialization process. Socialization at the level of 'public administration elites', a group located between the government and society at large, has been both very complex and quite effective. We shall examine this socialization process in two stages. Firstly, views of the civil servants who were heavily exposed to the EU are compared to the views of the less exposed ones. Secondly, we analyse interactions between Czech civil servants and civil servants from EU national administrations within the EU-sponsored *twinning programme*.

A stratum of the Czech civil service from a variety of ministries and state agencies gained significant experience with the EU during the accession process. They represent one the most EU-socialized segments of Czech society. Interviews with these civil servants provide several findings (Drulák et al., 2003). Firstly, the interviewees are strongly pro-European, with positive expectations of European integration. Secondly, civil servants appear as more pro-European not only more than Czech public opinion (less exposed to interactions with the EU) but also more pro-European than university-educated Czechs (more exposed to interactions with the EU). So generally, higher exposure to the EU coincides with better knowledge of the EU integration project. When this civil service stratum is broken down into two subgroups, based on their intensity of contacts with the EU, a general observation can be made about civil servants more exposed to the EU ('Europeanized') being stronger supporters of it, especially when having been less socialized into the domestic administrative structures ('domesticated'). On the one hand, officers who are both firmly domesticated and firmly socialized and those who are strongly Europeanized but weakly domesticated have a stronger conviction than representatives of EU institutions are with preference for EU interests and are stronger supporters of a European federation. On the other hand, those civil servants whose domestication and Europeanization are equally thin and those civil servants who are strongly domesticated but weakly Europeanized are found to be worse informed about European integration. Also these civil servants seem more sceptical to EU institutions' representatives acting as impartial professionals and less convinced of the idea of a federation. Finally, there seems to be a significant degree of institutional autonomy towards domestic politics: Civil servants in both of these subgroups tend to be more sensitive to signals from EU institutions than to signals from their political leadership. This sensitivity is most pronounced with officers most exposed to the EU. Professional concerns, considered as another source of institutional autonomy, are significantly less important than political signals.

Twinning programmes offer yet another way of looking into interactions between Czech civil servants and external actors in the EU pre-accession framework. The twinning programme was devised by the European Commission to help accession countries to develop the administrative capacity to cope with the *acquis* (*A Reference Manual on 'Twinning' Projects* 2001: 11). Experts from EU member states' administrations are seconded to the candidate countries under this programme to use their own administrative experience in the construction of administrative structures and procedures in the candidate countries. There has always been a clear adaptation pressure for norm (*acquis*) adoption, but no pressure for a *specific* procedural change as there is no 'European' public administration model for domestic administrations to adapt to.

Twinning projects are based on persuasion. There are no mechanisms of material/social sanctioning in twinning for either party. The key to twinning is the political will of the 'receiving institutions'. The aim is to develop long-term relationships between public administration bodies of the members and candidates on the national, regional and local levels. That, in turn, helps to build political support and consensus for reforms through consultation of a spectrum of stakeholders even outside the institution where possible.

Interviews with twinning participants and direct observation reveal several findings (Königová, 2004). Firstly, the early twinning projects suffered from distrust and lack of interest on both sides. Some of the tenders were flawed and Czech civil servants had unrealistic expectations. Over time and thanks to feedbacks, the situation improved on both sides; projects have grown less ambitious and more effective. Secondly, Czech civil servants found themselves in new, unfamiliar situations. Facing cognitive uncertainty and often acknowledging a lack of positive definitions of their new institutional identities, they were more open to persuasion. Thirdly, Czech civil servants faced ambiguity in the process of adaptation (unclear goals, unclear structures of participation and so on). This also provided for greater susceptibility to external influences and argumentative persuasion and sidelined rational bargaining. Fourthly, these civil servants were often 'novices', both in terms of age and seniority, who had fewer prior ingrained beliefs and thus were relatively open to persuasion and adaptation. Finally, the semi-private, weakly politicized setting of twinning interactions encouraged persuasion over social influence. Coercion was excluded altogether. What ultimately helped was the high intensity and sufficient duration of interactions/exposure to socialization.

In general, twinning brought voluntary selective domestication of some aspects of the experience, procedures and structures of member states through both rational bargaining and, to a much greater extent, persuasion and social learning with substantial value transmission effects.

## Conclusion

The Czech socialization into the West European normative order was always presented as a 'return to Europe'. This return started as a bottom-up process when societal structures became key agents of the democratic change, replacing the petrified and isolated Communist elite. The new elite identified itself with the West European normative order, which created conditions for the norm transfer. Even though the return to Europe then continued in a top-down way, a link between government and society endured: the return to Europe was not just a governmental project but a project endorsed by most societal forces with the exception of Communists and extremists. The link facilitated the acceptance of the new norms within the society.

Each of the West European institutions focused on different kinds of norms within the overall norm set contained in the liberal order: democracy and respect for human rights (CoE); liberal economy (OECD); modern army under democratic control (NATO); and *acquis communautaire* (EU). On the most general level these norms were not perceived as being imposed and there was a lot of self-socialization at work. Still, the nuts and bolts often proved tricky to deal with. Sometimes, pressure for the implementation of the mutually agreed targets had to be exercised by the international institutions. What proved most challenging was the practical implementation of norms at the level of courts, armed forces, ministries and state agencies. This relates to the fact that changes at this level implied changes in sedimented practices while no clear models or criteria were available to govern these changes. Compared to this, the attainment of quantitative NATO investment goals and legislative incorporation of the *acquis* were relatively easy.

Interestingly, it is persuasion, which tends to be used in dealing with the more complex implementation challenges reaching deeper and, in some cases, affecting the widely accepted 'political culture'. This is the case with the EU twinning programme as well as with NATO intensified dialogue and the NATO post-accession socialization. However, in both cases a successful change would not be possible without local subjects' readiness to change which was again conditioned by their previous self- and other-categorization processes and their significant degree of self-socialization.

## Notes

1. The Czech and Slovak Republic became members of the Council of Europe on 30 June 1993, following their 'peaceful divorce' in January 1993.
2. http://www.sv/cz; http://www.strasbourg-committee.org.

3. When people were asked which institutions can assist the development of the Czech Republic in 2000–1, not only does NATO trail behind the EU but also behind the UN, OECD and IMF (Gabal et al., 2002).
4. These included democracy and market economy; democratic control of armed forces; adherence to the OSCE standards of minorities' protection; good neighbourly relations; inter-operability within NATO.
5. The last Regular Report was published in 2003.
6. *České veřejné mínění v Evropských souvislostech* 2/2002, http://www.stem.cz, http://www.euroskop.cz, http://www.cvvm.cas.cz/.

# 8

# From Isolation to Integration: Internal and External Factors of Democratic Change in Slovakia

*Marek Rybář*

On 1 May 2004, Slovakia became a new member state of the European Union, together with seven other countries of the former Communist Europe as well as Malta and Cyprus. Yet only six years earlier, representatives of the European Union had expressed serious doubts and reservations about the commitment of the Slovak government to respect even basic procedural aspects of democracy. Lack of respect for political rights of the parliamentary opposition, violation of civic and ethnic minority rights, negligence of the country's Constitutional Court and thwarting of the referendum by the Ministry of Interior were the most frequently quoted reasons for exclusion of the country from negotiations on early accession to EU and NATO in late 1997. Yet Slovakia had not been excluded completely: no political sanctions had been imposed and a formal inclusion into the second 'Luxembourg' group of EU candidate countries had been granted. Moreover, within less than a decade, Slovakia was able to catch up with its neighbours (Bilčík, 2001) and not only became a full member of the NATO in early 2004, but also successfully concluded rather difficult negotiations on the EU accession and entered the EU in the same year. Clearly, Slovakia has undergone a process of transition to democracy that has been characterized by many twists and turns as well as difficulties, where the former semi-authoritarian political forces in control of the government were replaced by a government adhering to the basic principles of democracy. Within the period of 1998–2004 two parliamentary elections and two presidential ones were held, with the initial effect of keeping the semi-authoritarian parties out of power and later with the emergence of an opposition whose democratic credentials are beyond doubt. The aim of this chapter is to analyse the process of political change and to illuminate the role the European Union has played in this process. Following the theoretical framework of this volume, the domestic level is conceptualized here as consisting of two distinct and differently constructed social groups, the first being the state/elite level and the second being the nation/people level. The two levels are obviously located within a broader political context consisting of formal and informal procedures, and intermediary structures like political parties and interest groups, making the whole domestic level a rather complex entity.

The single most important theoretical difficulty of the present norm transfer model rests with the nature of the social norm to be transferred from the international institution (in this case the European Union) to the national context. Democracy, in this case the chief 'subject of transfer', can and does have important sources of origin other than transposition from the outside environment. Even though the importance of the European Union and of international factors more generally for the so-called third wave of democratization in the late twentieth century has been widely acknowledged (Huntington, 1991; Smith, 2001), it is difficult to argue that it has been the single most important source of successful democratization. With the possible exception of democratization through conquest by a foreign power, other successful instances of democratization contain important domestic sources of regime change and completed democratic transition. How then can we possibly speak of socialization of democratic norms in the international context? The answer rests in acknowledging the proximity of attitudes to democracy between the 'socializer' and the 'socializee' that reinforces the self-perception of the socializee as belonging to the social group of the socializer. The causal link between the social influence of the external socializer and norm recipient at the domestic level is thus relaxed to a reinforcing factor, the one that is not the main source of the norm origination, but one that works as a chief norm maintainer and norm promoter. In other words, the socializee's self-image as a social entity belonging to the outside group is reinforced by rhetoric, activities and assistance of the socializing agent. In the case of Slovakia, the state/elite level in the crucial period of 1994–8 was controlled by the coalition government under the leadership of Prime Minister Vladimír Mečiar. In that period the distance between the state/elite level and the European Union with regard to respecting democratic norms and procedures, had been progressively increasing, resulting in exclusion of Slovakia from the first group of EU (and NATO) candidate countries. On the other hand, the main representatives of the nation/people level (various non-governmental organizations as well as a majority of voters as reflected by public opinion polls) felt rather uneasy about the diminishing prospects of Slovakia's Euro-Atlantic integration, and so did the intermediary structures of opposition political parties and important interest groups, including the trade unions and churches. Slovakia thus represented a rather unique case of what is called in this volume an outgroup 3, where there was a significant variation between the distance of the socializing agent and the two domestic levels, with the nation/people level being considerably closer to the norm-promoting agent than the state/elite level. If at least a minimalist procedural democracy exists (basically amounting to competitive elections), there is a good reason to assume that a political change at the state/elite level can be brought about by a general election.

The prospects for change were very well understood by the European Union representatives, who progressively changed their strategy towards the Mečiar government from 'persuasion' to 'social influence' and towards the end of 1998 focused their main concern upon the need to hold free and fair parliamentary elections. At the same time, they carefully distinguished between the Slovak government of the day and the Slovak voters in their statements. This was accompanied by the EU institutions, international foundations, and both EU and non-EU nation-states donating substantial sums of money to Slovak nongovernmental organizations for their pre-election activities. Even though these activities were non-partisan, they were aimed at monitoring the free and fair character of the election and at increasing electoral turnout (Bútora and Demeš, 1999). Thus, they contained a 'hidden agenda', since it was widely acknowledged that the anti-Mečiar opposition parties would benefit from a higher turnout. This strategy proved to be effective and in the autumn of 1998 the Mečiar-led government was replaced by a broad left–right coalition of parties under the leadership of the Prime Minister Mikuláš Dzurinda. The trend was reinforced by the results of the 1999 presidential election, where Mečiar himself was defeated by a candidate representing the new coalition government. The September 2002 parliamentary elections brought a surprisingly clear-cut victory of Dzurinda and his allies along with further weakening of Mečiar's power base. This development secured the necessary political conditions for Slovakia's invitation to the EU and NATO later that year.

The rest of this chapter is divided into three parts. First, I shall outline the 'access points' of the EU to the domestic level, primarily embodied in the formal structure of the so-called EU–Slovakia political dialogue, accompanied by a thorough mechanism of the candidate country evaluation by the socializing agent. Second, the failure of social influence techniques (in the EU-state/elite level dialogue) will briefly be outlined together with accompanying developments at the nation/people level. Third, continuous involvement of the external socializing agent in the most critical instances of the domestic development (elections and major political crises) will be briefly analysed. However, since the formation of the new government following the 2002 parliamentary elections, the EU representatives basically refrained from giving their opinions about the general political situation in Slovakia, as it was acknowledged that the country's democratic commitments were indisputable. Similarly at the domestic level, worries about the democratic character of the political regime have given way to concerns over the quality of democracy, the performance of the economy and other 'everyday' political issues.

## The framework of EU–Slovak relations

Shortly after the regime change in East-Central Europe in 1989, Czechoslovakia, of which Slovakia was then a part, was considered a front-runner for early integration into Euro-Atlantic international political organizations. Even though a full membership in NATO and the European Community soon emerged as the strategic goal of leaders of these new democracies, a similar determination was lacking on the other side. Nevertheless, the EC/EU became the most significant donor to the East-Central European countries, with programmes like *Phare* aimed at helping transformation of the centrally planned economies into market ones. Moreover, Czechoslovakia, Poland and Hungary were the first post-Communist countries with which the EC concluded Association Agreements in 1991. However, before the association agreement between Czechoslovakia and the EC had been ratified, the Czechoslovak federation was divided into two successor states – the Czech Republic and Slovakia. Hence, new negotiations had to start formally and separate association agreements were concluded in October 1993. The Association Agreement (also called the 'Europe Agreement') between Slovakia and the EU entered into force in early 1995. Apart from listing detailed and lengthy specification of technical aspects of mutual trade and setting quotas on sensitive goods, the Association Agreement contained important provisions of the so-called political dialogue between the associate country and the EU. Even though the agreement did not express any commitment on part of the EU to future enlargement, the conditionality of any kind of support, including the benefits resulting from the agreement itself, was stated rather clearly. 'Respect for democratic principles and human rights established by the Helsinki Final Act and the Charter of Paris for a new Europe, as well as the principles of a market economy' were identified as the essential preconditions to the conclusion of the Association Agreement. Various kinds of financial and expert assistance were thus tied to compliance with the EU democratic norms, later labelled 'the political conditions'. What is important here is that respect for democratic norms had been officially acknowledged as the condition for support even before the EU agreed that the East-Central European countries would be invited to join the EU in the future. Hence, the EU policy of dealing with the post-Communist countries has from the very beginning been to support democratization and marketization for their own sake, and not just because these countries could distort the political and economic environment within the EU, if they were accepted without the necessary political stability and satisfactory economic performance. Democratic norm promotion by the EU has thus been its general policy strategy, not just a mechanism of its future-oriented self-protection.

The Association Agreement established a complex structure of a regular political deliberation process between the EU and Slovakia. It included regular bilateral consultations and meetings at the highest political level involving all topics of common interest. The Association Council, composed by the members appointed by the Slovak government as well as by the members of the Commission and the Council of the European Union, served as the principal access points through which the official positions of the two parties were transmitted. The Association Council met once a year, and its meetings, especially before the 1998 Slovak parliamentary elections, served as a forum where the EU representatives tried to persuade their Slovak counterparts to accept the EU perception of the state of democracy in Slovakia and to change their attitudes accordingly. More technical aspects of the EU–Slovak relations were dealt with in the Association Committee, composed according to the same criteria as the Council itself. The two forums represent an institutional embodiment of the relations between the EU and the domestic state/elite level. The composition of the Slovak delegation, and thus the views it expressed, represented an official position of the Slovak government controlled by a coalition of three political parties. However, as became increasingly clear, it did not express the views of the whole national elite. The main reason for this was that there was no cross-party consensus about how to deal with the democratic conditionality policy of the EU. While the parliamentary opposition basically accepted and even welcomed the opinions and criticism of the EU, the parties of the government generally rejected them as biased and ill-informed. Both views were represented in the Association Parliamentary Committee (APC), composed by an equal number of members of the Slovak and European parliaments. The Association Parliamentary Committee represented a parliamentary forum of the EU–Slovak political dialogue and met twice a year, once in Brussels and once in Slovakia. Formally, the APC was only informed of the decisions of the Association Council and could have only made recommendations to it. However, the parliamentary opposition was granted a proportional representation within the Slovak delegation to the APC, something that was not a common practice in other important political bodies set up exclusively by the Slovak parliament. As a consequence, the APC's meetings and conclusions received very close attention by the Slovak public, and also played an important role as a channel, through which the EU addressed the nation/people level of Slovak domestic politics. Hence, the APC's role in Slovak politics as well as in a broader context of EU–Slovak relations was much greater than its formal powers would normally suggest.

The structure of political dialogue was not the only means through which the EU communicated its position to Slovakia. The Commission's annual official 'Regular Reports' on progress of the candidate countries, and especially the first *avis* issued in July 1997 as a part of the *Agenda 2000* document, constituted a very important source of information on the EU position towards the candidates. The reports also attracted considerable attention domestically, with the opposition and the media focusing attention especially on the most criticized aspects of political, economic and administrative affairs. These documents were issued annually between 1997 and 2002. In the Slovak case, the 1997 and 2002 avis were the most important. The former recommended to the Luxembourg European Council not to start negotiations with the country due to its failure to meet the political criteria (Rybář and Malová, 2004), while the latter proposed to the Copenhagen European Council to formally conclude the accession talks and start ratification of Slovakia's full membership in the EU (Bilčík, 2003). The last formal document evaluating candidate states was issued under a slightly modified title 'The Comprehensive Monitoring Report' by the Commission in November 2003; its goal was to identify the main deficiencies and obstacles to be eliminated before candidates assumed full EU membership (European Commission, 2003). The main difference between the 'Comprehensive Monitoring Report' and previous 'Regular Reports' was twofold: While the former monitored countries that were already invited into the EU, the latter evaluated *candidate* countries. Second, regular reports were directed to candidate countries as separate documents (one document per country and year), while the 2003 Comprehensive Monitoring Report was a single document on the future member states as a group, even though 'warnings' about unsatisfactory progress were individually attributed. Hence, the story of Eastern enlargement is primarily the story of developments 'from Copenhagen to Copenhagen'. The 1993 Copenhagen European Council formally endorsed eventual membership of the post-Communist states as a goal and set up the minimal political criteria to be met by the candidates, while the 2002 Copenhagen Summit decided to conclude the accession negotiations and invite ten candidate states to the EU. As far as *political* conditions are concerned, the Copenhagen criteria were sometimes criticized for being too vague and difficult to measure: the framework criteria of guarantee of democracy, rule of law and respect for human and minority rights, do not provide for a comprehensive assessment of consolidated democracy (Pridham, 1999b, 2002a). In a retrospective view it seems that a country's state of democracy was more easily identified as negative rather than as positive, in the sense that for the EU representatives it was less problematic to say where democratic norms were lacking than where they appeared to have firm roots. The problem of monitoring and judging adherence to democracy, however, is not confined to candidate countries alone. Since the Amsterdam Treaty, the EU can impose sanctions and even suspend the rights of member states if due to internal political dynamics they fail to meet the democratic political conditions. However, the imposition of diplomatic sanctions against Austria after the far-right Freedom party became a member of the Austrian executive clearly shows how problematic the usage of this clause may be. Hence, it is yet another reason for the EU representatives to adopt *ex ante* 'democratic screening', whereby only stable and consolidated democracies are allowed to joined the EU.

Besides the specific institutional framework between the EU and candidate countries (the political dialogue) and a comprehensive monitoring of their progress, there are other, more traditional diplomatic means through which important messages are transmitted. Among them, the EU presidency statements, resolutions of the European Parliament and bilateral meetings between the Slovak government and representatives of the EU and its member states played a prominent role in EU–Slovak dialogue. Again, these have been directed primarily towards the state/elite level, but represented an important 'material' for interpretation at the nation/people level, especially by the opposition parties. In addition, transnational party linkages between major political parties of the EU countries and the Slovak (primarily opposition) parties complemented the existing structure of communication and norm-promotion (Pridham, 1999b). The character and content of this communication is analysed below; before doing that, it is important to introduce briefly the most important reasons why Slovakia under the Mečiar government of 1994–8 came to be seen as a country with a serious democratic deficit.

## Marginalization of the opposition

Following the early elections of autumn 1994, a new government was formed consisting of the Movement for a Democratic Slovakia (HZDS), the Association of Slovak Workers (ZRS) and the Slovak National Party (SNS). For Vladimír Mečiar, the founder and undisputed leader of the HZDS, it was his third term as prime minister. Two previous terms were terminated by a parliamentary vote of no-confidence. After his return to power in 1994, Mečiar tried to use all necessary measures to prevent a repetition of the same scenario. During the first working session of the newly elected parliament, the newly formed three-party coalition departed from the previous practices and assumed all the important positions within parliament as well as in the state administration. Within a single night session, the nominees of the opposition were dismissed from the supervisory bodies overseeing the public mass media and intelligence services. Similarly, no opposition nominees remained in the Supreme Auditing Office and the National Property Fund. The Attorney General was also replaced by a candidate who was close to the new government. Contrary to the previous practices, no opposition deputy was elected to chair any parliamentary committee and the ruling majority also voted against opposition candidates nominated for positions within the parliamentary leadership. Within a very short time, the new government also recalled a great deal of representatives of the state administration in Slovak regions and municipalities. Besides ostentatious demonstration of power, what surprised most was the denial to the parliamentary opposition of any formal opportunities to influence public policies. The opposition parties were portrayed by the government as an obstacle to effective policy-making. Parliamentary statistics for the entire 1994–8 period show that the opposition could not effectively propose any agenda for parliamentary sessions, let alone succeed in adopting more substantive policy proposals. Participation of the opposition deputies in government control became the recurrent topic of discussion between the EU and the Slovak government.

## Minority policies

About 14 per cent of Slovakia's population belongs to an ethnic minority group. Hungarians are the largest and politically also the most visible group. After the regime change in 1989 their political representation consisted of three political parties of liberal, Christian-Democratic and radical nationalist persuasion. While the former was a constituent part of the first post-1989 democratically elected government, the latter two remained in opposition. However, following the 1992 elections that subsequently led to the dissolution of Czechoslovakia, the Hungarian political representation became increasingly critical of governmental policies. The then HZDS–SNS coalition government led by Mečiar pursued 'nationalizing' policies aimed at strengthening the ethnic Slovak character of the newly independent state. Shortly after Slovak independence became a reality, the Hungarian minority parties jointly drafted a memorandum to the Council of Europe outlining their objections to the new Slovak constitution and to several laws specifying the position of ethnic minorities in Slovakia. Due to these objections, Hungary even threatened to veto Slovakia's entry into the Council of Europe. In May 1993, the Political Committee of the Council of Europe outlined a ten-point list of conditions that Slovakia was to fulfil in order to be admitted as a new member (Reisch, 1993: 37). These included guarantees for usage of Christian and family names in the mother tongue of minorities, as well as the reintroduction of legislation that would allow usage of street and locality names in minority languages. The appropriate legislation, however, was introduced only well after Slovakia was admitted as a new member in June 1993 and following serious tensions within the ruling parties. These tensions resulted in the downfall of the Mečiar government and a new left–right government assumed power with the parliamentary support of the Hungarian minority parties. Following the 1994 early elections, however, the third Mečiar cabinet was appointed and the Hungarian minority came under increasing attacks from the government. In late 1995 the parliament adopted a new law on state language that did not specify any conditions for the usage of minority languages in public bodies. It clearly contradicted the constitutional provisions guaranteeing that minorities may use their mother tongues under conditions specified by law. Moreover, the new law effectively outlawed publishing all non-Slovak periodicals. It was legalized only at the beginning of 1996, when the parliament amended the Law on Periodicals. Even though the government representatives on several occasions promised the EU representatives to prepare a law on minority languages, these promises were never honoured.

At the same time, the government tried to alter the system of education of ethnic minorities, whereby instead of full education in their mother tongue, minority schools would have to teach several subjects in the Slovak language even in Hungarian schools. Given its historical (the Communist regime unsuccessfully tried to introduce 'alternative education' in the 1970s and 1980s) and symbolic connotations (the language is the most significant element of national identification of the Hungarian minority in Slovakia), these measures met with fierce opposition from Slovakia's Hungarian community. Even though alternative education was eventually not introduced, the Ministry of Education managed to change the old practice (dating back to 1921) whereby bilingual certificates with final grades were replaced by certificates issued only in Slovak. This stirred unrest among members of the Hungarian minority, and strikes of the Hungarian teacher's association, students and their parents' organizations took place. In addition, the Ministry of Culture severely circumscribed subsidies to activities of Hungarian cultural associations and periodicals, redirecting them to organizations obviously more sympathetic to governmental policies (Dostál, 1996). None of these policies, however, had changed before the end of the Mečiar administration.

## Democratic decay

The most serious deviation from even procedural aspects of democracy took place at the end of 1996 and in the first half of 1997. When an HZDS deputy, dissatisfied by policies of his party, decided to leave his parliamentary faction, the parliamentary majority stripped him of his mandate. This was made on the basis of a dubious and undated 'letter of resignation' that reportedly all HZDS deputies had to sign before the 1994 elections. After the deputy announced his intention to leave the HZDS faction, the letter appeared in parliament as if sent by him. Even though he denied sending it and refused its content, the ruling majority 'accepted' his resignation. Moreover, the Constitutional Court later ruled that the parliament violated his constitutional rights and asked the parliament to change its decision on the matter. However, the ruling parties repeatedly refused to do so. The parliament thus openly ignored the ruling of the Constitutional Court. In a similar vein, a vacant parliamentary seat was given to a member of the SNS even though the law provided for the allocation of the seat to another member of the same party. Even in this case, the ruling of the Constitutional Court was ignored by the parliamentary majority. Both these events seriously discredited the democratic credentials of the Mečiar government. However, it was the circumstances accompanying the May 1997 referendum on NATO accession and the direct presidential election that represented a turning point in Slovak politics. The referendum was called by the president and consisted of two basic issues: the first three questions dealt with the (possible future) Slovak membership in NATO, the fourth question asked whether the president should be elected directly by the citizens. While the former were initiated by the parliamentary majority as a 'pre-emptive strike' (the wording was to elicit a 'no' vote and thus to relieve the government of its responsibility for its failure to secure an invitation from NATO), the latter was initiated by a popular petition and was to increase the opposition's chances to elect a president more to its liking. The government appealed to the Constitutional Court and asked about the constitutionality of the fourth question. The Court ruled that the constitution could not be changed by a referendum but upheld the right to have a referendum on the issue. However, the Ministry of Interior ignored the ruling and distributed the ballot papers with only questions on NATO. The opposition called for a boycott of the plebiscite and the Central Referendum Commission, the body in charge of the election process, declared the referendum thwarted by the unlawful action of the Ministry. The thwarted referendum represented a turning point in the political developments of the country. First, it documented that the free and fair character of the election process cannot be taken for granted. This prompted the opposition parties to co-operate more closely and even to create broad electoral alliances for the 1998 elections. Second, it was widely acknowledged that integration of Slovakia into the EU and NATO could be ruled out under Prime Minister Mečiar. Even representatives of the state/elite level acknowledged it. The official explanation was that international organizations, especially the EU and NATO, used double standards: one (more critical) for Slovakia, and another one for other countries of East-Central Europe. At times, Mečiar argued that the USA and Russia agreed not to invite Slovakia into NATO; at others the EU representatives were portrayed as over-critical towards the new Slovak state and dissatisfied with its independently pursued modernization policies. Finally, it also mobilized the nation/people level of the country. Representatives of 'civil society', including numerous non-governmental organizations and foundations, directed their attention towards one major goal: to secure free and fair parliamentary elections in 1998.

In March 1998, when Prime Minister Mečiar assumed some of the presidential powers (due to parliament's inability to elect a new president after the term of President Kováč had expired) his first step was to grant amnesty to the interior minister for his activities relating to the thwarted 1997 referendum. He also granted amnesty to all persons involved with the abduction of a Slovak citizen, attributed to the Slovak secret service headed by a close Mečiar ally. Mečiar claimed that his goal was to calm down the heated political controversies surrounding both affairs but his steps were perceived by the opposition as well as most of the public as a blatant misuse of powers (Velšic, 2001). Hence, Slovak politics between 1992 and 1998 had certainly come a long way: from a country generally perceived as a strong candidate for early NATO and EU accession to a pariah regime excluded from the mainstream integration in Europe. Let us now turn to on analysis of the changing strategies of the EU representatives towards the country.

## EU strategies vis-à-vis Slovakia

### Strategy 1: general diplomacy

After the break-up of the Czechoslovak federation, the two successor states formally enjoyed the same status in international relations. The Czech Republic as well as Slovakia were recognized by the major powers and established a whole network of bilateral relations. Both countries expressed equal foreign policy goals: early integration into the EU and NATO. However, their trajectories started to differ rather quickly: Slovakia, unlike the Czech Republic, encountered reservations about its internal (minority) policies already in early 1993, when the Council of Europe obliged Slovakia to comply with its recommendations on minority policy (Reisch, 1993). However, it was only after the early elections of 1994 that the EU representatives officially and critically commented on the state of democracy in Slovakia. Following the night parliamentary session in November 1994, the EU presidency issued a démarche to the Slovak authorities, expressing its concerns about the conditions accompanying the transfer of power to the new Mečiar government. The EU presidency even issued a second démarche to the Slovak government in October 1995, followed by a similar document from the US administration. All three documents stressed the need to respect plurality of political opinions, comply with the constitution and adhere to its international obligations (Mesežnikov, 1996). In November 1995 the European Parliament adopted a resolution where it called upon the Slovak government to respect basic democratic principles and human rights. It even warned that the EU might suspend the Association Agreement with Slovakia if there was no improvement of political practices (Mesežnikov, 1996). Similarly, in December 1996 the European Parliament adopted another resolution where it emphasized that 'respect for fundamental democratic principles, including the free exercise of parliamentary mandate, is a condition for entering into a developing cooperation with the EU' (European Parliament, 1997). Informally, the EU representatives were even more frank: the Reuters Press Agency quoted a senior EU diplomat as saying that Slovakia had no chance to be invited into the EU in the first round of enlargement, as the EU priorities did not include taking care of democratic processes of its member states (*Sme*, 20 December 1996). The EU representatives, however, insisted that Slovakia needed to embark upon major political reforms before it could be accepted as an EU member. The most obvious evidence that the Slovak government failed in its major foreign policy goal – start of the talks on NATO and EU accession – came with a decision of the July 1997 NATO Summit in Madrid, and the December 1997 Luxembourg European Council. NATO representatives decided not to invite Slovakia to join the Alliance. Similarly, the EU Council fully accepted the Commission's earlier evaluation of Slovakia, and refused to start direct negotiations on accession due to serious domestic problems in respecting democratic norms.

**Strategy 2: using structures of the EU–Slovak political dialogue**

As was outlined above, for the EU to express its opinions about Slovakia, the structure of political dialogue established by the Association Agreement supplemented more traditional diplomatic methods of démarches, resolutions and press conference statements. All meetings of the Association Council were marked by disagreements between the Slovak and EU officials concerning the state of democracy in Slovakia. For example, in February 1997 the EU representatives expressed their hope that the rights of the parliamentary opposition would be respected and the legislation on the use of minority languages would be enacted (*Sme*, 26 February 1997). Similarly, in April 1998 the EU Association Council members emphasized that concrete steps aimed at improving the situation in Slovakia needed to be taken before the Slovak integration aspiration could be fulfilled (*Pravda*, 29 April 1998). The Slovak representatives, on the other hand, claimed that the EU based its opinions on biased sources and that the Slovak government could not agree with the assessment of the EU (*Sme*, 19 March 1998). The Association Parliamentary Committee, due to the fact that it met more frequently than the Association Council, was even more outspoken in its critique. It regularly adopted resolutions calling for improvement of the state of democracy in Slovakia, only to state a lack of progress at the following meeting. Its top EU members openly expressed their frustration and disappointments with the fact that the Slovak government did not keep its promises to improve the situation (*Sme*, 22 April 1994).

### Assessing the results of the EU influence strategies

The two above-mentioned EU strategies towards Slovakia did not differ in the content of the message transmitted to the domestic (Slovak) level, but rather were complementary in their effort to warn the elite level of the consequences of its policies. The first strategy used a more general way of international communication based on resolutions, démarches and expression of opinions of the EU representatives on the state of democracy in Slovakia and its chances for early EU accession. The second strategy was to use the more specific EU–Slovak communication channels embodied in the structure of political dialogue. Here, the Association Council saw only limited political debates and exchange of political opinions between the EU and Slovak government representatives. On the other hand, the Association Parliamentary Committee attracted more attention within Slovakia and thus contributed more to the awareness of the general public about the different views of the Slovak government and the EU. The main reason for this was that the opposition deputies in the APC were able to communicate the EU views through the representatives of the media reporting on the APC meetings. The EU message was thus 'amplified' more vigorously to the Slovak public. In addition, resolutions of the APC were subsequently ignored by the Slovak parliament. For example, in spite of much urgency, the Mečiar government never prepared the law on minority languages, and the cabinet even officially announced in 1997 it had no intention of doing so. Government officials even criticized the APC's resolution, despite the fact that it was adopted unanimously with support of the coalition deputies (*Pravda*, 24 June 1997).

In late 1996/early 1997 it was crystal-clear to the EU representatives that the Slovak government was not willing to correct its policies towards national minorities and political opponents in parliament. Following the 1997 thwarted referendum, they repeatedly stressed the need for free and fair elections (parliamentary, local and presidential) and also emphasized that 'Slovakia had its destiny in her hands'. These assurances had a twofold meaning: first, they were to counter the official explanation of the Slovak government that EU was over-critical and unfair to Slovakia. This was the main message of various EU representatives, including German Foreign Minister Klaus Kinkel (May 1997), EU Commissioner Hans van den Broek (May 1997), co-chair of the EU–Slovak Association Parliamentary Committee and an Austrian MEP Herbert Boesch (June 1997), the EU Troika presidency (October 1997) and others. Second, it was a clear and unequivocal message to the Slovak citizens to choose their political representatives carefully in the 1998 parliamentary elections. In its reaction to the amnesties granted by Mečiar in March 1998, the EU presidency stated: 'The EU regrets that such a step might represent a set-back to the legitimate *aspiration of the Slovak people to international respect* and progressive integration into European structures' (European Council, 1998, emphasis added). Similarly, the EU Commissioner Hans van den Broek during his visit to Slovakia in June 1998 assured the Slovak citizens of 'an unconditional support of the EU' for their effort to join the EU (*Sme*, 18 June 1998). In March 1998, the European Parliament's resolution called upon the Slovak authorities to guarantee free and fair parliamentary elections (*Sme*, 13 March 1998). Romano Prodi, the then Italian prime minister, was only the second head of government of an EU member state to visit Slovakia during the 1994–8 period. In July 1998 he also stressed that the Slovak elections must be free and fair (*Pravda*, 31 July 1997).

From this short overview it should be clear that the overall strategy of the EU towards Slovakia had changed during the Mečiar government of 1994–8. In its strategy to influence Slovak democratic conditions, the EU representatives specified their main concerns and repeatedly stressed the failure of the Slovak government to comply. This was visible from the statements of the EU representatives in the Association Council and also from the conclusions of meetings of the Association Parliamentary Committee. Moreover, the European Parliament adopted several resolutions on the (unsatisfactory) state of Slovak democracy. The EU presidency issued two démarches to the Slovak authorities on the same matter, and individual representatives of the Commission as well as EU member states also reiterated the need to improve the state of democracy in Slovakia. Moreover, apart from visits of EU officials within the framework of the EU–Slovak political dialogue, international isolation of the country was clear by the fact that the highest Western political representatives, with only minor exceptions, avoided official visits to Slovakia. In the end, however, these strategies only had an effect of a 'negative social influence' as they did not elicit the required behaviour from the Slovak officials, but contributed to a widely accepted opinion in the Slovak public that EU accession with Mečiar was impossible. After it was clear that the Mečiar government lacked respect for even essential democratic procedures (thwarted referendum, disrespect for the Constitutional Court), the EU representatives focused on a minimalistic democratic criterion, that is, free and fair elections. At the same time, they tried to encourage the Slovak citizens, who were increasingly dissatisfied with the international isolation of their country, that EU integration was possible with another set of public officials. Two points should be added to this. The EU did not impose formal diplomatic sanctions against Slovakia and did not suspend the Association Agreement, even though it was one of the options considered. Instead, it made any further steps (that is, direct negotiations on EU accession) conditional on compliance (Schimmelfennig et al., 2003). Second, the EU representatives did not openly support parties of the anti-Mečiar opposition, even though their preference was rather obvious (Lombardini, 1999). Moreover, the transnational contacts of the opposition parties with their partners in the EU countries definitely contributed to the tactics of the EU representatives (Pridham, 1999b). A notoriously known weakness of Mečiar's HZDS was the lack of foreign contacts with respected political parties, a weakness which was fully exploited by the opposition representatives. They often argued that only internationally recognized political forces could guarantee successful integration into the EU (Mesežnikov, 1999). Thus, this was a way in which the opposition parties expressed their belonging to the norm-promoting EU and, at the same time, pointed to the outsider status of the government representatives.

## Mobilization of the nation/people level

It is generally acknowledged that for a democracy to flourish, a vibrant and active civil society must be in place. Similarly, a democratic attitude of a majority of the voters, a high level of interpersonal trust and other related conditions are seen as necessary if the democratic character of the regime is to stay (Diamond, 1999). Throughout the 1990s, the attitudes of the Slovak population concerning political democracy had been similar to those existing in other Central European countries (Szomolányi, 2003). What was significant for Slovak citizens was a prevalent feeling that democracy in the country was endangered. In January 1997, more than 50 per cent of the voters subscribed to that view (Velšic, 2001: 33). Even though more than 75 per cent of them wanted Slovakia to join the EU, only about a quarter of Slovaks believed that their country was indeed heading towards eventual EU membership (Bútorová, 1999: 67). This was a major disappointment, since 'return to Europe' had been one of the major slogans of the 1989 anti-Communist 'Velvet Revolution'. In the second half of the 1990s, however, a full realization of this dream started to disappear. For example, in late 1997, 60 per cent of the voters said the international position of Slovakia had worsened compared to 1994 (Bútorová, 1999: 63), and almost 40 per cent of voters claimed they were afraid of manipulation of the 1998 parliamentary elections (Bútorová, 1999: 71). It was clear that a gap between, on the one hand, the attitudes of the Slovak citizens as a whole, and democratic commitment of their government on the other had deepened.

The opposition parties, even though divided along left–right socio-economic issues, nevertheless started to co-operate on the basis of their agreement on the need to protect democracy, win the election and return the country on to the integration track. The most important impetus for their close co-operation was provided by the thwarted referendum of 1997. Shortly afterwards, five opposition parties, ranging from Christian Democrats to Greens and Social Democrats, decided to conclude an electoral alliance and run for the elections on a single party list. This newly formed Slovak Democratic Coalition (SDK) pledged to fulfil the EU political criteria within 100 days of coming to power (*Sme*, 15 December 1997). Three parties, representing the Hungarian minority, merged into a single Party of Hungarian Coalition (SMK), even though the move was in part forced by a change of the election law that in fact effectively prevented pre-election coalitions. Even the Communist-successor Party of the Democratic Left, in spite of its initial reluctance, agreed to co-ordinate some of its activities with other opposition parties. This effort of the opposition, however, was significantly boosted by activation of other intermediary structures of the domestic political system. The Trade Union Confederation (KOZ), at first hesitant to support any political party, decided to call upon the voters to support the opposition. The KOZ did not campaign on behalf of any political party but prepared an analysis of party electoral manifestos and concluded that the opposition parties were more supportive of the KOZ than the Mečiar government (Malová, 1999).

In traditionally religious Slovakia, a message from the two largest churches (Catholic and Lutheran) was at least symbolically very important. In April 1998, nine Catholic bishops sent a letter to the prime minister, where they expressed their concern about the political situation in the country. They singled out disrespect for the rulings of the Constitutional Court and a danger of manipulation of the parliamentary elections among the most serious issues. It was the most critical statement of the

Church representatives since 1989 (Kollár, 1999: 153). Both the Catholic and Evangelical Church called upon Slovak citizens to take part in the election and choose political representatives who cared about the common good.

Representatives of the opposition political parties, trade unions and churches not only tried to encourage Slovak citizens to mobilize against the government, they also agreed on regular meetings and consultations. This unique institution, called the 'Democratic Roundtable', was also composed of other important players of the nation/people level and represented the culmination of efforts to create a 'winning coalition'. The Democratic Roundtable also consisted of representatives of the independent media, and various non-governmental institutions. The latter, in paricular, represented a very significant force: In February 1998 there were almost 15 000 non-governmental organizations registered by the Ministry of the Interior, of which an overwhelming majority represented various civic associations, unions and clubs (Bútora and Demeš, 1999: 132). These organizations prepared almost sixty independent projects aimed at increasing citizens' awareness of the parliamentary elections, informing about programmes of political parties, the overall international situation and monitoring the election process. Specific projects were directed towards first-time voters, women and the Roma population (Bútora and Demeš, 1999). The realization of many of these projects would not have been possible without the financial help from international foundations and grants from governmental agencies of the EU member states as well as from the US. In addition, hundreds of volunteers took part in the pre-election mobilization, thus showing a considerable mobilization of ordinary Slovak citizens. Even though government representatives were very critical and sometimes even hostile towards these activities, the Slovak population overwhelmingly endorsed the information and mobilization campaign of the NGOs (Bútorová, 1999). Hence, the double pressure from the EU representatives and from the nation/people level upon the Mečiar government was a major contribution to the fact that the September 1998 elections were free and fair and no major problems were reported by the international observers.

## Developments after the 1998 elections

The elections brought a clear defeat to the parties of the Mečiar's government. One of them did not get into the parliament and both Mečiar's HZDS and the Slovak National Party lost a significant portion of their parliamentary representation. Moreover, the four opposition parties secured a majority of 93 out of 150 votes, hence securing enough mandates to pass constitutional amendments. A new government of Mikuáš Dzurinda was sworn in, and for the first time in the history of independent Slovakia representatives of the Hungarian minority (the SMK party) were a constituent part of the government. The main explanation for their acceptance by other parties was the fact that their participation was perceived as improving the *image* of Slovakia in the eyes of the EU representatives (Pridham, 2002b: 92–3). Catching up with Slovakia's neighbours in an effort to join the EU, as well as a desire to keep Mečiar out of power became the strongest glue of the Dzurinda 1998–2002 government. Even though important economic and social reforms were embarked upon, these frequently stirred considerable controversies and almost brought about the collapse of the government. In 2001, for example, the law on administrative reform so frustrated the SMK representatives that they seriously considered leaving the government. Only after appeals from liberal Slovak intellectuals and, perhaps even more importantly, after a series of warnings from EU and US representatives about the foreign policy consequences of such a move (Pridham, 2002b: 965), did the SMK change its position.

The trend of predominance of democratic political representatives in Slovak politics was reinforced in the 1999 presidential elections, when Vladimír Mečiar was defeated by Rudolf Schuster, a candidate supported by the Dzurinda government. Results of both the parliamentary and presidential elections were cautiously welcomed by the EU representatives, but it was only at the Helsinki European Council in December 1999 that Slovakia was invited to conduct direct negotiations on EU accession. This was preceded by the Commission's Regular Report in which the progress of Slovakia towards meeting the necessary democratic political criteria was acknowledged.

If the results of the 1998 parliamentary elections represented a necessary precondition for democratization changes in Slovakia, by the 2002 elections it was generally accepted that Slovakia was heading towards democratic consolidation. Yet the 2002 elections are sometimes regarded as a last test of democratic credentials of Slovak politics (Novotný et al., 2003). Significantly, even though Mečiar did his best to improve his public image and openly supported Dzurinda's 'pro-European' foreign policy orientation, the EU and US officials repeatedly warned against his return to power (Korba, 2003). International donors supported even more information and monitoring projects of Slovak NGOs than in 1998 (Novotný et al., 2003). Moreover, EU integration was one of the most important issues of the campaign (Pridham, 2003; Haughton, 2003). The major parties did not differ in their attitude towards integration itself, rather they argued about which party was more able to secure successful conclusion of the accession talks. The election results brought a surprisingly clear victory for the centre-right parties led by Dzurinda's Slovak Democratic and Christian Union (SDKU), while Mečiar's HZDS was again condemned to the opposition benches. This time, however, the inclusion of ethnic Hungarian SMK into the government was unproblematic and almost taken for granted (Mesežnikov, 2003). In November 2002, Slovakia was invited to join NATO at its Prague Summit and a month later at the Copenhagen European Council the EU accession talks were successfully concluded and the EU decided to invite ten new countries, including Slovakia.

## Conclusion

The present chapter has tried to analyse a unique case of a country where there had been a considerable gap between democratic commitment of the state/elite and nation/people level. In the period between 1994 and 1998, the former progressively deviated from generally accepted democratic norms and even resorted to blatant violation of constitutionally guaranteed democratic principles and procedures, while the latter became increasingly dissatisfied with the direction the country was heading in. The European Union representatives tried to influence the state/elite level by traditional techniques (démarches, resolutions, bilateral negotiations, and so on), making any further integration dependent on complying with the basic democratic requirements. Over time, however, their main effort was to commit the Slovak government to holding free and fair parliamentary elections. This clearly shows that not even 'negative social influence' can guarantee behavioural change, let alone ideational change, if an uncommitted elite controls the domestic level. At the same time, the EU tried to encourage the nation/people level by stressing that it is upon them (that is, the citizens voting in the election) to decide about the integration prospects of the country. The creation of the winning coalition of opposition parties, non-governmental organizations, media, trade unions and other societal players, represented a desire of a majority of Slovak citizens for democracy as well as for integration into the Euro-Atlantic international organizations. In that period, desire for democratization became intertwined with international recognition expressed by European integration. Almost unconditional popular support for early EU accession (preferably at the same time as

Slovakia's neighbours) later revealed its 'darker side' – almost no critical public discussion about the terms of EU accession and the role Slovakia could play in the EU (Bilčík, 2002). A desire for international recognition first prompted the actors of the nation/people level to unite and elect democratic representatives into the state/elite level positions, and later to prevent a return of the political personalities responsible for the initial failure to integrate Slovakia into the Euro-Atlantic institutional structures. Hence, democratic change in Slovakia was possible due to a double pressure upon the state/elite level: one coming from the external environment (the EU), the other exerted by the representatives of the nation/people level.

# 9

# The Socialization of Democratic Norms in Russia: Is the Glass Half-empty or Half-full?

*Mette Skak*[1]

## Why Russia matters

The whole enterprise of examining the role of international actors in socializing democratic norms throughout Europe builds upon a basic premise of the external environment's influence upon domestic developments in states. This analytical set-up logically implies a possible role not only for international organizations, but also for powerful state actors like Russia as another external factor capable of influencing the development and consolidation of democracy and security in the transforming societies of Europe. Indeed, due to its historical role in Europe, notably in the transforming societies of Baltic, Central and Balkan Europe in the recent past, Russia qualifies as 'perhaps the dominant external influence on the trajectories of change' (Breslauer, 1997: 5; Skak, 1996: 76–136). Russia is thus simultaneously an agent of socialization as well as an object for socialization. For better or worse – and many would focus on the latter seeing Russia as a nuisance, if not an outright threat to democracy and security in the region – Russia remains a key factor in the equation of Europe even though Russia has been decisively weakened through the collapse of Communism economically, militarily and politically. Therefore, Russia is no plain out-group 2 country[2] (if there ever was one) where *ceteris paribus* conditions prevail due to geopolitics and history: points I shall elaborate upon below.

The case of Russia and its possible socialization into a fully democratic political system deserves closer examination on Russia's own merits. Russia's actual dismantling of its Communist economic and political system is significant due to the insulation from the external world and repression it entailed. Therefore, the point of departure for this contribution is that the opening of the Russian state and society – in Karl Popper's sense of 'open society' (Popper, 1966) – marks the decisive change in Russia in relation to the larger question of democracy. Travel abroad is no longer subject to political restrictions, believers are free to practise religion, contact with foreigners is now a personal matter, and the media are no longer dull. Given Russia's Soviet past as a closed, totalitarian society, the very opening of Russia represents *the* change for the better in relation to which criticism of Russia's democratic achievements, market economic and foreign policy shortcomings have to be placed. It may thus be taken for granted that much of the change in Russia can be assumed to derive from its recent exposure to norms and practices of the democratic West as this represents a genuinely new dimension to Russia's developmental dynamics (Dawisha, 1997).

Accordingly, the focus of the analysis that follows is less on pinpointing the efforts of particular international actors in relation to Russia and more on the domestic structures and their embrace of these new developmental dynamics. I shall follow the analytical distinction into a nation/people level of popular political culture and the state/elite level of governmental or 'state political culture' (Hedetoft, 2003; Flockhart, this volume) with the aim of portraying Russia's overall development towards democracy. At the same time, however, it is also the basic axiom of this contribution that Russia's sheer territorial vastness and great power structure will limit the impact and power of external actors upon domestic developments in Russia compared to the small or medium state empirical cases of out-groups 1, 3 and 4 actors within this volume, a topic I shall return to shortly. Mainly for this geopolitical reason Russia has no prospect of becoming a full and normal EU and NATO member, a key factor serving to discipline other post-Communist states (Skak, 1997). This does not render the Russian case irrelevant. On the contrary: the implication is rather that change towards democratic norms in Russia can be considered *partly a case of ideational 'logic of arguing' socialization into democratic norms*, not just 'rational choice'-based change of behaviour (cf. Risse, 2000: 10; Flockhart, this volume).

As stated above, Russia itself is a factor influencing – negatively or positively – upon others rather than the opposite. Yet this heightens the positive significance of Russia's opening to the West as argued in the European Union's common strategy on Russia of June 1999. This document explicitly says that 'a stable, democratic and prosperous Russia, firmly anchored in a united Europe free of dividing lines, is essential to lasting peace on the continent' (Common Strategy, 1999). The comprehensively closed nature of Communist totalitarian societies (Skak, 1996: 18–21; Buzan and Segal, 1992) means that the transition agenda of Communism touches virtually each and every issue area – from culture, economics, law, military and domestic to foreign affairs – in stark contrast to the limited scope of right-wing authoritarianisms like Southern Europe's recent dictatorships (Greece, Portugal and Spain). The collapse of Communism thus marks a paradigmatic change of internal and external openness, that is, tolerance of intervention from actors and forces beyond the state itself. The point is the arrival in Russia of the dynamics of *transnationalism* defined as the uninhibited interaction among individual citizens, groups, and sub-state organizations within different countries.[3] Transnationalism breaks the power monopoly of state and government and is a *sine qua non* for building up democracy including political cultures of participation. Moreover, Russia's ambition of economic modernization presupposes democracy if it is to be sustainable, something that seems to be realized by Russia's president, Vladimir Putin, although his vision is the dubious oxymoron 'managed democracy'.

Russia's capacity for influencing or even thwarting the development towards democracy in its European neighbourhood results from Russia's geographic proximity combined with its historical record of intervening into the affairs of its Western neighbourhood – from the Tsarist interventions into Poland and Hungary to the far more drastic measures of Stalin, Khruschev and Brezhnev for the similar purpose of arresting political development. The record includes recent intimidations of the Balts (Oldberg, 2003). This led the EU to counteract through its Northern Dimension of 1997 extending co-operation to the northwestern regions of Russia in recognition of the need not to isolate Russia when its western neighbours enter the EU and NATO (The Northern Dimension, 2003).

Summing up, this chapter on the socialization of democratic norms in a transforming society argues the relevance of Russia as constituting both a deviant great power case and a critical case of possible ideational change of general importance for the study of the domestic–international nexus in processes of democratization. As for the empirical subject matter, Russia's overall political development in terms of democracy will be operationalized as an analysis of Russia's political culture. The enquiry is divided into, first, nation/people-level political culture and democratic norms and, second, state/elite-level political culture and participation traditions with only occasional references to the intervention of particular international actors in Russia. Foreign policy dimensions of Russia's changing domestic structure will be touched upon prior to the conclusion, which will highlight the contradictory pattern of democratic change leaving Russia in the ambiguous category of out-group 2 countries. Even so, the point is that any democratic change in Russia is qualitatively more interesting than, say, Romania's recent metamorphosis into an out-group 1 country because of the peculiar geopolitical and historical odds against democratic change in Russia. Before going into the empirical analysis, however, it is warranted to briefly consider where and why Russia differs from other transforming states and societies hereby making Russia a generally important, deviant, but critical case.

## Why Russia differs

Generally speaking, the idea of treating the international environment as a key causal factor behind actual democratizations is perfectly valid and an important objection to the way most students of comparative politics tend to frame their analysis of democratization, namely in entirely domestic terms[4] and as an internally determined process. As I have argued elsewhere (Skak, 1997) democracy and its consolidation are interactive processes that are best understood in the context of the workings of what the Swedish political scientist Kjell Goldmann dubs stabilizers, notably international stabilizers. International stabilizers may be structural forces like economic and strategic interdependence between a democratizing state and its international democratic surroundings; forces which clearly count in the case of contemporary Russia as seen in the European Union's combined role as Russia's most important trading partner. They may be specific actors like states or political leaders to which Russia attaches special importance or prestige, for example Germany, the United States, or the WTO, or they may be organizations, groups and individuals displaying particular zeal and efficiency in promoting democracy such as, for example, George Soros. Yet, as already observed, international forces of democratization will tend to carry less weight in Russia than in small transforming states. Their impact will be thinly spread as drops in the ocean of Russia's sheer vastness.

There is an important qualitative twist to this argument against the workings of international democracy stabilizers, namely Russia's great power identity. The crux of much of Russian foreign policy remains Moscow's quest for rank (like French foreign policy) as made explicit in the otherwise enlightened liberal foreign policy agenda of former Russian foreign minister Andrei Kozyrev (*Izvestia*, 2 January 1992). The obsession with prestige means that Russian pride is all too easily hurt when it comes to interventions from the outside into its political sphere – imagined or real. A further complicating factor is Russia's former role and partly surviving imperialistic political culture as centre of the Soviet empire (Skak, 1996: 2, 139–40 and *passim*). Many Russians are prone to nostalgia for the Soviet past in a way one never sees among Balts, Czechs, Poles and Romanians, the former subjugated subjects of the empire. They generally have no qualms about complying with harsh EU and NATO membership conditionalities as they are seen to guarantee their long-term independence from Moscow. There may thus be less ideational than rational change at work in their case (cf. Skak, 1997; Flockhart, this volume) compared to Russia who is bereft of similar membership prospects as international stabilizers of democracy. On top of this comes Russia's delinking from much of Europe's centuries-long history of pluralism and civil societies autonomous from state interference resulting in a highly ambivalent Russian attitude towards the West (Skak, 1993; Neumann, 1996).

The combined effect of all these structural and cultural factors is to turn Russia into a victim of its tragic domestic logic. Fortunately, there are at least two important factors pushing in another direction. The first one is Russia's increasingly strong aspiration to integrate itself with Europe rather than Asia, the only logical alternative in view of Russia's Eurasian geographical make-up, yet neither a realistic nor promising outcome (Trenin, 2002). The other one is the dynamic nature of political culture itself leaving room for processes of learning and change in norms and values as maintained by Hahn (1991). The latter takes issue with scholars like Richard Pipes who in his work *Russia under the Old Regime* insisted on the continuity of imperial Russian absolutist norms among Soviet street-level bureaucrats and thus precluded a development towards democracy in Russia.[5] Accordingly, a natural place to begin the empirical part is by comparing past and present Russian political culture, including the Soviet legacy.

## Nation/people-level socialization of democracy: half-empty or half-full?

The problem about Russia's history and political culture, so to speak, is the lack of significant lasting experiences with democracy and Russia's overwhelming record of autocracy, repression and authoritarianism.

According to Stephen White (1984: 66), pre-1917 Russian political culture was more centralist, state interventionist and collectivist than its major European and North American counterparts. The Bolshevik contribution was to drive this pattern into the extreme through indoctrination and terror. Apart from that, Soviet political culture was one of continuity with respect to nationalism and imperialism.

Judging from uncensored sources like the Prague Manifesto launched by the anti-Stalin Soviet defector General Vlasov during the Second World War, the Soviet experience seems to have been instrumental in nourishing a vision of a 'third way' for Russia between the extremes of capitalism and Communism (White, 1984: 89–90). Today, Russian analysts and politicians often argue the attraction for the citizenry of a Russian *Sonderweg* as a way of criticizing the perceived excesses of Russia's shock therapy of the early 1990s. Many Western observers share this unqualified myth of state paternalism as the essence of Russian political culture. Against this widespread perception it is worth remembering the continuing political fiasco of Russia's social democrats despite the brutality of Russia's economic transition from Communism. Social democratic parties have no following worth mentioning among Russian voters indicating an evolution of Russian political culture away from the Soviet legacy. One could argue that the lack of Marxist zeal within today's Communist party of Russia headed by Gennadi Ziuganov combined with the support he enjoys among the losers in Russia's transition makes his party the real proponent of the 'third way'. Yet, even the Communists' following crumbled during the December 2003 Duma elections, so it is increasingly difficult to identify a constituency behind an alternative to the economic reform agenda pursued by Putin. Not that Russians have turned into staunch neo-liberals, but they apparently fail to see a feasible alternative and in this willy-nilly way have become socialized into market economic conditions and norms as the reality of Russia today.

Russian and Soviet autocracy produced a lasting imprint of subject-orientations – a preoccupation with the implementation side of politics – among Russians at the expense of a participant political culture consonant with democracy (Hahn, 1991). Jeffrey Hahn thus found little confidence among his sample of voters from Yaroslavl in 1990 in their ability to influence governmental decision-making, but goes on to emphasize their support for democratic values – a clear majority favoured competitive elections. He confirms the validity of the insight from modernization theory that the younger and better educated form the critical mass of democracy with respect to Russia. The implication of this finding is important. All other things being equal, it means that Russia's democratic consolidation may be a simple question of time. M. Steven Fish (1995) is less optimistic, though, as he sees the late-Soviet years of Gorbachev and early post-Soviet years of Boris Yeltsin's presidency as the one and only mass-level peaceful political mobilization of Russians.

Since then enthusiasm for political activism and democracy among the Russian citizenry has clearly diminished and apathy has become more widespread,[6] but this cannot be taken as a sign that democracy was and is a non-starter in Russia. Here I should like to invoke a recent contribution by the former, politically influential CIA analyst Tom Bjorkman (2003: 18) who insists that empirical data from opinion surveys – Russian and non-Russian – undertaken in Russia show that:

- People want democratic institutions: voters' first priority at present is 'restoring order' but they do not equate order with authoritarianism. Support for democratic values is deeply rooted.
- Russians want to build democracy their own way: people are ready to back leaders who build stronger democratic institutions.
- Resistance to democracy is centred in a small segment of Russia's political and economic elite, not in society and not in the elite as a whole.
- Voters blame the failures of the first post-Soviet decade on leadership failures, not on democracy.
- Russia's leaders, not Russian society, must take the lead in building stronger democratic institutions.

True, the opinion surveys of the World Values Survey show that support for democracy in Russia ranks near the bottom of the countries included, much lower than in post-Soviet Estonia and lower than even in turbulent post-Soviet Georgia! (Bjorkman, 2003: 19). But the mere fact that a solid majority of Russians continue to support democracy, a growing portion does not support the military campaign in Chechnya, and the fact that originally, only a minority was prepared to back the pro-government and pro-Putin party United Russia in the December 2003 elections is no indicator of authoritarian inclinations. On the contrary:[7] another author who insists on a basically sound democratic political culture in Russia, claiming it has historical roots is Nicolai N. Petro (1995).

Russia's current economic situation should be a factor bolstering democracy as it contrasts the hardships the population had to suffer when democracy was launched around 1990/91. Real per capita incomes are said to have risen 32 per cent under Putin with inflation under control. Interestingly, recent evidence points to growing middle-class orientations (that is, how people perceive themselves) as a result of Russia's economic recovery after the August 1998 crash.[8] The middle class is the class which political scientists from Barrington Moore and onwards identify as the key social constituency behind liberal and democratic values. The reasoning goes that because of the moderate wealth gained by those belonging to the middle class, they will shy away from political extremism in order to protect themselves. Moreover, middle classers thrive in a culturally and politically lively society without violence – in short, they represent the moderate median voters, which are central to the theory of democratic peace (Snyder, 1996). In South Korea, Thailand and elsewhere democracy has been accompanied by a 'middle classinization' of class identity around 1990 whereas political scientists for a very long time bemoaned the lack of a middle class in Russia capable of shouldering democracy.

When identifying the enemies of democracy in Russia, analysts routinely include Russia's armed forces, for example Michael McFaul in his congressional testimony cited earlier (*Johnson's Russia List*, no. 7348, 2 October 2003). The Russian military's surprise seizure of Pristina airport in the summer of 1999 mentioned by McFaul did represent a dangerous lapse into adventurism, but it is not a clear-cut case of Bonapartism and lack of civilian control over the military. Nor is the general organizational and political culture inside the Russian army according to one thorough and highly acclaimed study of Russian civil–military relations by Brian D. Taylor (2003). The Pristina airport incident appears to have been approved in advance by Yeltsin, Russia's popularly elected president at the time (Taylor, 2003: 314). Similarly, Yeltsin and Russian intelligence shares responsibility for fatal decisions such as the first war against Chechnya (Lapidus, 1998; Bennett, 1999: 295–347, cf. Galeotti, 2000). Taylor sees Russian military organizational culture as having a powerful 'norm of civilian supremacy in sovereign power issues' concluding that 'with the fundamental basis of an apolitical military organizational culture in place, the potential for progressive and democratic change in Russian military affairs remains very much alive' (Taylor, 2003: 340).

The norm of civilian supremacy is a rare example of a positive legacy from the Soviet past. The Communist Party was superior to the army, not vice versa, as brutally established by Stalin's purges of his officers. Even so – and for the sake of returning to this volume's topic of external actors' aid in fostering democratic norms in other countries – I should like to dwell on one particular Danish project of technical assistance and know-how aimed at the mental-professional conversion of Russia's armed forces towards a career as potato farmers (Hansen, 2001). Denmark wanted to act as a constructive third party in persuading the Russian forces to withdraw from the Baltic States (which took place in 1993–4) without a Russian loss of face due to rehousing and employment problems once the retired officers returned to Russia. The project was launched as one of rehousing, but the vital element was the accompanying retraining of officers as farmers, which eventually became a commercial success. The Danish state invested in the building of the villages of Shotkusa and Rassvet (northeast of Sankt Petersburg) in the mid-1990s and the Danish Ministry of Agriculture allotted funds for the purchase of machinery and equipment. One Danish farmer, Lorens Simonsen spent years in Shotkusa as instructor and moderator for the twenty-four officers during their tortuous process of becoming dedicated farmers.

The officers, some of whom had served as nuclear physicists on submarines, shunned physical work and drove their tractors into the ditch in protest. Later, as they realized their above-average earnings from the production of potatoes they became interested and now have no difficulty in attracting customers (Hansen, 2001: 36–7). Judging from Bente Villum Hansen's survey of the demobilized officers' ethical, social and political attitudes one cannot speak of a participant political culture, nor of confidence in Russia's leaders except for Evgeni Primakov, the former boss of Russia's external intelligence, foreign and later prime minister 1996–9 (Hansen, 2001: 85ff.). The very conversion from a military to a civilian lifestyle, however, seems to have succeeded in the case of Shotkusa as the project opened the prospect of a sustainable life as a civilian (Hansen, 2001: 97ff., 105ff.). She also notices some trickle-down into the local surroundings such as a less prejudiced view of where farming may succeed. All in all then, even if the project remains a drop in the ocean of conversion, it probably helped to defuse Baltic–Russian tension as well as tension between the demobilized military and civil authorities in Russia at the federal and local level.

This glimpse into one of the thousands of projects aimed at helping Russia's transition cannot do justice to the field, but I shall finish this part of the analysis by introducing a recent, highly critical monograph on Western attempts to build democracy in Russia through support for Russian NGOs written by Sarah L. Henderson (2003). The disturbing finding of her in-depth examination of various projects launched by

Western NGOs – including efforts at building a functioning women's movement in Russia – is that current aid strategies have encouraged civic groups to adopt a vertically organized corporate-style bureaucratic structure that has centralized resources into the hands of a few Westernized NGOs, and all but disenfranchised a wide array of other important social service organizations (*Johnson's Russia List*, no. 7426, #11, 18 November 2003). Henderson urges Western aid agencies to radically rethink the NGO approach to fostering democracy in Russia. The narrow Western definition of what constitutes 'civil society' has created civic groups in Russia that are unable to sustain themselves, threatening not only long-term civic stability, but the promise for democracy in modern-day Russia (*Johnson's Russia List*, no. 7426, #11, 18 November 2003). Not even the otherwise enlightened assistance offered by the Soros Foundation that has poured huge amounts of money and expertise into Russia escapes this criticism.

In other words, Henderson sees the Western-sponsored NGOs as outcompeting whatever embryonic indigenous civil society elements Russia had on the eve of the Soviet collapse or which emerged later. Her view matches that of the influential Russian legal scholar Alexander N. Domrin (2003) of the legislation-drafting division of the federal Russian government who distances himself from rigorist conceptions of civil society autonomy – consonant with Putin's approach of 'managed civil society' as it were. Among other things, he hails Larry Diamond of the Hoover Institution for stressing that the 'single most important and urgent factor in the consolidation of democracy is not civil society but political institutionalization' (quoted from Domrin, 2003). Domrin notices the status of *grazhdanskoe obshchestvo* (civil society) as the new mantra of the Russian government and political elite, but leaves irony aside concerning Putin's meeting on 12 June 2001 (Russia's national holiday) with twenty-eight Russian NGOs that launched the Civic Chamber as a government-level sponsor and (presumably!) monitor of civil society.

In any event, although a majority of Russians cherish democratic rights and freedoms, their confidence in political parties is very low, they attach a high priority to the restoration of order and they have fewer qualms about restrictions on the media and their bosses, the oligarchs, than Westerners have (Domrin, 2003). In this respect Putin's policy matches voter preferences. A case in point is the contrast between the Western public outcry over the arrest in late 2003 of Mikhail Khodorkovsky, a tycoon sponsoring right-wing political parties rivalling Putin as well as human rights organizations and NGOs, and the muted

Russian reaction mixed with glee. Judging from the voter apathy and pro-Putin outcome of the December 2003 Duma elections Russians identify with Russia's strong presidentialism and other features of Russia's democratic political order in the 1993 Constitution. Although this outcome is bad news for Russian parliamentarianism it need not be less 'democratic' than the presidentialist political culture of the United States, albeit here there are additional contextual factors to take into consideration.

To conclude, mass-level Russian political culture is not inherently undemocratic nor is it an anti-open society as such, but frustrations and actual hardships mean that there is no vibrant participant political culture and enthusiasm. In my mind there is no doubt that ordinary Russian citizens love the freedom to travel abroad, which they now have, as these kinds of restrictions were felt by many as the overarching insult of the Soviet system upon their dignity as human beings. Few really wanted to emigrate, ordinary people just wanted to visit Paris or Italy, but even Warsaw Pact countries were off-limits for individual travel. Another infringement of human rights was the extremely rigid Soviet system of *propiska* ('licence to stay'), which controlled domestic mobility and turned people, notably peasants, into serfs rather than citizens. Sadly, 68 per cent of Russians nowadays prefer to keep *propiska*, only 23 per cent want it abolished (Domrin, 2003) – an outcome that may have to do with the topical threat of terrorism, but on this point paternalism survives.

## State/elite-level socialization of democracy: half-empty or half-full?

I believe it was Michael McFaul (1995) who pioneered the analysis of the Russian state as having been hijacked by enterprise managers and corporate interests when the economic reforms of the Yeltsin team unfolded in the aftermath of the failed August putsch in 1991. McFaul saw Yeltsin as missing a historical chance by focusing on economics at the expense of politics, that is state-building and democratic institution-building. McFaul later muted criticism of Yeltsin, but the notion of a 'captured democracy' in Russia has regained popularity and respectability (Reddaway and Glinski, 2001).[9] Without resorting to the untenable conspiracy theory reasoning of this approach, it is clear that Russia faces elite-level problems of political culture impairing Russian democracy. I am referring to the elites' general lack of responsiveness towards voters as pointed out among others by Sarah E. Mendelson (2001, see below).

Russian political culture remains one of Byzantinism and hierarchy, of arrogance, arbitrariness and lack of transparency on the part of leaders, often accompanied by indifference and cynicism towards those at the bottom.

The problem of elite unresponsiveness is illustrated by Sarah L. Henderson's observation about the insulation of Western-sponsored NGOs in Russia from the society they should serve. Similar diagnoses of alienated, if not clashing political subcultures can be inferred from Tom Bjorkman's (2003: 18) engaged contribution presented above, for instance when he urges Russia's leadership, not its society, to take on the task of building strong democratic institutions. Analysts often portray the relationship between the mass- and elite-level of Russian politics as hourglass-shaped, that is with the thinnest possible contact point between the masses and their demands and the ruling elite irrespective of the fact that nowadays the political elite is subject to free and fair elections. Thus, Oksana Gaman-Golutvina deplores the 'gulf between the aims and values of the elite and of the mass of the people' (2001: 304) and speaks indiscriminately of the entire elite's profound indifference to the idea of development and Russia's national interests. Her views are exaggerated in the light of, for example, Putin's strong commitment to modernizing Russia without alienating his electorate, but apart from that she has a point, not least concerning Russian foreign and security policy elites (Skak, 1996, 2005). In view of the possible 'middle-classization' of the greater part of the Russian electorate the isolation of Russia's elites from the daily concern of voters may certainly backfire.

This said, it is worth repeating Tom Bjorkman's point that resistance to deeper democracy is centred in a small segment of Russia's political and economic elite, not in society and not in the elite as such. This unalarmist view of Russia's elites is repeated in an in-depth monograph on the political culture of Russia's diverse elites by the Norwegian political scientist Anton Steen (2003). He conducted structured, face-to-face interviews with 980 respondents in leading positions in 1998 and another 605 interviews in 2000; interviews representing the 'core elite' (the Kremlin leadership), the 'national elite' (the remaining federal-level political elite such as Duma and Federation Council and leading ministerial officials) and the 'regional elite' (regional and republican-level leaders, politicians and officials). Given his comprehensive approach to the concept of the elite – also encompassing enterprise managers – it is surprising that he finds such broad support for Putin's recentralization resulting in a heightened legitimacy for the state's executive institutions (Steen, 2003: 47).

Steen thus rejects the widespread notion of fragmented elites (Steen, 2003: 173). The main problem he identifies is the scepticism towards non-government institutions and among the elites themselves – the low social capital to use another term – making Russia a difficult milieu for civil society, for instance a party system, to take root and prosper. As if anticipating the outcome of the 2003 Duma elections and the 2004 presidential elections, Steen comments: 'While freedom imperilled Yeltsin's democracy, stabilization is jeopardizing Putin's democracy' (Steen, 2003: 48). He sees a major problem for democracy in the way Russians 'deposit their destiny in the hands of a strong leader', but also displays empathy for the Russian longing for economic and political relief after the tumultuous Yeltsin years as reason for the demobilization of masses and elites nowadays. Steen's view of Putin and Yeltsin stresses the complexity of their situation, Yeltsin playing the historical role of laying 'the foundation for a pluralist structure with vested elite interests in democracy and decentralization even if many of them rejected Yeltsin's liberal economic policies' (Steen, 2003: 177). Contrary to the naive perception found in much criticism of shock therapy, 'the government's shift from Yeltsin's grand laissez faire plan to Putin's more state-oriented approach was a reaction to the opinion of the elite rather than that of the people' (Steen, 2003: 178).

An important contribution to the problem of elite unresponsiveness and its relation to the issue of Russia's socialization into democratic norms through Western democracy assistance is the one by the American political scientist Sarah E. Mendelson (2001) from the Fletcher School of Law. She stresses that the picture is mixed in that 'many ideas and practices related to parties, elections, and other democratic institutions have developed in Russia partly as a result of Western groups working with local activists' (Mendelson, 2001: 102–3). On the other hand, campaign skills did not lead to robust parties, nor did it lead parties to engage themselves in establishing contacts with NGOs and unions creating stable linkages between themselves and the surrounding society. The latter is a paramount shortcoming for Mendelson, blocking participant political culture beyond the narrow layer of activists. She hails the unprecedented deployment of domestic electoral monitors from parties other than Ziuganov's Communist Party in the 1999 elections, while also pointing to their passivity – using the occasion to read a book or take a nap – and questions their ability to detect voter fraud (Mendelson, 2001: 89). She exposes the arrogance of Putin and his entourage during elections, his abuse of power towards rival parties and stresses the federal authorities' harassment of political and social activists and their clamp-down on the media. Her criticism and conclusion of a backlash for democracy in Russia are reiterated by Freedom House, the New York-based democracy and human rights worldwide monitoring agency (www.freedomhouse.org).[10] Mendelson's main concern is Western passivity in the face of this backlash – she scorns the OSCE for having endorsed Russia's skewed electoral process during the 1999 and 2000 elections.

The 2003 Duma elections actually broke the pattern of Western tolerance of Putin's use of undemocratic measures – both the OSCE and the Bush administration were publicly critical. The OSCE said that the pre-election process was characterized by extensive use of the state apparatus and media favouritism to benefit the largest pro-presidential party, which resulted in voter apathy (OSCE, 2003). Despite Putin's apparently good intentions concerning Russia's modernization and integration into Europe, during his reign Russia has taken steps in the wrong direction. The promotion of actors representing Putin's background within Russian intelligence is ominous as they are often placed in power positions where they are not accountable: for example, Russia's seven 'super governors' overseeing regions and their bosses. To conclude, the good news about Russia's socialization of democratic norms is the democratic trends and persuasions at work both at the state/elite level and the nation/people level rendering the problem of Russian self- and other-categorization much less static than often perceived. The bad news is that the two levels tend to be separate spheres of potential 'logic of arguing' change implying a sharply reduced vertical transfer of norms.

## Democracy and foreign policy

Russia's ambiguous domestic structure of socializing democratic norms is not the last word on the topic, however. The introduction argued Russia's significance concerning the larger issue of consolidation of democracy elsewhere in Europe as a major external influence on other countries in transition. Therefore, a few final comments on the paradoxical relationship between Russia's foreign policy and democracy are warranted. Yeltsin's far more tolerant and in this sense democratic reign was one of relative indifference towards issues of foreign policy resulting in a loss of control over foreign policy-making (Skak, 1996, 2005). The initiative slipped to reckless elites pursuing an agenda of neo-imperialism against the 'near abroad' (Russia's post-Soviet neighbours) and of isolating Russia in world affairs through its balancing of US unipolarity. Both analysts and leading US politicians like Condoleezza Rice (2000) made it clear that Russia was sliding into irrelevance as a partner for the US. Yet, it took the terrorist attack upon the United States before Russia's dangerous self-marginalization could be decisively reversed. Until then Russian foreign policy-makers like Sergei Karaganov sought mostly in vain to draw attention to Russia's policy failure (Skak, 2005).

As far as European democracy and security is concerned it is a major and positive reversal that Russia has silently embraced the prospect of the Baltic States joining NATO and buried its anti-NATO campaign altogether now that Russia perceives an acute need for focusing on terrorism and threats emanating from its south. This development points towards a possible democratic peace and future security community between the three Baltic States and Russia akin to the *modus vivendi* established between the NATO member Poland and Russia as well as the rest of Central Europe and the Balkans. Similarly, Russia's ability ultimately to compromise on the issue of transit to and from its Kaliningrad exclave is telling for the advent of long-term economic considerations in the foreign policy calculus of Russia's elites when making difficult choices (Oldberg, 2003).

In other words, there are powerful trends of Russian foreign policy moderation of significance for the consolidation of democracy throughout Europe, albeit a highly selective moderation that does not include, for instance, Ukraine.[11] Apart from that and concerning the need for the Balts to build up a working relationship with Russia as part of their democratic consolidation, Russia may, in fact, have contributed to the socialization of democratic norms in Europe. There is, however, the terrible question of whether Putin's control over foreign and security policy and his more enlightened practices in some of his neighbourhood to the west comes at the price of Russia's own democracy at home.

## Conclusion

Needless to say, the above treatment of the immense topic of socialization of democratic norms in Russia and the input of external actors into this process has in no way exhausted the subject. I just hope to have delivered a useful review of some of the relevant literature and issues while presenting my own ideas and assessments and inviting further research and discussion. The point of departure was that Russia's opening for the dynamics of transnationalism is significant, but Russia is a problematic piece in the pan-European democratization and security puzzle. However, Russia's insulation from the rewarding prospect of full EU and NATO membership also makes it a theoretically important case of possible ideational change, even if change in Russia may seem slower and more fickle than in this volume's out-group 1 countries: actual post-Communist EU and NATO members by mid-2004.

Indeed, the overall finding is one of a contradictory Russian embrace of democratic norms, in other words the glass is both half-empty and half-full. Thus, the empirical analysis of the nation/people-level socialization of democratic norms found both changes and continuity. Russian mass-level political culture appears to have adapted to the open society environment of market economy and pluralism rather than the much-heralded orientation of the third-way orientation of Russians as precious few voters in Russia are social democrats. Still, one senses paternalism in the citizenry's focus on order at the expense of freedom when facing this hard choice. A participant political culture has failed to take root, but this cannot be taken as a sign that Russians are indifferent about their new democratic order and rights.

Probing external actors' efforts of socializing Russians into democratic norms, a Danish project on the mental conversion of officers into farmers was presented. The project is successful in the narrow sense of having turned soldiers into civilians – swords into ploughshares as it were – but not in developing strong pro-democracy participatory orientations. In relation to this, however, it was suggested that the Russian military may be much less of a Bonapartist actor than perceived. The culprits in bypassing democracy and broader societal interests are often the intelligence or the political leadership of Russia itself. The relationship between the masses of the Russian army and the elites heading Russia's 'power ministries' is reminiscent of the general hourglass-shaped relationship between the nation/people level and the state/elite level of political culture, implying depressingly little vertical transfer of norms irrespective of whatever fruitful indigenous change there may be.

Thus, the analysis of the state/elite-level of democratic change highlighted the problem of elite unresponsiveness; something that resurfaces in the insulation of Western-made Russian NGOs as observed by Sarah Henderson (2003). Nevertheless, the fashionable 'captured democracy' approach misses the complexity of this issue of political culture through its demonizing of Russia's elites as enemies of the people. On this account Tom Bjorkman's brief monograph is far more sound in its perception of Russia's elites and democracy. Anton Steen (2003) is equally balanced and unalarmist in his conclusions on the increasing legitimacy of governmental institutions following the coming to power of Putin. Steen's point is that Russia's diverse elites have vested interests in the continuation of democracy. Still, the combination of mass-level apathy and endorsement of Putin is problematic. Sarah Mendelson raises critical questions about the long-term outcome of Western efforts to cultivate democratic norms and practices among Russia's political elites. Commenting on the problem of elite responsiveness she observes that it blossoms only during elections, not in between elections (Mendelson, 2001) – not exactly an indicator of ideational change!

Notwithstanding the modernization and, by implication, the democracy ambition of Russia's current leadership, recent political developments in Russia do reveal arrogance and manipulations of democracy – so much so that the OSCE and the US feel it necessary to go public about this. This being said, one must also mention embryonic trends of democratic peace concerning the foreign policy level of political culture in Russia – the switch to playing into both NATO and EU enlargement in a constructive fashion (as far as the non-CIS NATO applicants are concerned). All in all, then, the conclusion to be drawn from this analysis of Russia's contradictory evolution towards democracy is that the glass is neither really full nor is it empty. Progress is patchy and paired with setbacks, for instance within foreign policy where Russia practises a highly selective democratic peace, yet in itself this is significant for the Baltic countries concerned. Russia does not belong to out-group 1, but somewhere lower down the list of out-group countries, but the fact and quality of Russia's changing norms should not be missed – for analytical and structural reasons. Given the paramount importance for Russia of integrating into Europe as adamantly held by the Putin leadership itself, the policy implication emanating from this contribution is that the West must pursue a policy towards Russia that mixes empathy with assertiveness. This principle applies not only to Russia's domestic democracy and reform performance, but also to foreign policy. The complexity and depth of the transition from Communism necessitates this as do security considerations of being proactive in building a democratic peace and a pan-European transatlantic security community, if possible embracing all of Eurasia. This is no easy task, but then, the alternative is worse – as Churchill observed about democracy in general.

## Notes

1. I would like to thank Bjarke Hammer Eriksen, a student of political science at the Department of Political Science, University of Aarhus, Denmark, who acted as a research assistant for me when collecting material for this contribution.

2. According to Flockhart (this volume), out-group 1 countries have an ideational fit at both the nation/people level and the state/elite level of socialization, allowing for a fruitful mixture of bottom-up and top-down transfers of democratic norms. Her *a priori* categorization of Russia as an out-group 2 country implying a more problematic pattern of self- and other-categorization is probably valid in itself. Yet it is misleading in connection with the categorization of, for instance, Romania as an in-group 1 country, hence presumably a case of ideational fit at both levels. Among other things I base this judgement on a recent study trip to Romania where Romanians themselves were the first to emphasize the highly superficial, opportunistic – that is, rational choice based – embrace of democratic norms at elite and popular levels as narrowly related to the prospect of EU entry.
3. In his seminal work on transnationalism and the related topic of interdependence, James N. Rosenau defined transnationalism as 'the processes whereby international relations conducted by governments have been supplemented by relations among private individuals, groups, and societies that can, and do, have important consequences for the course of events' (Rosenau, 1980: 1).
4. Notable exceptions are Pridham et al. (1994); Pridham and Vanhanen (1994); Dawisha (1997); and Grugel (this volume).
5. To be fair to Pipes one must add that he later changed his view so that it roughly matches that of another prominent historian, Martin Malia, who sees the Soviet era as the real climax of Russian despotism after which democratic freedoms may, in fact, take root.
6. Thus, *Vremya Novostei* on 11 August 2003 cited data from the Russian Public Opinion Foundation showing that almost half of the 1500 respondents – 44 per cent – make no plans for the future and over half believe they have no chance of becoming well-to-do. Apathy is most pronounced among people aged over 50 (68 per cent) with modest incomes (between 1000 and 2000 rubles a month). Here pessimism prevails and the majority (65 per cent) support Ziuganov's Communist Party. Conversely, less than 20 per cent of the respondents are optimists, most of these being under 35 years old and/or urban residents with college degrees (*Johnson's Russia List*, no. 7284, #1, 11 August 2003).
7. These formulations are taken from a testimony by Michael A. McFaul, a prominent political scientist, for the US House of Representatives Committee on International Relations, 30 September 2003, published in *Johnson's Russia List*, no. 7348, 2 October 2003. Both McFaul and VTsIOM director Yuri Levada believe that VTsIOM's evidence on the growing opposition to the war in Chechnya and the other uncomfortable poll data, is the reason for the Putin government's recent efforts to end the independence of VTsIOM (*Moscow Times*, 6 August 2003 and *Johnson's Russia List*, no. 7278, 6 August 2003).
8. According to one sociological study carried out by the Social Studies Institute of the Russian Academy of Sciences covering 2100 respondents in all of Russia's territorial-economic areas nearly *half of Russia's population ranks itself as middle class* – 48.9 per cent, an immense rise since 1999 which is matched by the doubling of the upper class and a reduction in the share of the lower classes (*RIA Novosti*, Moscow, 3 December 2003, here from *Johnson's Russia List*, no. 7451, #1, 4 December 2003).

As can be concluded from the figures on 'pessimists' vs. 'optimists' cited in note 7 above, the evidence on Russia's middle classes is contradictory. VTsIOM data show that as many as 80 per cent of Russians consider themselves to belong to the middle class, whereas when measured in income terms the majority of them would qualify as poor. The reason for this paradox seems to be the middle-class value orientations of, for example, teàchers and health workers who are poorly paid (*Johnson's Russia List*, no. 7378, #2, 21 October 2003). Others again stress the pessimism inside the middle class defined as people earning 7000 roubles a month in their reading of the Russian Academy of Sciences study cited above (*Kommersant*, 13 November 2003; *Johnson's Russia List*, no. 7418, 13 November 2003).

9. To be sure, Reddaway and Glinski do not deal primarily with democracy, as their work is designed as an indictment of Russia's economic reforms and hence is a work on Russia's political economy. The authors see shock therapy as the reason for the derailing of democracy in Russia, which I see as an utterly primitive understanding of the complexity of political change in Russia. The implication is that a gradualist, state *dirigisme* approach would have solved Russia's problems of political culture overnight and led to a strong party system and parliamentarianism, which it obviously would not. They further see Yeltsin as a puppet catapulted into power by greedy elites and also see him as the mastermind behind the bloody showdown of October 1993. Overall they argue that shock therapy was nothing but a way to seize economic and political power and in this way capture democracy; similarly, the war in Chechnya is depicted as instrumental for Yeltsin, hereby ignoring the role of misperception and the desperation of Yeltsin's entourage afterwards.
10. On the eve of US President Bush's visit to St Petersburg in the early summer of 2003 Freedom House released a report on the disturbing decline of democracy in Russia (www.freedomhouse.org/pdf docs/research/nitransit/2003/nitrussia2003.pdf).
11. In October 2003 a Russo-Ukrainian crisis evolved, provoked by Russia's unilateral construction of a dam to the Ukrainian island Tuzla in the Kerch Strait dividing the Black Sea from the Sea of Azov, accompanied by statements from the Kremlin according to which Russia no longer recognizes the island as Ukrainian but declares it disputed territory (Sperling, 2003; cf. *Johnson's Russia List*, no. 7465, #8, 12 December 2003).

# 10

# Belarus: an Authoritarian Exception from the Model of Post-Communist Democratic Transition?

*Clelia Rontoyanni and Elena Korosteleva*

Western commentators sometimes refer to Belarus as 'Europe's last dictatorship'.[1] This emotively charged description is certainly an exaggeration. It nonetheless captures the unique situation in which Belarus has found itself the target of consistent criticism on the part of Europe's main international organizations and the United States for failing to meet what most European nations recognize as international democratic standards. The administration of President Lukashenko, who has been in power for the last decade, finds itself in a state of confrontation with 'the West', primarily due to its non-espousal of these standards – at least as perceived by the country's critics. The Belarusian administration has proved remarkably insensitive to external pressure, giving rise to policy dilemmas for external actors wishing to encourage political liberalization and promote democratic norms in Belarus. By all accounts, the West's attempts to promote democratic norms in Belarus have failed. The considerable popular legitimacy of the Belarusian president, despite his authoritarian style of government, poses the questions of whether Belarusian society actually espouses democratic norms and, if not, to what extent it may be receptive to them.

This chapter will outline the evolution of the Belarusian political system, which is characterized by a very high concentration of power in the hands of the president. It will examine the main issues of international criticism and assess their effectiveness in encouraging the Belarusian leadership's adherence to democratic principles (state/elite level). Secondly, the chapter will consider the impact of Western efforts to socialize democratic norms in the Belarusian population (nation/people level). The authors will thereby seek to account for the non-conformity of Belarus vis-à-vis the socialized democratic norm set, now unique in the European context. Finally, they will attempt to gauge the extent to which this exceptionalism can be attributed to the Lukashenko leadership's non-identification with the West (the external socializing agents) as opposed to deeper-seated societal attitudes and underlying features of the country's transitional path.

## Authoritarian government and international pressure

For the first three years of its existence as an independent state, Belarus seemed to have been oriented towards the adoption of the democratic norms promoted by international organizations. International criticism of Belarus began in November 1996, when the country's first elected president, Aleksandr Lukashenko, organized a referendum (despite the objections of the Constitutional Court[2]) to amend the Constitution to establish a truly 'super-presidential' system. Lukashenko had won the first Belarusian presidential elections in 1994 with 80 per cent of the vote, defeating then Prime Minister Vyacheslav Kebich in what was internationally recognized as a free and fair contest. Lukashenko set out to undermine the credibility and the effective operation of the legislative and judicial branches of power, thereby weakening institutional checks and balances limiting presidential power. His first step was to sabotage the parliamentary elections of May 1995 (the first since the country gained independence in 1991), *inter alia* by calling a referendum on the same day. The elections were observed by the OSCE, which found them to have fallen short of the Copenhagen commitments regarding political campaigning and recommended the clarification of electoral legislation and the provision of increased media access to political parties and candidates.[3] More than half of the seats failed to be filled, preventing the parliament from functioning and allowing the president to rule single-handedly by decree.

Lukashenko combined the parliamentary elections with a referendum of consultative character on restoring Soviet-era state symbols; Russian as an official language; increasing economic ties with Russia; and giving the president the power to dissolve parliament. This was Lukashenko's first use of a popular referendum as an instrument of capitalizing on his personal popularity to remove institutional constraints on his power. His confrontation with parliament was exacerbated when he proposed another referendum to consolidate his *de facto* one-man rule by substantially strengthening the president's powers and reducing those of the parliament and the judiciary. Lukashenko's initiative caused a serious political crisis: parliament refused to approve the organization of such a referendum and started impeachment proceedings, accusing the president of attempting 'an unconstitutional seizure of power'.[4] Despite the parliament's fierce opposition, Lukashenko insisted that the results of a referendum should be legally binding. He used his popularity to compel parliament to call a referendum by appealing directly to the electorate on television to 'choose between chaos and anarchy or discipline, order and a change for the better'. Indeed, he succeeded in convincing the electorate, who voted in favour of the proposed constitutional amendments with 71 per cent.

The main features of the constitutional amendments adopted in November 1996 were that the president gained the right to dissolve parliament, to call referenda, to issue decrees with the force of law, to hire and fire ministers without parliamentary approval, to appoint half of the members of the Constitutional Court and the Supreme Court, and an eighth of the upper house of parliament. Parliament became bicameral with the creation of an upper house consisting of presidential and local government appointees, a change which severely weakened the influence of the directly elected lower chamber. Moreover, the size of the lower house was reduced to 110 deputies, but no new elections were organized to accommodate that change. Forty-two deputies of the anti-Lukashenko parliamentary opposition insisted that the new Constitution and the new parliament lacked legitimacy and refused to sit in the new parliament. Consequently the composition of the new, weakened parliament was the result of self-selection: the new lower house ended up consisting mainly of Lukashenko's supporters, thus neutralizing the legislature as a counterweight to presidential power.

## International criticism

The results of the referendum, and along with it the legitimacy of the new Constitution and Belarusian institutions of government, were not recognized by a number of international actors often collectively understood as 'the West'. The legitimacy of the referendum was questioned by international actors because it went ahead against the ruling of the Belarusian Constitutional Court and without the approval of parliament. Furthermore, legitimacy was called into question on the grounds of the conditions under which the referendum was held, notably that the opposition was not given a fair chance to present its arguments to the electorate. In addition, international institutions considered that the constitutional changes had eroded the powers of parliament to an extent that was viewed as incompatible with democratic principles by allowing the president to rule by decree 'without commensurate legislative controls'.[5] International organizations, notably the CoE and the OSCE, continued to recognized the previous parliament as the only legitimate parliament of Belarus for several years. In practice, this meant that only the forty-two opposition (former) deputies were admitted to European forums, even though the deputies that remained in the new House of Representatives had also been elected in 1995.

Lukashenko attracted further international opprobrium when he refused to hold presidential elections at the end of his first term of office in July 1999 on the grounds that the first two years of his term should not be counted because they were covered by the old Constitution.[6] At the same time, the international reputation of Belarus was clouded by the disappearances of former Interior Minister Yury Zakharenko, former Chairman of the Central Election Commission Viktor Gonchar, and businessman Anatoly Krasovsky. A cameraman working for a Russian television channel, Dmitry Zavadsky, was added to the list of disappeared persons in July 2000. Under international and domestic pressure, an investigation was launched leading to the arrest and conviction in March 2002 of two Belarusian former secret service agents for the abduction and murder of Zavadsky. However, this trial did not fully convince the international community and dispel concerns that the investigations may have stopped short of revealing the moral authors behind the disappearances.

The parliamentary elections of 2000 and the presidential elections of 2001 were criticized for their failure to meet international standards. In the run-up to the parliamentary elections of October 2000, the OSCE, the CoE and the EU held a joint assessment of political conditions in Belarus based on four criteria: the amendment of the electoral legislation to ensure full transparency of the electoral process, including the composition and the work of election commissions; guarantees of all political parties' access to the mass media; the restitution of meaningful parliamentary powers; and measures to restore confidence in the run-up to the elections, notably by ending harassment and intimidation of opposition politicians and their supporters by the law-enforcement agencies. The three institutions noted an improvement thanks to amendments introduced to the election law in June 2000, but found that the four criteria, which were considered as necessary preconditions for the elections to be deemed 'free and fair', had not been met. They therefore decided against a full election observation mission. The elections were observed by a small delegation of the Parliamentary Troika (OSCE and CoE Parliamentary Assemblies, European Parliament), which identified several flaws, including the abuse of candidate registration procedures to disbar many opposition candidates; lack of transparency in the counting and tabulations of the vote, especially due to extensive early voting;[7] and a heavy bias in the state media in favour of pro-Lukashenko parties and candidates.

Still European institutions recognized that the Belarusian authorities had made some efforts to respond to international criticism, for example by amending the election law and giving all candidates five minutes' free air time on state television. The report of the Parliamentary Troika explicitly presented the following year's presidential elections as an opportunity for the Belarusian authorities to regain international legitimacy and end the country's international isolation by meeting the four criteria.[8] However, this opportunity was missed. Despite the intention of the OSCE to deploy a full election observation mission, the relevant invitation from the Belarusian authorities came too late to organize such a mission. As a result, a limited mission was organized covering only the last three weeks in the run-up to the election as opposed to the normal OSCE procedure of four weeks. This prevented the OSCE from observing the formation of election commissions, the registration of candidates and the first week of campaigning and media coverage. It also led to an impression that Belarus accepted international scrutiny of the election process only reluctantly.[9] At any rate, it illustrated the Belarusian authorities' distrust of the OSCE and also of the EU, which had also called for a timely invitation to the OSCE. The verdict of the OSCE observers was once again that the elections, which resulted in the victory of President Lukashenko with 75 per cent in the first round, fell below international standards on account of essentially the same flaws as the previous year's parliamentary elections.

The pressure by the authorities on opposition-biased non-state media has been another point of international criticism. This has included the confiscation of equipment and/or publications and the temporary closure of printing facilities such as those of the 'Magic' publishing house (including during the 2000 and 2001 election campaigns), which prints several opposition newspapers. The closure of media outlets and the criminal prosecution of journalists and politicians have provoked further international censure of Belarus' failure to observe freedom of speech.[10] Media pluralism in Belarus remains limited due to state control over the distribution of the print media and also due to the monopoly position of the state-controlled electronic media with nationwide coverage.

European institutions have castigated Belarus for repressing civic liberties by arresting peaceful demonstrators, thereby violating the internationally accepted freedoms of expression and assembly. The Belarusian authorities have also been repeatedly criticized for imposing undue restrictions on the activities of NGOs, trade unions and religious organizations such as extensive controls on their sources of funding and on their publications. Most recently, in March 2004, the EU expressed concern over the Belarusian tax authorities' decision to impose a heavy fine on the Belarusian Helsinki Committee, a human rights organization, and threats to close the most prominent non-state educational institution, the European Humanities University.

## The international isolation of Belarus and its results

After the constitutional referendum of November 1996 and the controversial reform of parliament, the international ostracism of Belarus began with the suspension of the country's observer status in the CoE and with the OSCE Parliamentary Assembly's refusal to accept delegations from the new parliament. In early 1997, the European Union requested the Belarusian authorities to open consultations with the former deputies of the 13th session to establish a proper balance between the executive, the legislative and the judiciary branches of power and to establish mechanisms to guarantee human rights and the position of the non-state media. The EU offered Belarus assistance in meeting democratic standards, but the Belarusian authorities refused to acknowledge that their conduct was in any way deficient with regard to democratic norms. The Lukashenko administration did not accept the authority of any international organization to assess it against 'European or international standards'. As far as the president was concerned, the expansion of his powers had received the overwhelming support of the Belarusian people and was therefore legitimate.

From the point of view of the EU and other international organizations, however, Belarus was in breach of its international commitments arising from its membership in the OSCE. By joining the OSCE in 1992 Belarus signed up to the organization's principles, including acceptance of the 'Copenhagen commitments', which include specific requirements for the conduct of elections campaigns in a free and fair environment and access to the media for all candidates on a non-discriminatory basis. Belarus is the only European country that is not a member of the CoE, the guardian of major European conventions concerning human rights and democratic norms. With the exception of

Russia, Belarus is also unique among CEECs in not aspiring to join either NATO or the EU, two organizations whose admission criteria include benchmarking in relation to democratic norms, human rights and civic liberties. Instead, the economic relations and foreign policy of Belarus are overwhelmingly oriented towards the Commonwealth of Independent States and Russia in particular. Despite considerable tensions between the Putin and Lukashenko administrations, Russia has continued to provide political support for Belarus in international forums, not least because Russia also resents international scrutiny of issues such as the conflict in Chechnya, which it considers as undue interference in its internal affairs.

Having tried to use persuasion without success, the EU then resorted to a strategy of exclusion, conditionality and even 'shaming',[11] through a strategy of social influence aimed at modifying the behaviour of the Belarusian leadership. In September 1997, the EU's Council of Ministers decided to freeze the commencement of the two agreements the EU had concluded with Belarus: the comprehensive Partnership and Co-operation Agreement (PCA) and the more limited Interim Agreement; to refrain from any ministerial contacts with Belarus – with the exception of extraordinary contacts through the EU presidency or the EU troika; to suspend EC and member-states' technical assistance programmes with the exception of humanitarian projects or those directly supporting the democratization process; and to continue democratization programmes in co-operation with the OSCE and the CoE. Belarus has also missed out on trade preferences that the EU has since offered to its neighbours such as Russia and Ukraine. The United States adopted a policy of 'selective engagement', which consists of restricting interaction (including assistance and trade) with the official authorities to a minimum, while providing political, technical and financial support for the opposition and the 'democratically oriented' (anti-Lukashenko, pro-Western) media and civil society.

Seven years after the introduction of the policies that have resulted in the isolation of Belarus from the part of the international community known as 'the West', there is barely any evidence of progress towards political liberalization in Belarus. On the contrary, there are grounds for considering that the situation with regard to some of the criteria set by European institutions has deteriorated. Faced with the expiry of his current term in office in 2006, the Belarusian president has announced his intention to once again resort to a popular referendum to lift the constitutional restriction that prevents him from running for a third term. It is clear that European institutions' policy of isolation has failed in its norm-socializing mission – at least at the state/elite level in Belarus. The country is now barely closer to conformity with internationally endorsed democratic standards than it was in 1997.

Far from socializing the Lukashenko administration into international democratic norms, Western criticism and pressure have exacerbated the Belarusian leadership's suspicion of 'the West' and the sincerity of its criticism. The Lukashenko administration neither wished Belarus to integrate with the West nor did it value the approval of Western institutions. In the case of Belarus, the distance (in terms of self- and other-categorization) separating the norm promoting actors (EU, US, CoE, even the OSCE) and the would-be socializee (that is, the Belarusian leadership) was from the start too significant for the socialization effort to succeed. Changing the behaviour, let alone the values, of the Lukashenko administration may not have been a realistic goal. From the start of its wrangle with European institutions, Belarus has shown itself remarkably unresponsive to external criticism, prompting the European Union to describe the international isolation of Belarus as 'self-imposed'.[12]

Belarus has often attempted to brush of Western criticism by accusing its critics of applying 'double standards'. Western policy is to some extent vulnerable to this accusation. Both the European Union and the United States maintain contractual relations with countries such as Uzbekistan whose records on democracy and human rights are by all accounts significantly worse than those of Belarus. European and American policy-makers defend their tougher line on Belarus on the grounds that higher standards with regard to democracy and human rights should apply to European countries. The Belarusian leadership's aloofness to the process of European integration *inter alia* reflects the Lukashenko administration's non-adherence to the principles professed by major European organizations such as the EU and the CoE. The low identification with 'Europe' in Belarus and its correspondingly low interest in being admitted to European 'clubs', coupled with its overwhelming reliance on Russia, have severely limited the options available to European institutions to encourage political liberalization through any form of socialization. The Belarusian administration's interest in relations with the EU is limited to interaction, not integration. Belarus wants co-operation with the EU in selected areas: trade and investment, cross-border and justice and home affairs co-operation, which in the understanding of the Belarusian leadership do not imply Belarusian acquiescence to the EU's right to scrutinize or – in Belarusian diplomatic language – 'interfere in' the country's internal affairs. Unlike Putin's Russia, Lukashenko's Belarus has shown little interest in the approval of

European institutions: it has made hardly any efforts or even verbal commitments to be recognized as 'a good European' or a 'worthy member of the international community'.

Political conditionality, which lies at the heart of European institutions' policies of isolation and the US policy of 'selective engagement', is unacceptable in principle to the Belarusian leadership. For President Lukashenko and many Belarusian senior officials, changing the way the country is governed to satisfy the standards set by European institutions (let alone the US) would be one concession too far. To a large extent, this is a question of national or even personal pride in the sense of President Lukashenko's strong reluctance to be seen to be backing down under Western pressure.[13] Certain prominent Belarusian analysts, such as Leonid Zaiko, have suggested that Lukashenko's occasional craving for international legitimacy is outweighed by his fear that the steps required to regain international legitimacy could lead to his downfall.[14] The Belarusian president has often used confrontation with the West, especially NATO, to bolster his domestic legitimacy. This anti-Western rhetoric has contributed to similarly suspicious attitudes towards the norm-promoting actors at the nation/people level, an issue we return to below.

The most significant gesture of compromise on the part of the Belarusian leadership came in February 1998, when Belarus accepted the mandate of a special OSCE mission, the Minsk-based Advisory and Monitoring Group (AMG) headed by Ambassador Hans-Georg Wieck. The AMG's mandate was to assist the Belarusian authorities in promoting democratic institutions and in complying with OSCE commitments and to monitor progress in this process. Towards the end of 1999 the AMG had some success in convincing the Lukashenko administration to engage in dialogue with the opposition and contributed to the adoption in 2000 of amendments to bring the electoral legislation closer to international norms. However, consultations between the authorities and the opposition proved short-lived and no significant steps towards political liberalization followed, with the exception of former prime minister Chigir's release from prison.

Prior to the parliamentary elections of 2000 and especially the presidential elections of 2002, the AMG's relations with the Lukashenko administration deteriorated sharply, culminating in the Belarusian president's public threats to expel Ambassador Wieck. The Belarusian authorities accused the AMG of exceeding its mandate. The AMG's training of domestic election observers and provision of advice to the opposition were especially controversial and prompted the Belarusian authorities to insist on a modification of the AMG's mandate. The AMG eventually had to close at the end of 2002, after the Belarusian authorities declined to renew the visas of its expatriate personnel. A new OSCE mission was established as of January 2003 with an amended mandate, which includes institution-building, consolidation of the rule of law and authorities' relations with civil society, but also economic and environmental activities. Although broader, the new mission's mandate is considered significantly weaker, since it does not explicitly refer to Belarusian compliance with OSCE commitments.

Seven years after their decision to economically and politically isolate Belarus, all European institutions concerned (EU, CoE, OSCE) as well as the United States confirm that this policy will remain in place. Apart from avoiding political embarrassment, 'the West' has insisted on the policy of isolation in order to 'draw a line' and send a clear signal that it considers this kind of authoritarian behaviour unacceptable and hopefully deter other countries' leaders from caving in to the temptation to use authoritarian methods. In terms of promoting political liberalization in Belarus, however, the isolation of Belarus from the West offers almost no channels of influence. If anything, the restriction of economic links and political contacts between Belarus and the West has reduced European and American leverage over Belarus. As a result, the external norm-promoting actors have had little access to alternative access points at the domestic level, especially elite channels that could serve as 'intermediate agents' in the transfer of democratic norms and as sources of pressure on the Lukashenko administration to liberalize. Indeed, Olga Abramova, a Belarusian parliamentarian critical of the Lukashenko administration, has argued that a toughening of Western economic sanctions might even benefit Lukashenko, who could credibly blame the West for a possible deterioration in living standards at home.[15]

The effectiveness of Western criticism of the Lukashenko administration and assistance to Belarusian civil society in promoting societal adherence to democratic values also remains unclear. This question is addressed in detail in the latter half of this chapter with reference to substantial evidence from public opinion surveys. It could be argued that the international community has had a role in encouraging the Belarusian opposition to coalesce and form a distinct group identity. The opposition has indeed developed a certain sense of a common identity and some capacity for co-ordinated action. The most notable instance of solidarity among the opposition was the formation of a coalition that supported the candidacy of Vladimir Goncharik in the presidential elections of 2001. The need to return the country to the path of democratic development and normalize relations with the West are the two points of convergence among the ideologically and programmatically diverse political forces that make up the Belarusian opposition. However, this sense of group identity may have emerged irrespective of any external factors due to the hostile domestic political conditions. Moreover, so far the Belarusian opposition has failed to form 'winning coalitions' that could help transform Belarus from a country with a low identification with democratic norm-promoting actors at both state/elite and nation/people levels (out-group 4) to a Western-oriented society with a high level of socialization of democratic norms (out-group 3). There are, however, signs that some officials in the Lukashenko administration are covertly sympathetic to the opposition's agenda and could potentially form part of such a 'winning coalition'.[16] So far, however, the rather monolithic domestic political structure has meant that the cost of joining ranks with the opposition has been too high for a critical mass of the ruling elite to consider such an option.

President Lukashenko's overwhelming dominance of Belarusian political life and his considerable – albeit declining – popular support at home pose serious dilemmas for Western policy-makers. Until recently, the policy of the European institutions was to disregard the relevance of the Belarusian president's popularity as a consideration when formulating their criticism. However, Lukashenko's re-election in 2001 prompted a rethinking of this strategy in many European capitals and also in international organizations such as the EU and the CoE. It has been increasingly acknowledged that limited assistance to selected NGOs has failed to reach out to Belarusian society as a whole or even to key constituencies of 'opinion formers' such as journalists, scientists or the business community and 'future leaders' (students). Many leaders of the Belarusian opposition such as Sergei Kalyakin (Party of Belarusian Communists) and Vintsuk Vyachorka (Belarusian Popular Front) have long argued that it is important for Western institutions to develop contacts with these constituencies, which have the potential to act as 'intermediate agents' and expand the social base in support of democratic norms and a European orientation.

The approach now favoured by many European governments and institutions is to broaden European contacts with Belarusian society in order to promote wide socialization of democratic norms and pro-European attitudes among the Belarusian public – indeed, a strategy that is suggested in the complex socialization model in this volume. Relevant measures proposed include the expansion of student and scientific exchanges, the encouragement of co-operation among local authorities in Belarus and other European countries such as twinning programmes, cross-border co-operation and possibly business-to-business co-operation or even dialogue with Belarusian parliamentarians. Indeed, the Belarusian authorities have expressed a reserved interest in the European Union's 'Wider Europe' or 'European Neighbourhood policy', which was launched in March 2003 and which offers the prospect of increased co-operation and societal contacts with the neighbours of the enlarged European Union including Belarus (European Commission, 2003). However, the policy's Strategy Paper of May 2004 makes it clear that Belarus will not be able to reap the full benefits until 'fundamental reforms are carried out' (European Commission, 2003). This political conditionality is likely once again to limit Lukashenko's willingness to engage, even though many Belarusian officials are reportedly keen to see progress in the country's relations with the West and to take advantage of opportunities for co-operation.

It therefore seems that the external promotion of democratic norms so far has failed to bring any substantive results in the Belarusian leadership's adherence to these norms. To some extent, this can be explained by the lack of international consensus on the need to exercise pressure on Belarus, with Russia playing the role of the economic and diplomatic lifeline of Belarus. Simply put, Western efforts to modify the Lukashenko administration's behaviour have not been backed by sufficiently powerful 'carrots or sticks'. Like many authoritarian regimes, the Belarusian administration has shown a high level of resistance to external pressure and has proven rather insensitive both to the threat of sanctions and to potential incentives offered by the West. As the theoretical model of 'complex socialization' suggests, the ideational distance between the state/elite level in Belarus and the norm-promoting actors has been the key factor accounting for the country's 'exceptionalism' in terms of non-adherence to democratic norms in the European context. An eventual change of political leadership in Belarus could have a catalytic role in fostering the country's socialization into democratic norms, especially if it is combined with aspirations to join the process of European integration.

## Public opinion in Belarus

As mentioned in the theoretical chapter of this volume, effective socialization of international norms and ideals at the domestic level presupposes a two-level relationship – that is, an interaction between the 'we-concepts' of the state and the nation. Human rights norms and democratic standards cannot be simply implanted in a domestic setting through their promotion by the international agents and their communication with the state/leadership. The norms and ideals need to become *internalized* by way of behavioural and ideational change. Furthermore, it is clear from the literature and empirical evidence that in order for socialization of international norms to be effective and enduring, it is important to place equal emphasis on the diffusion of norms from the international level to both elites and the masses, in the latter case by way of building linkages between civil society and the population at large.

In this part of the chapter we will attempt to establish the popular orientation and the level of diffusion of democratic norms into the general public in Belarus. For this purpose we will, first, examine public attitudes and knowledge of international organizations in Belarus, and second, evaluate public understanding of the norms and ideals of democracy, without which progress to better governance and effective settlement of international norms and ideals will not be achievable. We will demonstrate that despite relatively high cognizance of democratic norms and rules by the electorate, and the growing acceptance of respective institutions and international organizations, the people of Belarus display little emotional attachment to and behavioural socialization of these norms, which naturally impedes the country's progress to democracy.

## Public opinion and international organizations

Given the legacies of Belarus' socialist past, its authoritarian government and the international isolation it has been surrounded with over the last nine years, it comes as no surprise that variable patterns of support for activities of foreign countries and international organizations emerge in Belarus. On the cognitive level, there have been some positive developments in popular impressions and public attitudes towards individual countries and international organizations, which seem to have reached their culmination by 2000. This was associated with a considerable shift of public opinion towards a more positive perception of Russia (+19 per cent), USA (+18 per cent), Germany (+8 per cent) and Poland (+8 per cent), as compared to earlier years, as well as the growth of confidence in estimating those countries' ability to act responsibly. This is shown by the fact that the proportion of Belarusians who believed that the USA would deal responsibly with international affairs had risen by 34 per cent, for Russia by 11 per cent and for Germany by 18 per cent

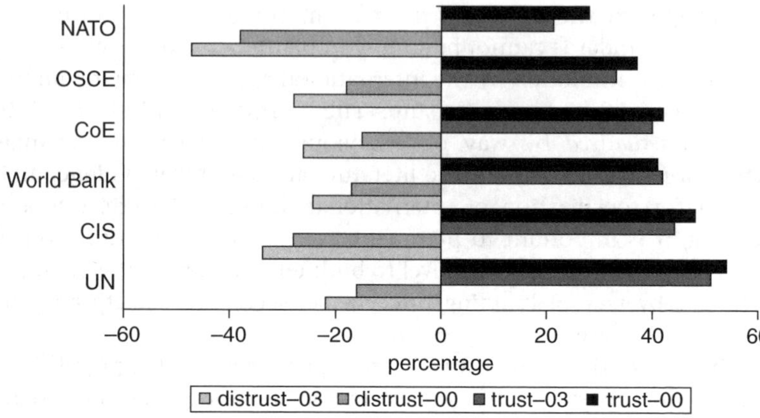


*Figure 10.1* Trust in international organizations, 2003

*Source*: Nationwide survey, conducted by NOVAK, 4–12 November 2003. Stratified random sample included 1096 respondents representing all adults over the age of 18.

respectively.[17] Three years on, however, the politics of international isolation and selective 'engagement' in a democratic dialogue with Belarus has finally reaped what the West carefully sowed under the headline of fostering democracy. Public trust in individual countries and international organizations has declined giving rise to the dangerous sense of exclusion coupled with limited choice and high confidence in the president. The overall decline of confidence in international institutions exceeded 5 per cent, whereas the level of distrust gained an additional 20 per cent also recruiting votes from the 'undecided' electorate. Out of all organizations, NATO enjoys the lowest level of confidence, dramatically outweighed (26 per cent) by lack of trust. This is followed by declining confidence in the CIS as a result of recent political frictions between the Putin and Lukashenko administrations.

Furthermore, when it comes to evaluating activities of international organizations *in relation to* Belarus, an even more poignant picture arises. For example, only one-fifth of the population feel that the West is trying to help their country to become prosperous and democratic, whereas a majority (63 per cent) believe Western nations are at least indifferent, and at most are acrimonious and malevolent in their intentions to the new states and Belarus in particular.[18] As another example of public controversial *modus operandi*, the OSCE is generally seen as a good-will organization helping to foster democracy worldwide; in practical terms, however, there is a rather mixed opinion in evaluating its

*Table 10.1* Confidence in AMG OSCE, Belarus

| Confidence in AMG OSCE mission (%) | Nov–99 | Apr–00 | Nov–00 | Apr–01 | Nov–01 | Apr–02 |
|---|---|---|---|---|---|---|
| Confident | 16.5 | 20.6 | 20.2 | 21.9 | 29.5 | 28.8 |
| Not confident | 20.7 | 20.5 | 22.4 | 23.4 | 28.8 | 31.4 |
| DK/DS | 62.8 | 58.9 | 57.4 | 54.7 | 41.7 | 39.8 |

*Source*: Oleg Manaev 'KNG OBSE v Belarusi: missiya nevozmozhna?', *Narodnaya volya*, 16 May 2002.

activity in Belarus, associated with varied levels of confidence and effectiveness of its mission. The Belarusians seem to be more open in their perception of the outside world, but remain rather cautious and often distrustful in their evaluation of the activities of international organizations in their own country.

An assessment of fear and images of enemies remaining from the Cold War period might be another indicator to help us evaluate change in public perception of foreign countries and international organizations. As a result, although the majority of the electorate (51 per cent) believes that no single country is an immediate threat to Belarus at present, the level of public anxiety in reference to international organizations has hardly altered. Over the past three years the EU seems to be the only organization that has enjoyed a 50 per cent decrease in levels of public anxiety, which is likely to be due to its politics of non-engagement into Belarusian affairs, whereas the OSCE – the only organization with a presence in Belarus – controversially emerges as causing a 3 per cent rise of public concern in relation to its activities in Belarus (which accidentally were termed 'subversive' by the state-controlled Belarusian media) (NISEPI News, 2003: 11). This seems to corroborate our initial hypothesis that Belarusians may remain positively minded and open in relation to those international organizations which have no immediate presence in the country. When, however, it comes to practical involvement into the country's affairs, the people display hostile and uncongenial attitudes to international organizations.

There has also been a decline in public attitudes towards the expansion of NATO since 1997, with rising concerns in relation to the safety of the Belarusian borders (+27 per cent) (NISEPI News, 2003: 11). Comparatively, Belarusians tend to be more open and positive in their attitudes to the EU and related organizations than to those led by the USA. For example, when asked what form of integration/co-operation with the international community Belarus should pursue, the choice of

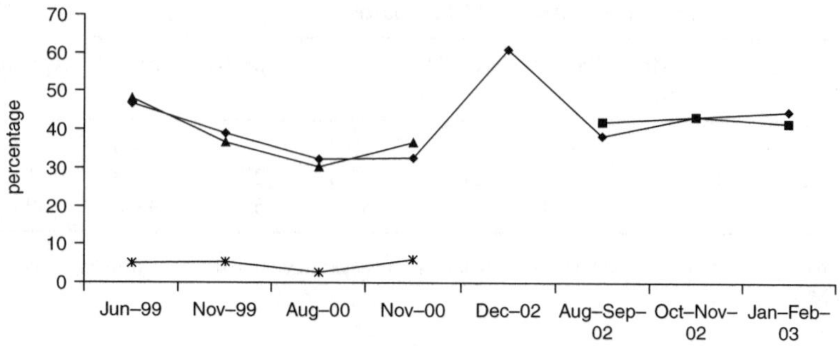


*Figure 10.2* Preferred forms of integration with the international community, 1999–2003

*Source*: The distribution is based on the question 'What form of integration would be preferable for the Belarusian people?' Compiled from Viktor Shadurskii, 'Otnosheniya Respubliki Belarus I Evropeiskogo Soyuza: vnutrennii I vneshnii kontekst', CENTIS seminar, BGU (www.centis.bsu.by, retrieved February 2004 and a survey of the Sociological Laboratory, NOVAK, 2003).

the EU positively dominated respondents' opinions. These attitudinal and behavioural preferences will be explored in greater detail below.

## The European Union and public opinion

On the question 'What are your impressions of the aims and activities of the European Union?' in White and Rose's 2000 survey (White and Rose, 2001: 49), 48 per cent of the respondents described their impressions as fair and very positive, 40 per cent remained undecided and only 13 per cent had reservations about the EU. This appears to be consistent with the findings of the New Democracies Barometer (Haerpfer, 2002: 118) that measured public attitudes to the EU's activities in 1994 (47 per cent as positive) and 1998 (49 per cent as positive). Furthermore, when in March 2003 the respondents were asked how they would vote if a referendum for the accession to the European Union were tomorrow, 56.4 per cent replied in favour (+ 3 per cent shift since September 2002), 12 per cent in opposition (+ 4 per cent), and 14 per cent confirmed they would refuse to vote at all (+ 1 per cent) (NISEPI News, 2003: 23).

Belarusians' attitude to any form of membership of the EU appears to be more than a simple expression of a policy preference. Given their socialist past, and the complex experience of regime change, for ordinary Belarusians the 'alignment with the West' could be regarded as an ideological choice in favour of political pluralism and market economy. The assessment becomes even more difficult when a choice is set between the liberal West and the Slavic East led by Russia. Thus, in September 2003, public opinion clearly split between those favouring the Russia–Belarus Union (38 per cent), those voting in support of Belarus' prospective association with the EU (23 per cent), and those who were in favour of both choices (23 per cent). Only a negligible percentage of respondents (7 per cent) rejected any of the above alternatives. The situation of choice was sharpened when the possibility of a dual answer was removed. It emerged that 48 per cent of the respondents were in favour of the Russia–Belarus Union, and 36 per cent expressed support for joining the EU (NISEPI News, 2003: 12).[19]

Amongst the incentives for a high number of those favouring prospective association with the EU appeared to be those of economic gains (58 per cent) and political stability (49 per cent), stable consumer prices (40 per cent) and higher personal income (36 per cent), as well as reduced levels of unemployment (29 per cent) (White and Rose, 2001: 49–50). Furthermore 54 per cent are convinced that the ten accession countries that joined the EU in May 2004 will undoubtedly benefit from their membership. The prospect of membership in the EU emerged as more likely to be favoured by younger generations between 18 and 39 years of age, those with higher education, students, those from western (border) regions, and by employees in the non-governmental sector (NISEPI News, 2003: 35–6).

## NATO and public opinion

Before one can evaluate public opinion towards NATO, it would be advisable to see what the Belarusians know about the organization. It appeared that about 49 per cent of the respondents believed NATO to be an American-led military alliance, 15 per cent thought it was a peacekeeping branch of the United Nations, 11 per cent were convinced that it was a trading bloc linking Western Europe and America, and 24 per cent refused to say anything or were undecided (White and Rose, 2001: 52).

Although tolerance and trust in NATO have positively changed over the past few years, and people's fears have diminished with the end of Cold War, NATO continues to be treated cautiously by the general public, especially on the grounds that it is American-led. Only 29 per cent of the respondents believe that becoming a member of NATO will be quite or a very good change (a fall of 7 per cent compared to 1998), 39 per cent are convinced that it is not 'such or not at all a good thing', whereas 33 per cent remain undecided, which runs in parallel with what has been discussed previously.

The above analysis of cognitive attitudes of the Belarusians to the West and various international organizations suggests a meagre shift towards a more positive appreciation of the activities of international organizations, especially those of the EU. This runs in parallel with cautious attitudes and declining trust in NATO, although muted by an overall openness of Belarusians to the international community. This picture, however, changes entirely when one comes to evaluate public judgements of immediate activities of international organizations present in Belarus. This might be pertinent to the official policy of 'non-co-operation' expressed by the Belarusian government, and hence ensuing official propaganda and discourse, as well as the level of low understanding of the workings of democracy by rank-and-file citizens of Belarus.

## Public opinion and democracy

As discussed above, the progress of a new regime towards democracy depends not only on the cognitive adoption of formal norms and rules of the game, but also on their successful socialization and emotional internalization to the very nucleus of society – that is, everyday practices of ordinary citizens. A brief look at the findings of the 2003 national surveys and focus groups[20] should be conducive to our evaluation of the true degree of cognitive and emotional acceptance of universal norms and rules of democracy and democratic assistance in Belarus.

It emerged that cognitively the citizens of Belarus are willing to foster democratic foundations, as shown by their openness to the international community and general refusal to accept media censorship, direct presidential rule, abuse of human rights, and manipulation of the law. A different picture, however, emerges when depicting people's 'attitudinal' or 'emotional' acceptance of democratic norms, which displays a continuing preponderance of 'authoritarian' judgements over their cognitive choice.

The 2003 national survey demonstrated that only 3 per cent of respondents, when asked what democracy meant for them, replied that it was 'government by the people'; and only 1 per cent pointed out that it could be an 'opportunity for people to affect decision-making in the country' as well as 'personal responsibility and more duties'. The leading majority, in contrast, associated democracy with 'crisis and complete anarchy' and 'something different from communism', 'life without looking back, free of fears', 'mission impossible' and 'the political regime of the USA'. A good one-fifth of respondents found the question difficult and abstained from answering.

Furthermore, comparison between 1998 and 2003 surveys revealed a definite increase in the number of subscribers to more authoritarian policies. For example, about half of the population in 2003 believed that 'society should not tolerate political views radically different from those of the majority' (49 per cent; +13 per cent), that 'freedom of expression can be harmful if it accommodates various extremists views' (49 per cent; +3) and that 'it is better to live in an orderly, firmly controlled society than allow for certain freedoms that can be used to destroy us' (48 per cent). Fewer (46 per cent; +1) were convinced that 'demonstrations and marches of protest should be banned as breeding extremism and disorder'. About two-thirds of the population stated that they did not care who was in power, as long as the situation improved; and about half of the sample noted that they would rather not interfere in politics, as there might be damaging repercussions. Paradoxically, despite their ostensible political passivity, a striking majority (56 per cent) were regular recipients of news (press and television), and believed that participation in politics was 'a duty' – a belief that seems to be inherited from Soviet-era civic education.

In summary, as opinion polls indicate, after nearly fifteen years of change and installation of a democratic framework, the citizens continue to display inconsistent views and contradictory evaluation of the democratic framework and its principles. Of greater concern, however, was the noticeable discrepancy between people's 'cognitive' and 'emotional' acceptance of democracy. They may abide with 'new' institutional settings but simultaneously confess intolerance of dissent and display explicit leniency towards strong leadership and governance by decree. They may welcome elections and a multiparty system, but entirely distrust all levels of government and abstain from voting, by that discarding the assumed partnership between the governed and their governors, and 'delegating' their choices and decisions to *appointed* officials. In other words, the Belarusian population was revealed as more cognitively rather than emotionally ready to embark on the ideas of democracy, but appeared to be more 'authoritarian' in judgements and, although well read, it felt they were more withdrawn from the actual process of politics.

Focus groups were designed to individualize nationally expressed judgements and attitudes to democracy and its ideals. The findings appeared to be consistent with the evidence revealed by national surveys reflecting diverging patterns of understanding and value orientation in people's evaluation of democracy, which may shed light on why democracy is not taking root in Belarus. The focus groups confirmed different understandings and interpretations of democracy. For many in Belarus democracy was 'difficult to fathom', and meant 'absolute order', 'compliance with rules', 'discipline, high morals', 'respect for others' and 'equality and education'. To others it was 'a mechanism of subordination of the minority by the majority' as well as 'power of repression', 'ineffective representation', 'public violence' and 'all-permissiveness'. The prevailing *leitmotif* was about 'order and obedience to rules', 'duties and responsibilities'.

Furthermore, many failed to reflect the current state of affairs, saying that they 'had never thought on such a grand scale' and should have been given time 'to do some reading and preparation beforehand'. On the question 'What needs to be done in order to improve national conditions?', respondents quoted the need for 'moral upbringing', 'education of our society', 'more discipline' and the 'state to invigilate the process (like in old times)', 'strong executives' and 'strong leadership'. Finally, a comparison between the 2000 and 2003 focus groups conveys that other forms of social and political engagement have not yet altered the intimate bond between the president and his people. Although a rise in critical thinking may be observed, it resembles more a critical appraisal than real criticism. For many Belarusians President Lukashenko still remains an icon.

This leads us to a conclusion that 'emotionally' respondents are not yet ready for democracy, advocating strong and single-handed leadership, and being uncertain about the rule and supremacy of law. After fifteen years of change, many post-Communist regimes may welcome institutional change and co-operation with the international community, but appeared 'morally' and 'emotionally' unready to adopt its principles and values. Belarus has revealed a striking discrepancy in its people's cognitive and emotional attitudes displaying little understanding of their rights and responsibilities, thus allowing for manipulation and dictate by their government.

It was once noted that Belarus had more 'democrats' (41 per cent) per head of population than the average for Eastern (30 per cent) and Northern Europe (29 per cent) (Haerpfer, 2002: 44), which nevertheless does not prevent her from remaining a transitional laggard amongst its neighbours. The above analysis does shed light on why such a discrepancy takes place, differentiating between cognitive and emotional socialization of democratic norms. As has been shown, although Belarusians may be seen as a democratically minded nation with respect to their attitudes and judgements, emotionally their allegiances remain committed to their non-democratic past.

## Conclusion

The emergence and endurance of an authoritarian mode of government in Belarus is the result of the complex and ineffective interaction between domestic and international agents, which found further stipulation in the legal, institutional and behavioral *modus operandi* in Belarus. Like in other post-Communist societies, especially in the former Soviet Union, the uncertainties of the early years of transition increased the appeal of a populist leader who promised 'a strong hand' and 'discipline and order' in society. Lukashenko's remarkable success in personalizing power and in marginalizing his political opponents has largely been the product of his own political skill and determination. Certain features of Belarusian society and of the country's transition path have facilitated the establishment of an authoritarian system. A high level of ethnic homogeneity and little elite change in the late Soviet period, in conjunction with a broad consensus on avoiding the social costs of reform and the lack of large-scale privatization and social disparities, have not been conducive to a pluralistic structure of societal interests. This apparent unity of interests coupled with the Lukashenko administration's authoritarian methods stifled political competition and curbed pluralism. The lack of informed opinion by the general population concerning the functioning of a democratic system entrenched by a nine-year international isolation further diminished the prospect of democratic change, leaving scope for demagogical manipulation and control by authorities.

International criticism, isolation and the politics of minimal engagement and incremental change have had little effect in modifying the conduct of the Belarusian leadership and promoting diffusion of democratic norms amongst the general population. In its present *modus operandi* Belarus remains a prototype of what at the outset of this volume has been conceptualized as a case of out-group 4. Interaction between the state, on the one hand, and the general population, on the other, with 'the external norm socializer' is minimal and reduced to negligible material support and a 'small amount of public shaming' (Flockhart, this volume).

It remains an open question whether societal internalization of democratic norms can develop from below and eventually result in a critical mass of popular pressure for democratization. External actors can hope to assist the formation of normative and social conditions necessary to support a pluralistic political system, for example through measures of support to an entrepreneurial class or young people's exposure to democratic norms. It is doubtful that the efforts of external actors would in themselves be sufficient to foster 'winning coalitions' within Belarus and successfully bring about norm change either directly at the elite/state level ('palace coup' scenario) or at the nation/people level. It is possible that, given enough time, the distance between the two domestic levels could increase: popular discontent with the Belarusian administration, coupled with the role of external norm-promoting actors, could expand popular adherence to democratic norms, making Belarus an 'out-group 3' country. However, a weak civil society and non-state media do not for the time being seem equipped to counteract the state's role as a filter impeding the transfer of democratic norms. An eventual change of political leadership could see the distance between Belarus and the external norm-promoting actors rapidly reduced. Were a Europe-oriented leadership to take power, Belarus could make up much of the lost ground and catch up with its European neighbours in terms of adherence to democratic norms.

## Notes

1. See for example the *Wall Street Journal Europe*, 7 September 2001; BBC News, 10 September 2001 at http://news.bbc.co.uk/1/hi/world/europe/116265.stm; *The Times (UK)*, 16 November 2002; speech by US Senator John McCain at the International Republican Institute Conference on Democracy in North-eastern Europe, Riga, 6 February 2004 (text published on www.iri.org/sp-mccain-latvia.asp).
2. On 4 November 1996, the Constitutional Court ruled that the results of such a referendum should be consultative, that is, have no legal force.
3. ODIHR Activity Report, 1995: 5.
4. Open Media Research Institute, 1996, OMRI Daily Digest, 23 November 1996.
5. OSCE Statement of Preliminary Findings and Conclusions on the Presidential Elections in Belarus, 10 September 2001: 2.
6. Declaration by the Presidency on behalf of the European Union on Belarus, CFSP Statement, no. 99/234, 1999.
7. Only nationwide official results were publicized; no detailed breakdown by region or polling station was given.
8. Report by Parliamentary Troika on the Political Situation in Belarus in the light of the parliamentary elections of October 15, 2000: 4.
9. The Belarusian authorities' refusal to issue visas to two members of the OSCE long-term observation team reinforced this impression.

10. The OSCE and the EU condemned the convictions of journalists Ivashkevich, Markevich and Mozheiko in 2002 as intimidation of the media by the Belarusian authorities.
11. EU declarations condemning human rights and civil liberties violations committed by the Belarusian authorities could be seen as an attempt to 'shame' the Belarusian leadership.
12. Declaration of the presidency on behalf of the European Union on the presidential decree on foreign aid and the by-elections in Belarus, 2001, CFSP Statement, 01/064.
13. Confidential interview by Clelia Rontoyanni with a senior Belarusian diplomat, April 2002.
14. Interview with Clelia Rontoyanni, April 2002.
15. Ibid.
16. Examples include former high-ranking officials who have openly joined the opposition such as former prime ministers Chigir, Mikhail Marynich (former ambassador) and formerly pro-Lukashenko deputy Vladimir Frolov.
17. *Opinion Analysis*, Office of Research, 20 September 2000, Department of State, Washington DC 20520, 5.
18. *Opinion Analysis*, Office of Research, 20 September 2000, Department of State, Washington DC 20520, 5.
19. See also Figure 10.2 for comparative detail.
20. In Belarus a national survey and focus groups were commissioned by the authors in March–April 2003 (BA SG-35130) led by the Centre for Social and Political Research, BGU. A nationwide sample included 1000 in Belarus of the adult population aged 18 and upward. Interviews were face-to face. The confidence interval is 99.47 per cent. The results were also corroborated by survey evidence gathered by authors in December 2000–January 2001 under EU–INTAS research (99-0245).

    Two focus groups were conducted in Belarus in 2003. The sample of respondents reflected the general socio-demographic profiles of leaders' group loyalties (established from opinion polls). The interview groups included 8–9 people, who were selected on the basis of positive answers to the following questions: (1) Do you support this leader, and (2) Did you vote for this leader in recent election? The participants were selected by a snowball method. Group interviews lasted for two hours in average, and were both audio taped and video-recorded.

# 11

# Turkey and the Eternal Question of Being, or Becoming, European

*Bill Park*

A transformation is taking place in much of today's Europe through a process that may be described as 'complex socialization'. This process, which arguably began in the western half of Europe soon after 1945 and which, with the demise of the continent's Cold War divisions, is now percolating into its former Communist eastern half, is associated with the transfer, adoption and entrenchment of shared democratic norms between the states and across the societies of the region. It is generally assumed that the multiplicity of overlapping international organizations that has characterized post-1945 Europe functions as a powerful agency of this process.

On the other hand, if we are to regard the very idea of 'Europe' as reflecting something more than a mere geographical expression, then, in some form or another, processes of norm transference across and within European political boundaries have long occurred. Notions of 'Europe' have for centuries been rooted in the identification of a shared core culture, often synonymous with or self-categorized as 'Christendom'. In other words, 'Europe' has historically existed as something more than a mere geographical region, even in the presence of conflict between its component parts and preceding the spread of democratic norms.

This 'older' Europe, Europe as Christendom, typically identified the Islamic world generally, and the Ottoman (Turkish) Empire specifically, as the 'other', as the 'out-group'. Modern day European Christian Democrats frequently maintain this categorization, and argue that Turkey cannot be European existentially, by virtue of its Islamic cultural roots. Ottoman rulers too generally saw themselves as central to the Islamic world and reciprocated European attitudes by regarding

Christendom as the 'other', the infidel world, notwithstanding the late Ottoman Empire's participation in Concert of Europe diplomacy. Even late Ottoman reformers sought to learn and borrow from Europe in order to compete more successfully with Europe rather than join it. It was only with the emergence of the Turkish Republic in 1923 following the break-up of the Ottoman Empire and (paradoxically) the loss of its Christian and European territories, that the elite in Ankara, presiding over a largely backward, rural, illiterate and now almost exclusively Islamic population, began to aspire to 'become' one of, rather than simply to emulate, the West.

The paradox that permeates these reflections becomes still more marked when we consider the Turkish case post-1945. Turkey has been an integral participant in Europe's post-1945 institutionalization. Turkey was a founder member of the Organization for Economic Co-operation and Development (OECD) in 1948, a member of the Council of Europe since 1949, and since 1991 has recognized the right of its citizens to make individual applications to the European Court of Human Rights. Turkey joined the North Atlantic Treaty Organization (NATO) in 1952, became an associate member of the EEC in 1963 and has been an applicant state since 1987, a West European Union (WEU) associate member since 1991, and on 1 January 1996 became the only state to enjoy a customs union with the EU. Since 1993, Turkey has been a regular contributor to 'peacekeeping' and other multilateral military missions, and has been active in Balkan, Black Sea and Islamic world diplomatic arrangements. Few countries are members of as many multilateral organizations as is Turkey, and at the diplomatic level at least, Turkey has un-disputably been part of the post-1945 US-sponsored Euro-Atlantic world, and hence institutionally at least, been part of the 'we' group. Indeed, attachment to the primacy of this particular definition of 'we' goes some way towards explaining British (and US) support for Turkey's EU membership.

Turkey is not, however, a member of the European Union, and indeed finds itself lagging in the race for EU accession behind former Communist states such as Poland, the Czech Republic and Hungary, and even the former Baltic states of the Soviet Union. Until the early 1990s, these states had been trapped behind an 'iron curtain' that served to minimize contact with the western half of Europe. They had been enveloped by a military alliance pitted against a NATO that incorporated Turkey and a majority of the EU member states. They had laboured under centralized, state-owned, command economic systems. Democratic norms were marked by their absence. Yet within a decade of the end of the Cold War, such states had been deemed more ready for, and more acceptable to, the EU club, than was Turkey. Particularly in the case of Poland, the Czech Republic and Hungary, but possibly also including the Baltic states and Slovenia, these states and societies were rapidly, and one might say naturally, categorized and self-categorized as belonging to the core European 'we' group.

It would appear, then, that Turkey's decades of membership of a wide range of European institutions did not sufficiently 'socialize' Turkey to render it a prime candidate for EU membership. This may in part be explained by features of the Turkish political, social and cultural landscape that have served as counterweights to pressures for socialization into (West) European democratic norms. It is also the case that the EU, at least since its 1993 adoption of the Copenhagen criteria for membership, insists on entry standards that are higher or different than those that were then required by the institutions that Turkey did join, which raises the question of the relevance to EU accession of Turkey's broader post-1945 institutional entanglement in the Euro-Atlantic world. Turkey's membership of a Cold War Euro-Atlantic 'in group' does not in and by itself qualify it as a member of the post-Cold War Copenhagen criteria-based EU 'in group'.

However, even NATO requires new post-Cold War members to pass a set of tests – civilian control of the military, and transparent defence sector budgetary arrangements, for example – that Turkey might be unable to pass even today. We might even speculate whether Turkey's high visibility in Europe's Cold War security arrangements did not reinforce the domestic prestige and power of the country's military, and thereby perhaps thwart more than encourage Turkey's fragile democracy. Turkey's soldiers, and its Euro-Atlantic alliance solidarity, have long been appreciated. The domestic political behaviour of its military and civilian elites, and the norms and nature of its domestic society, have been less well regarded in the West.

## Turkey and the EEC/EC/EU – over forty years, and what have we got?

Turkey's association with the EU has been a long one (Kramer, 1996; Buzan and Diez, 1999; Muftuler-Bac, 1999; Onis, 2001; Avci, 2003). The European Economic Community (EEC) accepted Turkey as an applicant member as long ago as 1959. Notwithstanding the difficulties caused by the Turkish military coup of 1960, in 1963 the Ankara Agreement was signed and came into force in December 1964. This was an Association Agreement between the EEC and Turkey, and was designed to enable

Turkey to progress gradually towards meeting the (then primarily economic) criteria for membership via a phased establishment of a Turkey–EU customs union. Turks have often regarded the Ankara Agreement as tantamount to a firm promise of eventual full membership. In November 1970, flesh and greater purpose were added to the Turkey–EEC engagement by the signing and annexing to the Ankara Agreement of the Additional Protocol, which more concretely specified a programme for bringing the proposed customs union into being. Associated with this, additional funds were released to enable Ankara's domestic economic reform and development programme to progress.

However, relations were again strained in the wake of the 1974 invasion of northern Cyprus by Turkey's armed forces, and in 1980 another military coup occurred in Turkey, as a consequence of which the European Community (EC) froze political relations with Ankara and suspended the Ankara Agreement. Relations were not properly resumed until 1986, opening the way for the free market-oriented reforming government of Turgut Ozal to apply for full Turkish membership of the EC in 1987 – an application that took Brussels by surprise. Significantly, Greece had already become a member in 1981, a development that did not assist Turkey's case in Europe's corridors. In any case, the European Commission's Opinion on Turkey's request for accession, delivered in December 1989, declared that all EU enlargements would be delayed until the single market came into operation in 1992.

However, the Commission also drew attention to the particular economic difficulties Turkey had, even in the wake of Ozal's market reform programme of the 1980s that had aimed to dismantle much of the Kemalist economic statism that had hitherto characterized Turkish economic management. The Commission's Opinion drew attention to Turkey's over-regulated and protected domestic economic market, its overblown and intrusive state sector, and the low level of economic and social development relative to the EU average. Traces of these observations can be found in the Commission's more recent (November 2003–October 2004) Progress Report on Turkish accession. However, the 1989 Report did recommend continued progress towards the establishment of a Turkey–EU customs union, so as to associate Turkey more closely with the operation of a single market.

Following years of close and detailed work between Ankara and Brussels, the EU and Turkey entered into a customs union with effect from 1 January 1996, heralding the closest economic relationship hitherto created between the EU and any non-member country. This abolished trade barriers between Turkey and the EU, established a common external tariff to imports from third countries, and envisaged almost total harmonization of Turkey's economic regulations with those of the EU's internal market. In December 1997, however, Turkish relations with the EU were again plunged into deep freeze with the rejection of Turkey's bid for accession status at the EU's Luxembourg summit. The other eleven applicant states, none of which enjoyed a customs union with the EU, were granted formal accession status. Of these, ten were former Communist entities, and the eleventh was a (Greek) Cyprus empowered to negotiate on behalf of the Turkish north of the island which had not been consulted and where its writ did not run. In response to this rejection, Ankara suspended political dialogue with Brussels, and Turks were strongly inclined to the interpretation that the EU's behaviour was based more on its unwillingness to categorize Turkey as a potential 'in-group' member than on any failure to meet the criteria.

Turkey's eligibility for eventual membership was nevertheless confirmed at Luxembourg, thus the door remained open to grant accession status to Turkey. This was done at the Helsinki summit in 1999. US pressure, the work done by Germany's EU presidency during the first half of 1999, and the depth of Ankara's sulk, all contributed to this outcome. Even so, the Helsinki summit left Turkey as the only candidate with which accession negotiations were still deemed premature. This prospect was delayed until after December 2004 (Eralp, 2000; Onis, 2000; Park, 2000; Rumford, 2000).

## Resistant to socialization?

In 1993, the EU adopted the so-called 'Copenhagen criteria', outlining the conditions aspirant countries were required to meet before membership could be granted. They emphasize political criteria such as respect for human and minority rights, the rule of law, and stable democratic institutions, as well as economic criteria such as a functioning market economy. The Copenhagen criteria reflected both the EU's insistence that enlargement into newly post-Communist Central and Southeastern Europe would only occur if these candidate states had fully embarked on the road to democratization and market reform, and also the EU's internal deepening and transformation into something more than the 'common market' of the EEC. In other words, it offered an opportunity, but not a guarantee, that others could become part of the 'we' group.

For Europe's post-Communist states, determined to 'return to Europe' in any case, the Copenhagen criteria offered both guidance and incentive regarding the direction their internal transformations should take. Unlike post-Communist Europe, however, Turkey in the 1990s did not experience a critical juncture. Rather, in the Turkish case the Copenhagen criteria confronted a fully formed, long-standing and entrenched political culture and system that, many Turks believed, had served the country well in its endeavours to modernize and democratize their country. Nor was Turkey seeking to 'return' to a Europe to which it was seen to properly belong. Turkey had not been isolated from Western Europe during the Cold War. Notwithstanding Turkish claims that they had been part of Europe since Ottoman times, Turkey's aspirations were rather to be accepted as part of, rather than to 'return' to, a Europe that civilizationally had long held them at arm's length. Turkey had never been regarded as a 'we' part of that centuries-old definition of European civilization as something akin to 'Christendom', and the country's Cold War western affiliations had not fully dispelled the impact of this. Countries such as Poland and the Czech Republic, on the other hand, were deemed integral parts of 'Europe', as pre-eminently 'we' in this more deeply rooted sense, and the isolation and diverging paths imposed by the Communist experience had done nothing to destroy this perception (Aras, 1997; Pesmazoglu, 1997; Buzan and Diez, 1999; Onis, 1999).

Nor did the Turkish elite rapidly and readily appreciate the shift in the EU's nature and expectations. The 'Europe' that Turkey sought to associate itself with back in 1959 was essentially an economic one, underpinned by Cold War security arrangements into which Turkey was already incorporated. In Ankara, Turkey's NATO membership and its non-Communist and democratized political features, certainly when combined with Ozal's market-oriented economic reforms of the 1980s, were regarded as broadly sufficient to qualify the country for EU membership. Indeed, Turkey's value as a security partner was regarded in Ankara as one of its major qualifications for acceptance. The 'in-group' that Ankara believed it was part of, and was regarded as part of, was a strategic, Euro-Atlantic, grouping. The revelation of the Copenhagen criteria looked to many Turks like a moving of the goalposts. Why, though, had Turkey's socialization to what were becoming the norms of the new Europe apparently made such limited progress, particularly in the light of Turkey's extensive multilateralism?

## Kemalism

Turkey's single-minded determination to be accepted as European dates back to the Republic's founder, Kemal Ataturk, in 1923. 'Kemalism', the state doctrine to which Ataturk gave birth and which has underpinned the Turkish Republic ever since, enabled Turkey to raise itself from the ashes of the Ottoman Empire. It has, many Turks believe, proved itself an effective vehicle for the country's modernization, and one might add democratization and Europeanization, unmatched elsewhere in the Islamic world. However, Kemalism has statist, nationalist, militarist and authoritarian characteristics. The Europe that Kemal Ataturk aspired to was the Europe of the 1920s and 1930s, a Europe that included Mussolini, Hitler, Franco, Pilsudski, Stalin, and countless Balkan dictators, a Europe strongly tinged with the forces of authoritarianism, atavistic nationalism, and economic autarchy. It bore little resemblance to the social welfare, highly democratized and liberalized, denationalized, economically integrated and mobile Europe of today.

Thus, post-1945 Western Europe explicitly rejected its authoritarian and nationalistic past, and progressively adopted and internalized more liberal, democratic, internationalist and free market values. In doing so, it shifted the criteria for self-categorization as part of the 'we'. To date, democratization and free market economics have softened rather than transformed Turkey's centralization and authoritarianism. Furthermore, the extent to which such norms have been internalized by either Turkey's elite or its society more broadly can be contested. Many would argue that both the state and political cultures of the Turkish Republic remain largely rooted in a Kemalist ideology, and a set of social norms and political practices that constitute barriers to effective norm transfer and ideational shifts, and that therefore resist adoption of EUs Copenhagen criteria beyond the rhetorical level (Landau, 1984; Poulton, 1997; Jung and Piccoli, 2001; Cooper, 2002).

## Secularism and Islam

Since its inception, political change in the Turkish Republic has been brought about largely by top-down rather than bottom-up processes. An example of this is the country's official secularism, enshrined in its constitution and which, with the principle of the indivisibility of nation and territory, forms the heart of Kemalism (Rouleau, 2000). Ataturk set Turkey on a secular path, regardless of the wishes of its people. The Republic's founder regarded religious influence in public and political life, and even its presence in private life, as a reactionary force that served to obstruct economic, social and political modernization and 'Europeanization'. However, it has sometimes been deemed necessary to subvert democratic norms to preserve the country's secular nature.

Thus, from time to time, Islamic parties have been banned and Islamic political leaders silenced, whilst the wearing of the headscarf and the growing of beards remain officially shunned. Thus, the Islamic challenge to Kemalist Turkey's official secularism has in the past provided a major source of the Turkish state's democratic transgressions. Furthermore, because the military is seen as the guardian of the country's constitution and protector of Ataturk's legacy, it has served as just one of the justifications behind the military's interference in domestic politics. Turkey's treatment of its Islamic activists, and their freedom to engage in politics, are regarded in Europe as a test of Ankara's commitment to democratic norms. In other words, the Kemalist elite has believed that it qualifies itself as part of the European 'we' group by imposing secularism on the Turkish body politic. For the European 'we' group that Ankara has aspired to join, however, the banning of political parties, and the associated limitations on freedom of speech and assembly, serve only to exclude Ankara's elite from such inclusion.

Rightly or wrongly, the Kemalist elite believes that Turkey's high levels of personal freedom, democratization and economic development relative to that of much of the rest of the Islamic world are at least in part explained by the general banishment of religious tenets from the nation's political life. In Kemalist Turkey's self-categorization, the 'we' that Turkey primarily belongs to clearly cannot be an Islamic world 'we'. European debates over, for example, the right of its Muslim citizens to wear headscarves in its secular schools, and the arguments of the late Pym Fonteyn and his followers in the Netherlands, suggest that West European governments and peoples too share concerns over the compatibility of political Islam with democracy and liberalism of the nation's political life. In Western Europe, the political freedoms of far-right groups and the dissemination of racist ideology have at times similarly been curtailed, precisely because such beliefs and activities can be seen as incompatible with democratic norms and as reminders of a discredited past.

The November 2002 elections resulted in victory for the Justice and Development Party (AKP), which represented moderate Islamist opinion in its most recently legally sanctioned guise, its predecessors having been banned for threatening the constitutionally imposed secularity of the Turkish Republic (Yesilada, 2002; Jenkins, 2003; Robins, 2003). It is seems highly unlikely that the November 2002 elections heralded the emergence of a popular Islamic 'fundamentalism' in Turkey, although many Turkish secularists do indeed fear for the country's secular future as a consequence of it. It is also worth noting that the AKP's election victory served to remind some Europeans of Turkey's Islamic roots. For Christian Democrats in particular, Europe's 'we' is synonymous with 'Christendom' and, as a Muslim country, Turkey can therefore never become European. For Europe's fundamentalist opponents of Turkish membership, no amount of democratization will help Turkey's case. The Europe that is being 'created' on the basis of democratic norms will nevertheless have boundaries to it, boundaries that are based on older notions of what Europe is. Morocco has already served notice that it aspires to join the EU. Israel, and even Russia or Canada, could similarly raise questions in the future concerning who or what it is that enables the European 'in-group' to categorize others as potentially inside or outside the group. Norm transfer will not serve as the sole criterion, and Turkey represents a test case for this fact.

An ironic twist to this development is that the moderate Islamists currently in power may have internalized Europe's norms more fully than its Kemalist predecessors – although Turkey's secular modernizers would contest this – and may be better placed to promote these norms in society as a whole. Their political experiences at the hands of the Kemalist regime, and the suffering of their constituents as a consequence of Turkey's economic and political failings, may have inculcated the values of democracy, the rule of law and the marketplace more deeply. The same could apply to the country's Kurdish leaders. Still more ironic is the AKP's self-identification as an Islamic version of Europe's Christian Democrats.

## The Kurdish problem

The Turkish Republic was created as an act of political will out of the largely Muslim and non-Arab residue of the multinational Ottoman Empire, which had been dismembered by a combination of internal ethnic separatism and external sponsorship of it. Ataturk led the resistance to the 1920 Treaty of Sèvres drafted by the Allies and which threatened to further dismember even this rump and still-embryonic state. This historical experience has resulted in a strong national attachment to sovereignty and suspicion of foreign intentions towards Turkey. The new Republic's approach to citizenship – that to be a citizen of the Turkish Republic is in some way to be a Turk, regardless of the fact that up to 20 per cent of the population is ethnically Kurdish – was derived from and is akin to the French model. Kurds are not necessarily discriminated against as a consequence of their ethnicity, and many have risen to the very highest ranks in the Republic. But the Kurds of Turkey are not expected to resist 'Turkification'. Hence, teaching and broadcasting in the Kurdish language have been outlawed (as, for example, Welsh once was), the use of Kurdish names forbidden, and Kurdish political parties and cultural expression banned.

However, in 1984, the persisting Kurdish sense of distinctiveness gave rise to a violent separatist war, involving the radical and terroristic Kurdish Workers Party (PKK) (Olsen, 1996; Kirisci and Winrow, 1997; Barkey and Fuller, 1998; Robins, 2000). This conflict, fought by the security forces with little apparent supervision by politicians, has been associated with the silencing and detention of journalists and political activists, covert assassinations, torture, scorched earth policies that have emptied suspect Kurdish villages of their inhabitants, and military incursions into neighbouring Iraq. As a consequence, the war has served as an additional and major source of discomfort in Turkish relations with its Western allies and prospective EU partners, who have seen the problem as one of respect for minorities rather than as a terrorist challenge to Turkey's tranquillity.

The Kurdish issue is thus important when considering the development of democratic norms in Turkey and the country's EU accession prospects. It not only raises the issue of the protection of minorities, but is also the major source of many of Turkey's other imperfections. However, even the most democratic of European states can experience slippage in their democratic norms when confronted with terrorism and separatism. Political bans and human rights abuses, and even extra-judicial killings, have taken place in both Spain and the UK, for example, in the context of their respective domestic campaigns against violent separatism, although both the separatist violence, and the democratic transgressions, have been on a far smaller scale than in the Turkish case.

Furthermore, it is conceivable – though hard for the liberal West to accept – that a soft approach to Kurdish separatism might not forestall Turkey's territorial dismemberment. Furthermore, given Kurdish minorities in Iraq, Iran and Syria, a broader regional tension and prospective fragmentation could be the downstream outcome of Kurdish self-determination. Indeed, the international community might be about to learn just these lessons via the medium of an unstable post-Saddam Iraq. In this context, is the question primarily one of Turkey's incomplete socialization, or rather of the absence of preconditions that enable that process of complex socialization to fully take root? Does the construction of Europe based on socialization and the adoption of democratic norms depend on a prior regional or neighbourhood stability? Or could it even be that, for example, unacceptable treatment of the Roma by 'we' groups in Central Europe (or of Basque and Irish Nationalist separatists) is more tolerable than unacceptable treatment of the Kurds by non-'we' Turks?

## Neighbourhood difficulties

Turkey's foreign policy problems, and its difficulties with the EU, are also unique in light of the relationship with an existing EU member, Greece. The Helsinki requirement that Turkey resolves its territorial differences with EU member Greece would – not least in light of the absence of any concomitant pressure from the EU on Greece – probably involve the extension of Greek waters and air space right up to the entire Turkish Aegean coastline (Wilson, 1980). For economic, security and historical reasons this would be difficult for Ankara to accept.

With (Greek) Cypriot accession to the EU agreed, the division of that island took on a still greater urgency in Turkish–EU relations. The 1974 Turkish military intervention in Cyprus, the continued occupation of the northern one-third of the island since that summer, the 1983 creation and Ankara's recognition of the Turkish Republic of Northern Cyprus (TRNC) as a 'sovereign' entity, and the perceived intransigence of the TRNC leadership (and by extension, Ankara) in its approach to a settlement and reunification of the island's division, have all grumbled on as a souring backdrop to Turkey–EU relations throughout these decades. Until relatively recently, Greece has been prepared to deploy its EU membership against Turkey's cause. Indeed, the Helsinki summit opaquely linked eventual Turkish membership to a settlement of its Aegean differences with Greece, and required Turkey to both accept and act upon its primary responsibility for achieving a settlement on Cyprus.

Without wishing to delve into the complexities of the Cyprus imbroglio (Brewin, 2000; Diez, 2002; Tocci, 2002; Suvarierol, 2003), it would appear that some combination of the impact of the international economic and political isolation of the people of the TRNC, the heavy hand of the mainland Turkish state, and the glittering prospect of EU membership and probable escape from the island altogether, has persuaded a majority of Turkish Cypriots of the desirability of a settlement of the island's division based on the UN plan unveiled in November 2002. The present AKP government, in its readiness to achieve a settlement, has had to confront the obstructiveness of the Kemalist state elite in the foreign ministry and the military, the TRNC's leadership, and the more nationalist politicians in Ankara. Many regard their posture as illustrative of a confrontational and uncompromising approach that marks Turkey out from modern Europe's consensual approach to diplomacy, and as affording an additional rationalization for excluding Turkey from the European 'in-group'.

However, it should be noted that the Greek Cypriot side, for long a front runner for EU membership, was similarly profoundly unhappy with the UN plan. Although EU membership, and such democratic norms that have taken root in Greece and Greek Cyprus, should afford the Turkish Cypriot minority sufficient protection and confidence, the often brutal history of Greek attempts to fully Hellenize the island, and the sheer difficulties of governance in societies that are torn by ethnic division, should give pause for thought. A unified Cyprus that is harmonious is a far from foregone conclusion, and the Greek inclination to regard Cyprus as properly Hellenic is hard for the Turkish side to accept. After all, if Greeks did not regard the island of Cyprus as essentially Hellenic in its entirety regardless of the ethnicity of the population, there would be no pressure for reunification, and either double *enosis* or the establishment of two sovereign states on the island could instead have emerged as preferred options.

The security-conscious, military-dominated and nationalistic Turkish side has undoubtedly been far too uncompromising on the Cyprus issue, but Europe's readiness to internationally isolate the people of the TRNC combined with the one-sided threat to Turkey, but not Greece or Cyprus, should a settlement remain elusive, suggests to many Turks that the protection of minorities is a far from universally internalized norm in mainstream Europe. A Europe prepared to militarily intervene to protect Bosnian Muslims and Kosovans from ethnic cleansing by more powerful and atavistic neighbours, and now trapped in place by the political immobilism of ethnically divided and antagonistic communities there, might usefully revisit the evolution of its position on Cyprus. In short, from a Turkish perspective, the EU's approach to the Cyprus issue is as complacent as it is hypocritical, and is explained not by the details of the case but by Europe's *a priori* exclusion of Turks, and inclusion of Greeks, as part of their 'we'.

## The role of the military

The military coups of 1960 and 1980, and the behind-the-scenes exercise of intense political pressure by the military in 1971 and 1997, all served as reminders of the enormous political power wielded by the Turkish military (Heper and Guney, 2000; Karaosmanoglu, 2000; Ozbudun, 2000; Narli, 2000; Jenkins, 2001; Demirel, 2003), and introduced an additional rockiness into Turkey–EU relations. In fact, the military's role in Turkey's domestic politics has deep-seated causes and explanations that include Ottoman legacies, Kemalist political legitimization, a weak political culture and party system, the occasional threat of social disorder, separatism, the country's troubled neighbourhood, and the military's widespread popularity.

In short, the relationship between Turkey's state culture on the one hand, and its political or societal culture on the other, is symbiotic. Turkey's corrupt political class, clientalist political practices, weak civil society, low levels of economic development, its social and regional disparities, and rapid social and economic transformation, have not provided ideal raw material for the internalization by the population of West European norms. In so far as elements of the Turkish state elite, including the General Staff, may in fact have adopted European norms, it doesn't follow that a more 'European' political and social culture would inevitably take root in the country as a whole.

Only time will tell whether the institutional reforms called for by the EU and incorporated into the AKP government's reform programme, such as a reduction of the military's presence on the National Security Council (NSC) and a shift in the role of that body, can seriously dent the Turkish military's domestic political power. More contentiously, it is not self-evident that any removal of the military from the domestic political sphere would necessarily produce an enrichment and entrenchment of Turkish democracy. Indeed, in the wake of the Helsinki Agreement and until the November 2002 election, the military's role in domestic politics had arguably been increasing as the country's political life became more fragmented and chaotic. In other words, the military's role might also be an effect of as much or more than a cause of Turkey's imperfect democratization

## Can Turkey change in time?

In order to meet the short- and medium-term conditions of the EU's Accession Partnership for Turkey, issued in December 2000, the Turkish coalition government adopted its National Programme in March 2001. It envisaged far-reaching reform in both the political and economic spheres (Park, 2001). Both the coalition government led by Prime Minister Bulent Ecevit, and to an even greater degree the moderate Islamist government of the Justice and Development Party (AKP) that came to power in the November 2002 elections, vigorously undertook programmes of constitutional, political and economic reform that – on paper at least – tackled most of the more problematic features of Turkey's political and social landscape, such as minority language rights, the death penalty, and the role of the military-dominated National Security Council (NSC). Indeed, the energy of the AKP government's lobbying abroad, and the courage, speed and breadth of its reform programme, impressed many onlookers.

That these reforms have only been undertaken in the light of the Accession Partnership document issued in the wake of the Helsinki decision, and that Turkey's National Programme, produced as it was by Ecevit's coalition government, was a much fought-over document that did not quite meet the EU's expectations, have raised questions in some minds about how sincere Ankara's intentions are, and how truly ideational is the shift. Although welcomed by Brussels and by many of the governments of the EU's constituent states, reservations concerning the Turkish government's willingness or capacity to fully implement the reforms remained pungently tangible.

At the time of writing it is not possible to assess the outcome of the reform programme (Kardas, 2002; Hale, 2003). Clearly great strides have been made, and it might appear paradoxical that the AKP government that came to power in the November 2002 elections has been responsible for most of the measures taken. On the other hand, there has been considerable resistance from the state institutions and from the AKP's political opponents, and many of the constitutional and legal changes that have been passed in the General Assembly have left in place get-out clauses that appear to give wide scope for the notoriously conservative judiciary to restrict in practice many of the freedoms that the EU would expect to see in place. Furthermore, the EU has learned to distinguish between reform and its implementation in the Turkish case, and the capacity of the regional and central bureaucracies, the courts, the law enforcement agencies and the like to obstruct and delay should not be underestimated (Onis, 2003). The 2003 Progress Report drew attention to these difficulties, and in particular demonstrated scepticism with respect to implementation.

Although most Turkish political parties, and a substantial majority of its public, pay lip service to the goal of EU accession, it is far from clear that the bulk of Turkey's political spectrum is truly prepared or able to pay the price that accession demands. Given the volatility of the Turkish electorate, it also seems reasonable to wonder whether the current AKP government will necessarily be representative of future Turkish governments. A nationalistic suspicion of the EU, and a fierce and prickly attachment to the country's sovereignty, remain powerful forces amongst the Turkish electorate, across its political parties, and in the institutions of state.

What appears to have occurred post-Helsinki, perhaps reinforced by the winter economic crises of 2000–1, is an intensification of the Turkish debate on EU accession, and an intensification of divisions. To some extent, EU accession is now most genuinely supported by the most 'Eastern', least 'European' elements of Turkish society, the Islamists and the Kurds, in combination with its most modern, the transnational business community. Although the Kemalist establishment and political parties pay lip service to EU accession, which is seen as part and parcel of the longer-term aspiration to become a part of Europe, in practice Turkey's traditional 'modernizers' remain reluctant to meet the EU's terms, and have led much of the resistance to it.

## Conclusion

Turkish society has transformed itself massively in recent decades. It is far more urbanized, more educated, more worldly, more democratic, more critical, more enterprising, than it was when Turkey made its first steps towards Europe's institutions in the immediate aftermath of the Second World War. Its economy is more open, its media freer, and its civil society – not least if measured by the ballooning number and activities of its non-governmental organizations (NGOs) – far more sophisticated. Much of this development derives from internal social, political and economic dynamics. Turkey is a modernizing and Westernizing society, and Kemalism, as well as broader externally derived processes of complex socialization – of 'Europeanization' and 'globalization' – should share some of the credit.

On the other hand, with a population that could be the EU's largest by the time Turkish accession eventually takes place, a GNP per head that is likely to remain substantially lower than the average even of an enlarged EU, a massively agriculturally and regionally undeveloped economy that could threaten to drain such funds as the EU makes available for such programmes in the future, and the reasonable likelihood of persisting problems of governance, the translation into actual membership of Turkey's formal acceptance as an accession candidate might not be a foregone conclusion. Furthermore, an unhappy outcome (although any such 'outcome' might well be put off indefinitely by the EU) might not hinge exclusively upon the energy, or lack of it, with which Ankara endeavours in its domestic political arrangements to meet the EU's membership criteria. Turkey has knocked on Europe's door, and in response the door has at best been left only slightly ajar, and with transparent reluctance. This is only partly explained by the negative features of Turkey's social, economic and political landscape. It also reflects European struggles to incorporate Turkey as part of a broader 'we'.

The notion of a Europe constructed on the basis of a shared regional adherence to democratic norms such as those created in its Western, Christian, stable, and economically developed half during the Cold War, implies either that such socialization does not greatly depend for its progress on the existence or otherwise of regional stability, security, economic well-being, or any specific cultural traits and historic circumstances, or that the Europe that is being built remains exclusive, confined to those states able to enjoy the requisite happy circumstances. The Copenhagen criteria are designed not only to raise standards, but also to raise barriers, and to define what it is that makes the European 'we' distinct. It is a template, a 'take-it-or-leave-it' one-size-fits-all set of requirements, which do not take into account peculiar and special circumstances. They may (or may not) have helped Turkey raise its democratic standards, but in threatening to withhold membership because Turkey insufficiently resembles the character and circumstances of the secure and prosperous states of Northwestern Europe, they may also in time serve to set back Turkish progress, and generate new fault lines across Europe.

The Turkish case raises questions not raised by other EU (and NATO) accession candidates. Perhaps there are some similarities with the Russian example – another large, former imperial and Eurasian state that historically followed a trajectory at odds with much of the rest of Europe. However, and unlike Russia, Turkey has been a member or associate of most of (Western) Europe's post-1945 institutions. Yet it is only in the wake of the Helsinki Agreement, or even of the AKP election victory in November 2002, that it is possible to present a convincing case that Turkey's domestic political arrangements are being brought into line with those of existing EU states. How can this be explained? Is it because 'soft' Europe has overlooked how vital is the precondition of security and stability before full democratization can take place? Is it because for 'democratic norms' to take root, a deeper cultural root, and one that Turkey lacks, is required? Is it because democratic norms spread not as a result of institutional affiliation, which Turkey has experienced abundantly, but via informal processes of integration – trade, travel, inward investment – which have often passed Turkey by, notwithstanding its customs union with the EU? Or is it simply because Turkey has evolved a unique and powerful political culture that has embedded itself deeply into the Turkish psyche and that resists the country's complete 'Europeanization'? Is Turkey doomed to remain on the fringes of Europe's 'in-group', 'westernistic' (Buzan and Diez, 1999) rather than Western, and – at least in any foreseeable time scale – unalterably so?

# Bibliography

*A Reference Manual on 'Twinning' Projects 2001*, http://www.europa.eu.int/comm/enlargement/pas/twinning/index.htm.

Abbott, Jason, 2001, 'Fall from Grace: the Political Economy of Indonesian Decay and Decline', paper presented at the conference on The Global Constitution of 'Failed States': the Consequences of a New Imperialism? University of Sussex, 18–20 April.

Abbott, Kenneth, Robert Keohane, Andrew Moravcsik, Anne-Marie Slaughter and Duncan Snidal, 2000, 'The Concept of Legalization', *International Organization*, 54(3): 401–19.

Abrahamsen, Rita, 2000, *Disciplining Democracy Good Governance and Development Discourse in Africa*, Zed Press.

Adler, Emanuel, 1997, 'Imagined (Security) Communities: Cognitive Regions in International Relations', *Millennium*, 26(2): 249–77.

Adler, Emanuel, 1998, 'Seeds of Peaceful Change: the OSCE's Security Community-Building Model', in Emanuel Adler and Michael Barnett (eds), *Security Communities*, Cambridge University Press.

Adler, Emanuel and Michael Barnett (eds), 1998, *Security Communities*, Cambridge University Press.

Alderson, Kai, 2001, 'Making Sense of State Socialization', *Review of International Studies*, 27(3): 415–33.

Almond, Gabriel, 1950, *The American People and Foreign Policy*, Harcourt Brace.

*An Agenda for Democratization* (A/51/761 December 1996) and supporting documents from 1995 and 1996 (A/50/332 and Corr.1) and (A/51/512).

Aras, Bulent, 1997, 'Turkey's Insecure Identity from the Perspective of Nationalism', *Mediterranean Quarterly*, 8(1): 77–91.

Avci, Gamze, 2003, 'Turkey's Slow EU Candidacy: Insurmountable Hurdles to Membership, or Simple Euro-scepticism?', *Turkish Studies*, 4(1): 149–70.

Avery, Graham and Fraser Cameron, 1998, *The Enlargement of the European Union*, Sheffield Academic Press.

Baldwin, Richard, Joseph François and Richard Portes, 1997, 'The Costs and Benefits of Eastern Enlargement: the Impact on the EU and Central Europe', *Economic Policy*, 24: 125–76.

Barkey, Henri J. and Graham E. Fuller, 1998, *Turkey's Kurdish Question*, Rowman and Littlefield.

Barnes, James, M. Carter and M. Skidmore, 1980, *The World of Politics*, St. Martin's Press.

Baros, M., 2001, 'The UN's Response to the Yugoslav Crisis: Turning the UN Charter on its Head', *International Peacekeeping*, 8(1): 44–63.

Baros, M., 2003, 'Macedonian Conflict and International Law: Self-Determination or Self-Defence?', *International Peacekeeping*, 10(3): 60–78.

Beetham, David, 1992, 'Liberal Democracy and the Limits of Democratisation', *Political Studies*, Special Issue No.40: 40–53.

Beetham, David, 1999, *Democracy and Human Rights*, Polity Press.

Bennett, Andrew, 1999, *Condemned to Repetition? The Rise, Fall, and Reprise of Soviet-Russian Military Interventionism, 1973–1996*, MIT Press.

Bennett, G. and K. Hamilton (eds), 1997, *The Conference on Security and Cooperation in Europe 1972–75*, Documents on British Policy Overseas, Series III, Volume II, HMSO and FCO.

Berger, Peter and Thomas Luckmann, 1966, *The Social Construction of Reality*, Penquin Books.

Bilčík, Vladimír, 2001, 'Can Slovakia Catch Up? The Implications of EU Accession Talks a Year After the Helsinki Summit', *Working Paper 2001/1*, Danish Institute of International Affairs.

Bilčík, Vladimír, 2002, 'Slovensko a Diskusia o budúcnosti Európskej únie', in Anton Marcinčin and Martina Lubyová (eds), *Monitoring integrácie Slovenskej republiky do Európskej únie I*, Slovenská Spoločnosť pre Zahraničnú Politiku a Friedrich Ebert Stiftung.

Bilčík, Vladimír, 2003, 'Slovakia's Integration to the European Union', in Grigorij Mesežnikov, Miroslav Kollár and Tom Nicholson (eds), *Slovakia 2002: a Global Report on the State of Society*, Institute for Public Affairs.

Billig, Michael and Henry, Tajfel, 1973, 'Social Categorization and Similarity in Intergroup Behaviour', *European Journal of Social Psychology*, 3(1): 27–52.

Bjorkman, Tom, 2003, *Russia's Road to Deeper Democracy*, Brookings Institution.

Bloed, Arie, 1993, *The Conference on Security and Co-operation in Europe: Analysis and Basic Documents, 1972–1993*, Kluwer.

Boland, Frank, 2002, 'Military Matters. Mapping the Future', *Nato Review, Spring 2002*, on-line version.

Brenner, Michael (ed.), 1998, *NATO and Collective Security*, Macmillan.

Breslauer, George W., 1997, 'The Impact of the International Environment: Theoretical and Methodological Considerations', in Karen Dawisha (ed.), *The International Dimension of Post-Communist Transitions in Russia and the New States of Eurasia*, M. E. Sharpe.

Brewin, Christopher, 2000, *The European Union and Cyprus*, Eothen Press.

Bugge, Peter, 2000, 'Czech Perceptions of the Perspective of EU Membership: Havel vs. Klaus', *EUI Working Papers, RSC NO. 2000/10*.

Burnell, Peter, 1997, *Foreign Aid in a Changing World*, Open University Press.

Bútora, Martin and Demeš Pavol, 1999, 'Občianske Organizácie vo Vol'bách 1998', in Martin Bútora, Grigorij Mesežnikov and Zora Bútorová (eds), *Slovenské Vol'by 1998: Kto? Prečo? Ako?*, Inštitút pre Verejné Otázky.

Bútorová, Zora, 1999, 'Vývoj Postojov Verejnosti: Od Nespokojnosti k Politickej Zmene', in Martin Bútora, Grigorij Mesežnikov and Zora Bútorová (eds), *Slovenské Vol'by 1998: Kto? Prečo? Ako?*, Inštitút pre Verejné Otázky.

Buzan, Barry and Diez Thomas, 1999, 'The European Union and Turkey', *Survival*, 41(1): 41–57.

Buzan, Barry and George Segal, 1992, 'Introduction: Defining Reform as Openness', in George Segal (ed.), *Openness and Foreign Policy Reform in Communist States*, Routledge.

Buzan, Barry, Ole Wæver and Jaap de Wilde, 1998, *Security: a New Framework for Analysis*, Lynne Rienner.

Cammack, Paul, 2002, 'The Mother of all Governments: the World Bank's Matrix for Global Governance', in S. Hughes and R. Wilkinson (eds), *Engaging Global Governance: Towards a New Agenda*, Routledge.

Carothers, Thomas, 1991, *In the Name of Democracy: US Policies Toward Latin America in the Reagan Years*, University of California Press.

Carothers, Thomas, 1994, 'The NED at 10', *Foreign Affairs*, Summer: 123–38.

Carothers, Thomas, 1996, *Assessing Democratic Assistance: the Case of Romania*, Carnegie Endowment.

*České veřejné mínění v evropských souvislostech*, 3/2002.

Checkel, Jeffrey, 1998, 'The Constructivist Turn in International Relations Theory', *World Politics*, 50(2): 324–48.

Checkel, Jeffrey, 1999, 'Social Construction and Integration', *Journal of European Public Policy*, 6(4): 545–60.

Checkel, Jeffrey, 2000, 'Building New Identities? Debating Fundamental Rights in European Institutions', *ARENA Working Paper*, no. 12.

Checkel, Jeffrey, 2001, 'Why Comply? Social Learning and European Identity Change', *International Organization*, 55(3): 553–88.

Chilton, Patricia, 1995, 'Mechanics of Change: Social Movements, Transnational Coalitions, and the Transformation Processes in Eastern Europe', in Thomas Risse-Kappen (ed.), *Bringing Transnational Relations Back In: Non-State Actors, Domestic Structures and International Institutions*, Cambridge University Press.

Clapham, Christopher, 1996, *Africa and the International System*, Cambridge University Press.

Clark, Ian, 1999, *Globalization and International Relations Theory*, Oxford University Press.

Colas, Alejandro, 2001, *International Civil Society: Social Movements in World Politics*, Polity Press.

Collier, David and James Mahoney, 1996, 'Insights and Pitfalls: Selection Bias in Qualitative Research, *World Politics*, 49(1): 56–91.

Collier, David and R. Adcock, 1999, 'Democracy and Dichotomies: a Pragmatic Approach to Choices about Concepts', *Annual Review of Political Science*, 2: 537–65.

Common Strategy, 1999, 'Common Strategy of the European Union on Russia', *Official Journal of the European Communities*, 24(6): L/159/1–9.

*Compilation of General Comments and General Recommendations Adopted by Human Rights Treaty Bodies*, HR1/Gen/1/Rev.3, 15 August 1997.

*Conference on New or Restored Democracies*, Philippines (A/43/358 August 1988).

*Conference on New or Restored Democracies*, Romania (A/52/334 September 1997).

Cooper, Malcolm, 2002, 'The Legacy of Ataturk', *International Affairs*, 78(1): 115–28.

Cortell, Andrew and James W. Davis, 1996, 'How do International Institutions Matter? The Domestic Impact of International Rules and Norms', *International Studies Quarterly*, 40(4): 451–78.

Cottey, Andrew, Timothy Edmunds and Anthony Forster (eds), 2002, *Democratic Control of the Military in Post-Communist Europe: Guarding the Guards*, Palgrave Macmillan.

Cox, Michael, 2000, 'Wilsonianism Resurgent? The Clinton Administration and American Democracy Promotion in the late 20th Century', Paper presented at the ISA 41st Annual Convention, Los Angeles (CA) 14–18 March 2000.

Cox, Michael, G. John Ikenberry and Takashi Inoguchi, 2000, *American Democracy Promotion*, Oxford University Press.

Cox, Robert, 1987, *Production, Power and World Order: Social Forces in the Making of History*, Colombia University Press.

Cox, Robert, 1997, 'Democracy in Hard Times: Economic Globalization and the Limits to Liberal Democracy', in Anthony McGrew (ed.), *The Transformation of Democracy? Globalization and Territorial Democracy*, Polity Press.

Crawford, Gordon, 1997, 'Foreign Aid and Political Conditionality', *Democratization*, 4(3): 69–108.

Crawford, J., 2001, 'Right of Self-Determination in International Law', in Philip Alston (ed.), *Peoples' Rights*, Oxford University Press.

Dawisha, Karen (ed.), 1997, *The International Dimension of Post-Communist Transitions in Russia and the New States of Eurasia*, M. E. Sharpe.

De Witte, Bruno, 2000, 'Politics Versus Law in the EU's Approach to Ethnic Minorities', *EUI Working Papers RSC 2000/4*, European University Institute.

Demirel, Tanel, 2003, 'Civil–Military Relations in Turkey: Two Patterns of Civilian Behaviour towards the Military', *Turkish Studies*, 4(3): 1–25.

Deutsch, Karl et al., 1957, *Political Community and the North Atlantic Area*, Princeton University Press.

Diamond, Larry, 1999, *Developing Democracy: Toward Consolidation*, Johns Hopkins University Press.

Dienstbier, Jiří, [1986] 1990 (ed.), *Snění o Evropě*, Lidové Noviny.

Dienstbier, Jiří, 1992, *Dialog o národních zájmech*, ÚMV.

Diez, Thomas (ed.), 2002, *The European Union and the Cyprus Conflict: Modern Conflict, Postmodern Union*, Manchester University Press.

Domrin, Alexander, N., 2003, 'Society, "Civil Society", and the Russian State', *Russian Review*, 62(2): 193–211.

Donnelly, Chris, 2001, 'Civil–Military Relations in the New Democracies', in David Betz and John Löwenhardt (eds), *Army and State in Postcommunist Europe*, Frank Cass.

Dostál, Ondrej, 1996, 'Menšiny', in Martin Bútora and Péter Hunčík (eds), *Slovensko 1995: Súhrnná Správa o Stave Spoločnosti*, Nadácia Sándora Máraiho.

Doyle, Michael, 1983, 'Kant, Liberal Legacies and Foreign Affairs', Parts 1 and 2, *Philosophy and Public Affairs*, 12(3): 323–53.

Doyle, Michael, 1986, 'Liberalism and World Politics', *American Political Science Review*, 80(4): 1151–69.

Drew, N. S., 1995, *NATO from Berlin to Bosnia: Trans-Atlantic Security in Transition*, National Defence University.

Druckmann, Daniel, 1994, 'Nationalism, Patriotism and Group Loyalty: a Social Psychological Perspective', *Mershon International Studies Review*, 38(1): 43–68.

Drulák, Petr, 2000, 'Deset let československé a české zahraniční politiky jako (re)produkce politické identity', in *Společnost v přerodu. Češi ve 20. století*, Masarykův ústav AV ČR.

Drulák, Petr, 2004, 'Constructing Europe: European Integration in the Czech and Slovak Political Discourse', paper presented at ARENA Workshop in Avila, 7–8 May.

Drulák, Petr, Jiří Česal and Stanislav Hampl, 2003, 'Interactions and Identities of Czech Civil Servants on Their Way to the EU', *Journal of European Public Policy*, 10(4): 637–54.

Drulák, Petr, Lucie Königová and Petr Kratochvíl, 2004, *Podíl obecních a krajských samospráv na zahraniční politice ČR*, Praha: ÚMV.

Eralp, Atila, 2000, 'Turkey in the Enlargement Process: From Luxembourg to Helsinki', *Perceptions*, 5(2), www.mfa.gov.tr/grupa/percept/v-2/aeralp.htm.

European Commission, 2003, *Comprehensive Monitoring Report of the European Commission on the State of Preparedness for EU Membership of the Czech Repuplic, Estonia, Cyprus, Latvia, Lithuania, Hungary, Malta, Poland, Slokia and Slovenia,* European Commission, 5 November.

European Council, 1998, 'Presidency Statement on Behalf of the European Union', *Bulletin of the EU,* 9.

European Parliament, 1997, 'Resolution of the European Parliament on the Case of Frantisek Gaulieder, Member of the Slovak Parliament', *Official Journal of the EU,* C 020.

Evangelista, Matthew, 1997, 'Domestic Structure and International Change', in M. Doyle and G. J. Ikenberry (eds), *New Thinking in International Relations Theory,* Westview Press.

Fajkusová, Blanka, 1999, 'Přístup nových členských států do OECD na příkladu České republiky', *Mezinárodní vztahy,* 34(1): 80–90.

Falk, Richard, 2001, 'Self-Determination Under International Law: the Coherence of Doctrine Versus the Incoherence of Experience', in Wolfgang Danspeckgruber (ed.), *The Self-Determination of Peoples, Community, Nation and State in an Interdependent World,* Lynne Rienner.

Farrell, Theo, 2001, 'Transnational Norms and Military Development: Constructing Ireland's Professional Army', *European Journal of International Relations,* 7(1): 63–102.

Fierke, Karin M. and Antje Wiener, 1999, 'Constructing Institutional Interests: EU and NATO Enlargement', *Journal of European Public Policy,* 6(3): 721–42.

Finnemore, Martha, 1996, *National Interest in International Society,* Cornell University Press.

Finnemore, Martha and Kathryn Sikkink, 1998, 'International Norm Dynamics and Political Change', *International Organization,* 52(4): 887–917.

Fish, M. Steven, 1995, *Democracy from Scratch: Opposition and Regime in the New Russian Revolution,* Princeton University Press.

Flockhart, Trine, 2001, 'Democracy, Security and the Social Construction of Europe', *Perspectives on European Politics and Society,* 2(1): 27–53.

Flockhart, Trine, 2003, 'Critical Junctures and Social Identity Theory: Explaining the Gap between Danish Mass and Elite Attitudes to Europeanization', *Series of Occasional Papers, European Research Unit,* no. 37, Aalborg University, available at http://www.ihis.aau.dk/eru/publications.html#2003.

Flockhart, Trine, 2004a, 'Masters and Novices' Socialization and Social Learning in NATO's Parliamentary Assembly', *International Relations,* 18(3): 361–80.

Flockhart, Trine, 2004b, 'Uses and Abuses of Hegemony: Socialisation of Democratic Norms in Post-War Germany and Post-War Iraq', paper presented at International Studies Association, Montreal.

Flockhart, Trine, 2004c, '"Complex Socialization": a Rational and Ideational Framework for Understanding Norm Transfer', unpublished manuscript.

Flynn, Gregory and Henry Farrell, 1999, 'Piecing Together the Democratic Peace: the CSCE and the "Construction" of Security in Post-Cold War Europe', *International Organization,* 53(3): 505–35.

Forster, Antony, Timothy Edmonds and Andrew Cottey (eds), 2002, *Soldiers and Societies in Post-communist Europe. Legitimacy and Change,* Palgrave Macmillan.

Franck, Thomas, 1990, *The Power of Legitimacy among Nations,* Oxford University Press.

Fučík, Josef, 1999, 'Civilní tvář NATO', *Česká republika v NATO*, Czech Atlantic Commission, ÚMV, 37–48.

Fukuyama, Francis, 1992, *The End of History and the Last Man*, Hamish Hamilton.

Gabal, Ivan, Lenka Helsusova and Thomas S. Szayna, 2002, *The Impact of NATO Membership in the Czech Republic: Changing Czech Views of Security, Military & Defence*, RAND.

Gaddis, John L., 1998, 'History, Grand Strategy and NATO Enlargement', *Survival*, 40(1): 145–51.

Galeotti, Mark, 2000, 'The "Power Ministries" and Russian Foreign Policy', in Jakub M. Godzimirski (ed.), *New and Old Actors in Russian Foreign Policy*, Norwegian Institute for International Affairs.

Gaman-Golutvina, Oksana, 2001, 'Modernization and the Value System of the Russian Elite', in Archie Brown (ed.), *Contemporary Russian Politics: a Reader*, Oxford University Press.

Ghebali, Victor-Yves, 1989, *La diplomatie de la détente: la CSCE, d'Helsinki à Vienne (1973–1989)*, Bruylant.

Ghebali, Victor-Yves, 1996, *L'OSCE dans l'Europe post-communiste, 1990–1996. Vers une identité paneuropéenne de sécurité*, Bruylant.

Ghebali, Victor-Yves, 2004, 'OSCE Regional Policy in Central Asia: Rationale and Limits', in Farian Sabahi and Daniel Warner (eds), *The OSCE and the Multiple Challenges of Transition: the Caucasus and Central Asia*, Ashgate.

Gheciu, Alexandra, 2002, 'Security Institutions as Agents of Socialization? NATO and Post-Cold War Central and Eastern Europe', paper presented at IDNET workshop, European University Institute, Florence, 22–23 February.

Gill, Stephen, 1992, 'Economic Globalization and the Internationalization of Authority', *Geoforum*, 23(3): 269–83.

Gill, Stephen, 1995, 'Globalisation, Market Civilisation and Disciplinary Neoliberalism', *Millennium*, 24(3): 399–423.

Gills, Barry, 2000, 'The Crisis of Postwar East Asian Capitalism: American Power, Democracy and the Vicissitudes of Globalisation', *Review of International Studies*, 26(3): 381–403.

Goulding, M. 2002, *Peacemonger*, John Murray.

Grabbe, Heather, 1999, 'A Partnership for Accession? The Implications of EU Conditionality for the Central and East European Applicants', *EUI Working Papers RSC 99/12*, European University Institute.

Grugel, Jean (ed.), 1999, *Democracy Without Borders: Transnational and Non-state Actors in Eastern Europe, Africa and Latin America*, Routledge.

Grugel, Jean, 2000, 'Romancing Civil Society: European NGOs in Latin America', *Journal of Interamerican Studies and World Affairs*, 42(2): 87–108.

Grugel, Jean, 2002, *Democratisation: a Critical Introduction*, Palgrave Macmillan.

Grugel, Jean, 2003, 'Democratization Studies and Globalization: the Coming of Age of a Paradigm', *British Journal of Politics and International Relations*, 5(2): 258–83.

Grugel, Jean, 2004a, 'Democratisation: IPE and the Realm of Politics', in N. Phillips (ed.), *Globalising IPE*, Palgrave Macmillan.

Grugel, Jean, 2004b, 'New Regionalism and Modes of Governance: Comparing US and EU Strategies for Latin America', *European Journal of International Relations*, 10(4): 603–26.

Haas, Peter, 1992, 'Introduction: Epistemic Communities and International Policy Coordination', *International Organization*, 46(1): 1–35.

Haerpfer, Christian, 2002, *Democracy and Enlargement in Post-Communist Europe: the Democratization of the General Public in Fifteen Central and East European Countries, 1991–98*, Routledge.

Haggard, Stephen and Robert Kaufman, 1995, *The Political Economy of Democratic Transition*, Princeton University Press.

Hahn, Jeffery, W. 1991, 'Continuity and Change in Russian Political Culture', *British Journal of Political Science*, 2: 392–421.

Hale, Bill, 2003, 'Human Rights, the European Union, and the Turkish Accession Process', *Turkish Studies*, 4(1): 107–26.

Hansen, Bente Villum, 2001, 'Fra sværd til plovskær: Værnskultur under forandring? Holdningsanalyse af postsovjetisk militært personel i et dansk genhusningsprojekt, MA Thesis, Slavonic Department, University of Aarhus.

Hansen, Lene and Wæver, Ole (eds), 2002, *European Integration and National Identity*, Routledge.

Harbeson, John, 2000, 'Externally-Assisted: Theoretical Issues and African Realities', in John Harbeson and Donald Rothchild (eds), *Africa in World Politics: the African State Sytem in Flux*, Westview Press.

Harris, Geoffrey, 2002, 'The Democratic Dimension of EU Enlargement: the Role of Parliament and Public Opinion', in Ronald H. Linden (ed.), *Norms and Nannies: the Impact of International Organizations on the Central and East European States*, Rowman and Littlefield.

Harvey, Mark, 2000, 'Developing the Agent: Towards a Constructivist Theory of Identity', paper presented at the British International Studies Association conference, Edinburgh.

Haughton, Tim, 2003, ' "We'll Finish What We've Started": the 2002 Slovak Parliamentary Elections', *Journal of Communist Studies and Transition Politics*, 19(4): 65–90.

Havel, Václav, 1978, 1990 (ed.), *Moc bezmocných*, Lidové noviny.

Havel, Václav, 1990a, *Do různých stran*, Lidové noviny.

Havel, Václav, 1990b, *O lidskou identitu*, Lidové noviny.

Havel, Václav, 1991, *Letní přemítání*, Odeon.

Hedetoft, Ulf, 2003, 'Cultures of States and Informal Governance in the EU: an Exploratory Study of Elites, Power and Identity', *Series of Occasional Papers, European Research Unit*, no. 35, Aalborg University, Denmark.

Held, David, 1995, *Democracy and Global Order: From the Modern State to Cosmopolitan Governance*, Polity Press.

Held, David, Anthony McGrew, David Goldblatt and Jonathan Perraton (1999), *Global Transformation: Politics, Economics and Culture*, Polity Press.

Henderson, Sarah L., 2003, *Building Democracy in Contemporary Russia: Western Support for Grassroot Organizations*, Cornell University Press.

Heper, Metin and Guney Aylin, 2000, 'The Military and the Consolidation of Democracy: the Recent Turkish experience', *Armed Forces and Society*, 26(4): 635–57.

Heraclides, Alexis, 1993, *Helsinki-II and its Aftermath: the Making of the CSCE into an International Organization*, Pinter.

Herman, Margarate and Kegley, Charles, 1995, 'Re-thinking Democracy and International Peace: Perspectives from Political Psychology', *International Studies Quarterly*, 39(4): 511–33.

Higgins, R., 1994, *Problems and Process, International Law and How We Use It*, Oxford University Press.

Higley, John and Richard Gunther (eds), 1992, *Elites and Democratic Consolidation in Latin America and Southern Europe*, Cambridge University Press.

Hogg, Michael and Dominic Abrams, 1988, *Social Identifications: a Social Psychology of Intergroup Relations and Group Processes*, Routledge.

Hopf, Ted, 2002, *Social Construction of International Politics: Identities & Foreign Policies, Moscow, 1955 and 1999*, Cornell University Press.

Huntington, Samuel P., 1991, *The Third Wave: Democratization in the Late Twentieth Century*, University of Oklahoma Press.

Husák, Petr, 1997, *Budování kapitalismu v Čechách. Rozhovory s Tomášem Ježkem*, Volvox Globator.

Ikenberry, G. John and Charles A. Kupchan, 1990, 'Socialization and Hegemonic Power', *International Organization*, 44(3): 283–315.

*Informace o výsledcích analýz a srovnání provedených podle usnesení Vlády České Republiky ze dne 25. června 1997 č. 383*, MZV, září 1997.

Isaacs, Maxine, 1998, 'Two Different Worlds: the Relationship between Elite and Mass Opinion on American Foreign Policy', *Political Communication*, 15(3): 323–46.

Jayasuriya, K., 2003, 'Embedded Mercantilism and Open Regionalism: the Crisis of a Regional Political Project', *Third World Quarterly*, 24(2): 339–55.

Jelin, Elizabeth, 1996, 'Citizenship Revisited: Solidarity, Responsibility and Rights', in Elizabeth Jelin and E. Hersberg (eds), *Constructing Democracy: Human Rights, Citizenship and Society in Latin America*, Westview Press.

Jenkins, Gareth, 2001, *Context and Circumstance: the Turkish Military and Politics*, Adelphi Paper 337, International Institute for Strategic Studies.

Jenkins, Gareth, 2003, 'Muslim Democrats in Turkey?', *Survival*, 45(1): 45–66.

Johnston, Alastair, 2001, 'Treating International Institutions as Social Environments', *International Studies Quarterly*, 45: 487–515.

Joyner, C., 1999, 'The United Nations and Democracy', *Global Governance*, 5(3): 333–57.

Jung, Dietrich and Wolfgang Piccoli, 2001, *Turkey at the Crossroads: Ottoman Legacies and a Greater Middle East*, Zed Books.

Kant, Immanuel, 1795/1991, 'Perpetual Peace. A Philosophical Sketch', in Hans Reiss (ed.), *Kant's, Political Writings*, 2nd edition, Cambridge University Press.

Karaosmanoglu, Ali L., 2000, 'The Evolution of National Security Culture and the Military in Turkey', *Journal of International Affairs*, 54(1): 199–216.

Kardas, Saban, 2002, 'Human Rights and Democracy Promotion: the Case of Turkey–EU Relations', *Alternatives*, 1(3), www.alternativesjournal.net/kardas.htm.

Katzenstein, Peter, 1976, 'International Relations and Domestic Structures: Foreign Economic Policies of Advanced Industrial States', *International Organization*, 30(1): 1–45.

Keck, Margaret and Kathryn Sikkink, 1998, *Activists Beyond Borders*, Cornell University Press.

Kemp, Walter A., 2001, *Quiet Diplomacy in Action: the OSCE High Commissioner on National Minorities*, Kluwer.

Ken Wang, Qingxin, 2003, 'Hegemony, Socialization and US–Japanese Policy Cooperation', *Review of International Studies*, 29(1): 99–119.

Keohane, Robert and Joseph Nye (eds), 1971, *Transnational Relations and World Politics*, Harvard University Press.

Kidd, Warren, 2002, *Culture and Identity*, Palgrave Macmillan.

Kirisci, Kemal and Gareth M. Winrow, 1997, *The Kurdish Question and Turkey: an Example of a Trans-state Ethnic Conflict*, Frank Cass.

Klaus, Václav, 1991, *Ekonomická věda a ekonomická reforma (statě, eseje)*, GENNEX & TOP Agency.

Klaus, Václav, 1993, 'Europas zukunft aus tschechischer Sicht' (speech, 7 January), in *Česká zahraniční politika – Dokumenty*, Ministerstvo zahraničních věcí ČR.

Klaus, Václav, 1994, *Česká cesta*, Profile.

Klotz, Audie, 2001, 'Can We Speak a Common Constructivist Language?' in Karin M. Fierke and Knud Erik Jørgensen (eds), *Constructing International Relations*, M. E. Sharpe.

Kollár, Miroslav, 1999, 'Cirkvi a Volby 1998', in Martin Bútora, Grigorij Mesežnikov and Zora Bútorová (eds), *Slovenské Vol'by 1998: Kto? Prečo? Ako?*, Bratislava: Inštitút pre Verejné Otázky: 151–6.

Königová, Lucie, 2004, 'Geneticky modifikované organizace? Twinning jako případ transnacionální interakce', *Mezinárodní vztahy*, 39(1): 7–26.

Korba, Matúš, 2003, 'Zahraničná politika', in Grigorij Mesežnikov, Olga Gyárfášová and Miroslav Kollár (eds), *Slovenské Vol'by 2002: Výsledky, Dôsledky, Súvislosti*, Inštitút pre Verejné Otázky.

Koslowski, Rey and Fridrich Kratochwil, 1995, 'Understanding Change in International Politics: the Soviet Empire's Demise and the International System', in Richard Lebow and Thomas Risse-Kappen (eds), *International Relations Theory and the End of the Cold War*, Columbia University Press.

Kramer, Heinz, 1996, 'Turkey and the European Union: a Multidimensional Relationship with Hazy Perspectives', in Vojtech Mastny and R. Craig Nation (eds), *Turkey between East and West: New Challenges for a Rising Regional Power*, Westview.

Krasner, Steven, 1978, *Defending the National Interest: Raw Materials, Interests and US Foreign Policy*, Princeton University Press.

Kundera, Milan, 1984, 'The Tragedy of Central Europe', *The New York Review of Books*, 26 April.

Lake, David, 1992, 'Powerful Pacifists: Democratic States and War', *American Political Science Review*, 86(1): 24–37.

Landau, J. M. (ed.), 1984, *Ataturk and the Modernisation of Turkey*, Westview.

Lapid, Yosef, 1997, 'Culture's Ship: Returns and Departures in International Relations Theory', in Yosef Lapid and Friedrich Kratochwil (eds), *The Return of Culture and Identity in IR Theory*, Lynne Rienner.

Lapidus, Gail W., 1998, 'Contested Sovereignty: the Tragedy of Chechnya', *International Security*, 23(1): 5–49.

Latawski, Paul, 2002, 'Democratic Control of Armed Forces in Post-communist Poland: the Interplay of History, Political Society and Institutional Reform', in Andrew Cottey et al. (eds), *Democratic Control of the Military in Post-Communist Europe: Guarding the Guards*, Palgrave Macmillan.

Lavenex, Sandra, 1998, ' "Passing the Buck": European Union Refugee Policies towards Central and Eastern Europe', *Journal of Refugee Studies*, 11(2): 126–45.

Leff, Carol Skalnik, 1998, *The Czech and Slovak Republics: Nation Versus State*, Westview.

Legro, Jeffrey, 1997, 'Which Norms Matter? Revisiting the "Failure" of Internationalism', *International Organization*, 51(1): 31–64.

Levy, Jack, 1994, 'Learning and Foreign Policy: Sweeping a Conceptual Minefield', *International Organization*, 48(2): 279–312.

Linz, Juan and Alfred Stepan, 1996, *Problems of Democratic Transition and Consolidation: Southern Europe, South America and Post-Communist Europe*, Johns Hopkins University Press.

Locher Birgit and Elizabeth Prügel, 2001, 'Feminism: Constructivism's Other Pedigree', in Karin M. Fierke and Knud Erik Jørgensen (eds), *Constructing International Relations*, M. E. Sharpe.

Lombardini, Veronika, 1999, 'Reakcia Zahraničia na Priebeh a Výsledky Slovenských Volieb 1998', in Martin Bútora, Grigorij Mesežnikov and Zora Bútorová (eds), *Slovenské Vol'by 1998: Kto? Prečo? Ako?*, Inštitút pre Verejné Otázky.

Lose, G. Lars, 2001, 'Communicative Action and the World of Diplomacy', in Karin M. Fierke and Knud Erik Jørgensen (eds), *Constructing International Relations: the Next Generation*, M. E. Sharpe.

Lucarelli, Sonia, 2002, *Peace and Democracy: the Rediscovered Link. The EU, NATO and the European System of Liberal-Democratic Security Communities*, NATO-EACP Final Research Report (available at: http://www.nato.int/acad/fellow/00–02/f00–02.htm).

Ludwig, R., 2001, *Letting the People Decide the Evolution of United Nations Electoral Assistance*, Academic Council on the United Nations System.

MacFarlane, Neil, 2003, 'International Organizations in Central Asia: Understanding the Limits', *Helsinki Monitor: Quarterly on Security and Cooperation in Europe*, 14(3): 287–99.

Malová, Darina, 1999, 'Od Váhania k Premyslenej Stratégii: Konfederácia Odborových Zväzov SR', in Martin Bútora, Grigorij Mesežnikov and Zora Bútorová (eds), *Slovenské Vol'by 1998: Kto? Prečo? Ako?*, Inštitút pre Verejné Otázky.

Marcussen, Martin, 2000, *Ideas and Elites: the Social Construction of Economic and Monetary Union*, Aalborg University Press.

Marenin, Otwin, 1998, 'The Goal of Democracy in International Police Assistance Programs', *Policing: an International Journal of Police Strategies and Management*, 21(1): 159–77.

Maresca, John J., 1987, *To Helsinki: the Conference on Security and Cooperation in Europe 1973–1975*, Duke University Press.

Martin, Hans Peter and Harold Shumann, 1997, *The Global Trap: Globalization and the Assault on Prosperity and Democracy*, Zed Books.

Mayall, James, 2000, 'Democracy and International Society', *International Affairs*, 76(1): 61–75.

McCalla, R. B., 1996, 'NATO's Persistence After the Cold War', *International Organization*, 50(3): 445–75.

McFaul, Michael 1995, 'State Power, Institutional Change, and the Politics of Privatization in Russia', *World Politics*, 47(3): 210–43.

McGrew, Antony, 1997, *The Transformation of Democracy*, Polity Press.

McGwire, Michael, 1998, 'NATO Expansion: a Policy Error of Historical Importance', *Review of International Studies*, 24(1): 23–42.

Mendelson, Sarah E., 2001, 'Democracy Assistance and Political Transition in Russia: Between Success and Failure', *International Security*, 25(4): 68–106.

Menotti, Roberto, 1999, *Mediatori in Armi. L'allargamento della NATO e la politica USA in Europa*, Guerini e associati.

Merlingen, Michael, 2003, 'Governmentality: Towards a Foucauldian Framework for the Study of IGOs', *Cooperation and Conflict*, 38(4): 361–84.

Merlingen, Michael and Rasa Ostrauskaitė, 2003, 'Die internationale Sozialisierung post-sozialistischer Länder: Die Rolle des Europarats und der OSZE', in Institut für Friedensforschung und Sicherheitspolitik an der Universität Hamburg (ed.), *OSZE-Jahrbuch 2003*, Nomos.

Merlingen, Michael and Rasa Ostrauskaitė, 2005, 'A Dense Policy Space? The Police Aid of the OSCE and the EU', in Institut für Friedensforschung und Sicherheitspolitik an der Universität Hamburg (ed.), *OSZE-Jahrbuch 2004*, Nomos.

Mesežnikov, Grigorij, 1996, 'Vnútropolitický Vývoj a Politická Scéna v roku 1995', in Martin Bútora and Péter Hunčík (eds), *Slovensko 1995: Súhrnná Správa o Stave Spoločnosti*, Nadácia Sándora Máraiho.

Mesežnikov, Grigorij, 1999, 'Volby 1998 a Vývoj Systému Politických Strán', in Martin Bútora, Grigorij Mesežnikov and Zora Bútorová (eds), *Slovenské Vol'by 1998: Kto? Prečo? Ako?*, Inštitút pre Verejné Otázky.

Mesežnikov, Grigorij, 2003, 'Parlamentné Vol'by 2002 a Vývoj systému Politických Strán', in Grigorij Mesežnikov, Olga Gyárfášová and Miroslav Kollár (eds), *Slovenské Vol'by 2002: Výsledky, Dôsledky, Súvislosti*, Inštitút pre Verejné Otázky.

Meyer, John, John Boli, John Thomas and Francisco Ramirez, 1997, 'World Society and the Nation State', *American Journal of Sociology*, 103(1): 144–81.

Mineshima, Dale, 2002, 'The Rule of Law and EU Expansion', *Liverpool Law Review*, 24(1–2): 73–87.

Mittleman, James, 2000, *The Globalisation Syndrome: Transformation and Resistance*, Princeton University Press.

Moravcsik, Andrew and Milada Vachudova, 2003, 'National Interests, State Power and EU Enlargement', *East European Politics and Societies*, 17(1): 42–57.

Morphet, Sally, 1989, 'Article 1 of the Human Rights Covenants: Its Development and Current Significance', in D. Hill (ed.), *Human Rights and Foreign Policy, Principles and Practice*, Macmillan.

Morphet, Sally, 1993, 'UN Peacekeeping and Election Monitoring', in A. Roberts and B. Kingsbury (eds), *United Nations, Divided World: the UN's Role in International Relations*, Oxford University Press.

Morphet, Sally, 2000, 'States Groups at the UN' in P. Taylor and A. J. R. Groom (eds), *The United Nations at the Millennium: The Principal Organs*, Continuum.

Morphet, Sally, 2002, 'Current International Civil Administration: the Need for Political Legitimacy', *International Peacekeeping*, 9(2): 140–62.

Morton, Adam, 2002, 'La Resurrecion de Maiz: Globalisation, Resistance and the Zapatistas', *Millennium*, 31(1): 27–52.

Muftuler-Bac, Meltem, 1999, 'The Never-Ending Story: Turkey and the European Union', in S. Kedourie (ed.), *Turkey Before and After Ataturk: Internal and External Affairs*, Frank Cass.

Munck, Ronaldo (ed.), 2000, *Labour in the Global Economy: Challenges and Prospects*, Althone Press.

Murphy, Craig, 2000, 'Global Governance: Poorly Done and Poorly Understood' *International Affairs*, 76(4): 789–803.

Narli, Nilufer, 2000, 'Civil–Military Relations in Turkey', *Turkish Studies*, 1(1): 107–27.

Neumann, Iver B., 1996, *Russia and the Idea of Europe: a Study in Identity and International Relations*, Routledge.

Neumann, Iver B., 2000, 'Forgetting the Central Europe of 1980s', in Christopher Lord (ed.), *Central Europe: Core or Periphery?*, Copenhagen Business School Press.

Nicolai, Petro, 1995, *The Rebirth of Russian Democracy: an Interpretation of Political Culture*, Harvard University Press.

Novotný, Peter, Daniel Forgács and Marián Velšic, 2003, 'Mimovládne Organizácie a Vol'by', in Grigorij Mesežnikov, Olga Gyárfášová and Miroslav Kollár (eds), *Slovenské Vol'by 2002: Výsledky, Dôsledky, Súvislosti*, Inštitút pre Verejné Otázky.

O'Brien, Robert, Anne Marie Goetz, Jan Aart Scholte and Marc Williams, 2000, *Contesting Global Governance: Multilateral Economic Institutions and Global Social Movements*, Cambridge University Press.

O'Donnell, Guillermo, Phillippe Schmitter and Laurence Whitehead (eds), 1986, *Transitions from Authoritarian Rule*, Johns Hopkins University Press.

Oakes Penelope J., S. Alexander Haslam and Katherine J. Reynolds, 1999, 'Social Categorization and Social Context: Is Stereotype Change a Matter of Information or of Meaning?', in Dominic Abrams and Michael A. Hogg (eds), *Social Identity and Social Cognition*, Blackwell.

Oldberg, Ingmar, 2003, *Reluctant Rapprochement: Russia and the Baltic States in the Context of NATO and EU Enlargements*, FOI/Swedish Defence Research Agency, FOI-R-0808-SE, February.

Olsen, Robert (ed.), 1996, *The Kurdish Nationalist Movement in the 1990s: its Impact on Turkey and the Middle East*, Kentucky University Press.

Onis, Ziya, 1999, 'Turkey, Europe and the Paradoxes of Identity', *Mediterranean Quarterly*, 10(3): 107–36.

Onis, Ziya, 2000, 'Luxembourg, Helsinki and Beyond: Towards an Interpretation of Recent Turkey–EU Relations', *Government and Opposition*, 35(4): 463–83.

Onis, Ziya, 2001, 'An Awkward Partnership: Turkey's Relations with the European Union in Comparative-Historical Perspective', *Journal of European Integration History*, 7(1): 105–19.

Onis, Ziya, 2003, 'Domestic Politics, International Norms, and Challenges to the State: Turkish–EU Relations in the Post-Helsinki era', *Turkish Studies*, 4(1): 9–34.

Organization for Security and Co-operation in Europe (OSCE), 2002a, *Assistance to Border Services in the Southern Caucasus*, Project Report.

Organization for Security and Co-operation in Europe (OSCE), 2002b, *Assistance to Border Services in Central Asia*, Project Report.

Organization for Security and Co-operation in Europe (OSCE), 2003, 'State Duma Elections Well Organized but Failed to Meet International Standards', downloaded 17 December 2003 from www.osce.org./news/show_news.php?id = 3757.

Ort, Alexandr, 1993, 'Česká republika v měnící se Evropě', in Alexandr Ort (ed.), *Česká republika v měnící se Evropě*, Středisko mezinárodních studií Jana Masaryka.

Owen, J., 1994, 'How Liberalism Produces Democratic Peace', *International Security*, 19(2): 87–125.

Ozbudun, Ergun, 2000, *Contemporary Turkish Politics: Challenges to Democratic Consolidation*, Lynne Rienner.

Packer, John, 2000, 'Making International Law Matter in Preventing Ethnic Conflict: a Practitioner's Perspective', *New York University Journal of International Law and Politics*, 32(3): 715–24.

Paquette, Laure, 2001, *NATO and Eastern Europe after 2000: Strategic Interaction with Poland, the Czech Republic, Romania and Bulgaria*, Nova Science Publishers.

Park, Bill, 2000, 'Turkey's European Union Candidacy: From Luxembourg, to Helsinki – to Ankara?', *Mediterranean Politics*, 5(3): 31–53.

Park, Bill, 2001, 'Turkey and the European Union: Over the Horizon?', *World Today*, 57(6): 25–7.

Park, Bill, 2003, 'Strategic Location, Political Dislocation: Turkey, the United States, and Northern Iraq', *Middle East Review of International Affairs*, 7(2): 11–23.

Pei, Minxin, Samia Amin and Seth Garz, 'Why Nation-building Fails in Mid-course after US Intervention', *International Herald Tribune*, 17 March 2004.

Pesmazoglu, S., 1997, 'Turkey and Europe, Reflections and Refractions: Towards a Contrapuntal Approach', *South European Society and Politics*, 2(1): 138–59.

Petro, Nicolai N., 1995, 'Policy-making in a Rapidly Changing World: the Soviet Union and Eastern Europe', in Kenneth W. Thompson (ed.), *Revolutions in Eastern Europe and the USSR: Promises vs. Practical Morality*, University Press of America, 3–20.

Piper, Nicola Anders Uhlin (ed.), 2003, *Transnational Acitivism: Strategies, Issues and Organizations*, Routledge.

Pipes, Richard, 1997, *Russia Under the Old Regime*, Penguin Books.

Pithart, Petr (ed.), 1990, *Osmašedesátý*, Lidové noviny.

Popper, Karl R., 1966, *The Open Socieity and its Enemies*, Vols 1 and 2, Routledge & Kegan Paul.

Poulton, Hugh, 1997, *Top Hat, Grey Wolf, and Crescent: Turkish Nationalism and the Turkish Republic*, Hurst.

Pridham, Geoffrey (ed.), 1991, *Encouraging Democracy: the International Context of Regime Transition in Southern Europe*, Routledge.

Pridham, Geoffrey (ed.), 1993, *Securing Democracy: Party Politics and Democratic Consolidation in Southern Europe*, Routledge.

Pridham, Geoffrey, 1999a, 'The European Union, Democratic Conditionalty and Transnational Party Linkages: the Case of Eastern Europe', in J. Grugel (ed.), *Democracy without Borders: Transnationalization and Conditionality in New Democracies*, Routledge.

Pridham, Geoffrey, 1999b, 'Complying with the European Union's Democratic Conditionality: Transnational Party Linkages and Regime Change in Slovakia, 1993–1998', *Europe-Asia Studies*, 51(7): 1221–44.

Pridham, Geoffrey, 2002a, 'EU Enlargement and Consolidating Democracy in Post-Communist States – Formality and Reality', *Journal of Common Market Studies*, 40(5): 953–73.

Pridham, Geoffrey, 2002b, 'Coalition Behaviour in New Democracies of Central and Eastern Europe: the Case of Slovakia', *Journal of Communist Studies and Transition Politics*, 18(2): 75–102.

Pridham, Geoffrey, 2003, 'The Slovak Parliamentary Election of September 2002: Its Systemic Importance', *Government and Opposition*, 38(3): 333–56.

Pridham, Geoffrey and Ágh Attila, 2001, *Prospects for Democratic Consolidation in East-Central Europe*, Manchester University Press.
Pridham, Geoffrey and Vanhanen Tatu (eds), 1994, *Democratization in Eastern Europe: Domestic and International Perspectives*, Routledge.
Pridham, Geoffrey, Eric Herring and George Sandford (eds), 1994, *Building Democracy? The International Dimension of Democratisation in Eastern Europe*, Leicester University Press.
Provazník, Dušan, 1995, 'OECD v kostce', *Ekonom*, 39(38): 35–9.
Przeworski, Adam, 1999, 'Minimalist Conception of Democracy: a Defence', in Ian Schapiro and Cassiano Hacker-Cordon (eds), *Democracy's Value*, Cambridge University Press.
Ratner, Steven R., 2000, 'Does International Law Matter in Preventing Ethnic Conflict?', *New York University Journal of International Law and Politics*, 32(3): 591–698.
Reddaway, Peter and Dmitri Glinski, 2001, *The Tragedy of Russia's Reforms. Market Bolshevism Against Democracy*, United States Institute for Peace.
Reilly, B. and A. Reynolds (eds), 1999, 'Electoral Systems and Conflict in Divided Societies', in *Papers on International Conflict Resolution No. 2*, National Academy Press.
Reisch, Alfred A., 1993, 'Slovakia's Minority Policy under International Scrutiny', *Radio Free Europe/Radio Liberty Research Report 2*, No. 49, 10 December.
Remmer, Karen, 1997, 'Theoretical Development and Theoretical Decay: the Resurgence of Institutional Analysis', *World Politics*, 50(1): 34–61.
Rice, Condoleezza, 2000, 'Promoting the National Interest', *Foreign Affairs*, 79(1): 45–62.
Risse, Thomas, 2000, ' "Let's Argue!": Communicative Action in World Politics', *International Organization*, 54(1): 1–39.
Risse, Thomas, Stephen Ropp and Kathryn Sikkink (eds), 1999, *The Power of Human Rights: International Norms and Domestic Change*, Cambridge University Press.
Risse-Kappen, Thomas, 1992, 'Public Opinion, Domestic Structure and Foreign Policy in Liberal Democracies', *World Politics*, 43(4): 479–512.
Risse-Kappen, Thomas, 1994, 'Ideas do not Float Freely: Transnational Coalitions, Domestic Structures, and the End of the Cold War', *International Organization*, 48(2): 185–214.
Robertson, Roland, 1992, *Globalization: Social Theory and Global Culture*, Sage.
Robins, Philip, 2000, 'Turkey and the Kurds: Missing Another Opportunity?', in Morton Abramowitz (ed.), *Turkey's Transformation and American Policy*, Century Foundation Press, 61–9.
Robins, Philip, 2003, 'Confusion at Home, Confusion Abroad: Turkey between Copenhagen and Iraq', *International Affairs*, 79(3): 547–66.
Robinson, William, 1996, *Promoting Polyarchy: Globalisation, US Intervention and Hegemony*, Cambridge University Press.
Robinson, William, 2000, 'Neoliberalism, the Global Elite and the Guatemalan Transition', *Journal of Interamerican Studies and World Affairs*, 42(4): 89–107.
Robinson, William, 2002, 'Globalisation as a Macro-Structural-Historical Framework for Analysis: the Case of Central America', *New Political Economy*, 7(2): 242–9.
Rosenau, James N., 1980, *The Study of Global Interdependence: Essays on the Transnationalisation of World Affairs*, Nichols.

Rouleau, Eric, 2000, 'Turkey's Dream of Democracy', *Foreign Affairs*, 79(6): 100–14.
Ruggie, John C., 1998, *Constructing the World Polity*, Routledge.
Rumford, Chris, 2000, 'From Luxembourg to Helsinki: Turkey, the Politics of EU Enlargement, and the Prospects for Accession', *Contemporary Politics*, 6(4): 331–43.
Rupert, Mark, 2000, *Ideologies of Globalization*, Routledge.
Russett, Bruce, 1993, *Grasping the Democratic Peace: Principles of a Post-Cold War World*, Princeton University Press.
Russett, Bruce and Maoz Zeev, 1993, 'Normative and Structural Causes of Democratic Peace', *American Political Science Review*, 87(3): 624–38.
Russett, Bruce et al., 1995, 'Correspondence: the Democratic Peace', *International Security*, 19(4): 164–84.
Rybář, Marek and Darina Malová, 2004, 'Exerting Influence on a Contentious Polity: the European Union's Democratic Conditionality and Political Change in Slovakia', in Antoaneta Dimitova (ed.), *Driven to Change: the European Union's Enlargement Viewed from the East*, Manchester University Press.
Šafaříková, Vlasta et al. 1996, *Transformace české společnosti 1989–1995*, Doplněk.
Sandel, Michael, 1996, *Democracy's Discontent*, Harvard University Press.
Sarvaš, Štefan, 1997, 'Pohledy české veřejnosti a vojáků z povolání na vstup ČR do NATO', *NATO* [information bulletin of the Czech Ministry of Defence], August: 41–56.
Schimmelfennig, Frank, 1998/9, 'NATO Enlargement: a Constructivist Explanation', *Security Studies*, 8(2/3): 198–234.
Schimmelfennig, Frank, 2000, 'International Socialization in the New Europe: Rational Action in an Institutional Environment', *European Journal of International Relations*, 6(1): 109–39.
Schimmelfennig, Frank, 2001a, 'Conditionality, Costs, and Commitment: Domestic Conditions of Adaptation to Fundamental European Norms in the CEECs and Turkey', discussion paper presented at the Robert Schuman Centre for Advanced Studies/European Forum, 11 October.
Schimmelfennig, Frank, 2001b, 'The Community Trap: Liberal Norms, Rhetorical Action, and the Eastern Enlargement of the European Union', *International Organization*, 55(1): 47–80.
Schimmelfennig, Frank, 2002, 'Introduction', in Ronald H. Linden (ed.), *Norms and Nannies: the Impact of International Organizations on the Central and East European States*, Rowman and Littlefield.
Schimmelfennig, Frank, 2003, *The EU, NATO and the Integration of Europe: Rules and Rhetoric*, Cambridge University Press.
Schimmelfennig, Frank and Ulrich Sedelmeier, 2005, 'Introduction: Conceptualizing the Europeanization of Central and Eastern Europe', in Frank Schimmelfennig and Ulrich Sedelmeier (eds), *The Europeanization of Eastern Europe*, Cornell University Press.
Schimmelfennig, Frank, Stefan Engert and Heiko Knobel, 2003, 'Costs, Commitment and Compliance: the Impact of EU Democratic Conditionality on Latvia, Slovakia, and Turkey', *Journal of Common Market Studies*, 41(3): 495–518.
Schimmelfennig, Frank, Stefan Engert and Heiko Knobel, 2005, 'The Impact of EU Political Conditionality', in Frank Schimmelfennig and Ulrich Sedelmeier (eds), *The Europeanization of Eastern Europe*, Cornell University Press.

Schlotter, Peter, 1999, *Die KSZE im Ost-West-Konflikt: Wirkungen einer internationalen Institution*, Campus.

Schmitz, Hans Peter, 2002, 'When Networks Blind: Human Rights and Politics in Kenya', in T. Callaghy, R. Kassimir and R. Latham (eds), *Intervention and Transnationalism in Africa: Global-Local Networks of Power*, Cambridge University Press.

Schmitz, Hans Peter and Kathryn Skikkink, 2002, 'International Human Rights', in T. Risse and B. Simmons (eds), *Handbook of International Relations*, Sage.

Scholte, Jan Art, 2000, *Globalization: a Critical Introduction*, Palgrave Macmillan.

Schwellnus, Guido, 2005, 'Non-discrimination and Minority Protection in the EU Enlargement Process', in Frank Schimmelfennig and Ulrich Sedelmeier (eds), *The Europeanization of Eastern Europe*, Cornell University Press.

Sedelmeier, Ulrich and Helen Wallace, 2000, 'Eastern Enlargement: Strategy or Second Thoughts?', in Helen Wallace and William Wallace (eds), *Policy Making in the European Union* (4th edition), Oxford University Press.

Šedivý, Jiří, 1995, 'Známe atlantické hodnoty?', *Mezinárodní politika*, 19(12): 10–11.

Šedivý, Jiří, 2001, 'The Puzzle of NATO Enlargement', *Contemporary Security Policy*, 22(2): 1–26.

*Selected Documents Relating to Problems of Security and Cooperation in Europe 1954–77*, Miscellaneous No. 17 (1977), Cmnd, 6932, 212.

Simmons, Beth, 2003, 'Why Commit? Explaining State Acceptance of International Rights Obligations', unpublished manuscript.

Simon, Jeffrey, 2004, *NATO and the Czech and Slovak Republics: a Comparative Study in Civil-Military Relations*, Rowman and Littlefield.

Sinclair, Iain, 1976, 'Principles of International Law concerning Friendly Relations and Co-operation among States', in M. Nawaz (ed.), *Essays on International Law in Honor of Khrishna Rao*, A. W. Sitjthoff – International Publishing.

Skak, Mette, 1993, 'Rusland og Europa', *Økonomi og Politik*, 66(4): 13–21.

Skak, Mette, 1996, *From Empire to Anarchy: Postcommunist Foreign Policy and International Relations*, Hurst and Co.

Skak, Mette, 1997, 'Stability of Democracy and Institutions and the Rule of Law', in Peter-Christian Müller-Graff (ed.), *East-Central Europe and the European Union: From Europe Agreements to a Member Status*, Nomos.

Skak, Mette, 2005, 'Russian Security Policy after 9/11', in Roger E. Kanet (ed.), *The New Security Environment: the Impact on Russia, Central and Eastern Europe*, Ashgate.

Smith, Hazel, 2000, *Democracy and International Relations*, Palgrave Macmillan.

Smith, Karen E., 2001, 'Western Actors and the Promotion of Democracy', in Jan Zielonka and Alex Pravda (eds), *Democratic Consolidation in Eastern Europe, Vol. 2: International and Transnational Factors*, Oxford University Press.

Smith, Steve, 2003, 'Singing our World into Existence', Presidential Speech at the International Studies Association Convention, Portland.

Snyder, Jack, 1996, 'Democratization, War and Nationalism in the Post-Communist States', in C. A. Wallander (ed.), *The Sources of Russian Foreign Policy after the Cold War*, Westview.

Solomon, Gerald B., 1998, *The NATO Enlargement Debate, 1990–1997: Blessing of Liberty*, Praeger.

Sperling, James (ed.), 1999, *Two Tiers or Two Speeds? The European Security Order and the Enlargement of the European Union and NATO*, Manchester University Press.

Sperling, Vibeke, 2003, 'Frygt for det russiske demokrati', *Politiken*, 5, December.

Steen, Anton, 2003, *Political Elites and the New Russia: the Power Basis of Yeltsin's and Putin's Regime*, Routledge and Curzon.

Stiles, Kendall, 2003, 'The Role of Domestic Elites and Masses in the Diffusion of International Norms', paper presented at the Annual Meeting of the International Studies Association, Portland, Oregon

Stoudmann, Gérard, 2003, 'Turkmenistan, a Human Rights "Black Hole" ', *Helsinki Monitor: Quarterly on Security and Cooperation in Europe*, 14(2): 117–24.

Strange, Susan, 1992, 'States, Firms, Diplomacy', *International Affairs*, 68(1): 1–15.

Stroehlein, Andrew, 1999a, 'Czech Intellectuals and Post-Communism', *Central Europe Review*, 1(14): http://www.ce-review.org/99/14/stroehlein14.html.

Stroehlein, Andrew, 1999b, 'Three Vaclavs', *Central Europe Review*, 1(10): http://www.ce-review.org/99/10/stroehlein10.html.

Suvarierol, Semin, 2003, 'The Cyprus Obstacle on Turkey's Road to Membership in the European Union', *Turkish Studies*, 4(1): 55–78.

Szomolányi, Soňa, 2003, 'Vol'by v Krajinách V4: Čo Vypovedajú o Stave Demokracie v Regióne', in Grigorij Mesežnikov, Olga Gyárfášová and Miroslav Kollár (eds), *Slovenské Vol'by 2002: Výsledky, Dôsledky, Súvislosti*, Inštitút pre Verejné Otázky.

Tajfel, Henri, 1978, *Differentiation between Social Groups: Studies in the Social Psychology of Intergroup Relations*, Academic Press.

Tajfel, Henri, 1982, *Social Identity and Intergroup Relations*, Cambridge University Press.

Tajfel, Henri and John Turner, 1979, 'An Integrative Theory of Intergroup Conflict', in W. G. Austin and S. Worchel (eds), *The Social Psychology of Intergroup Relations*, Brooks/Cole.

Tajfel, Henri and John Turner, 1985, 'The Social Identity Theory of Intergroup Behaviour', in S. Worchel and W. G. Austin (eds), *Psychology of Intergroup Relations*, Nelson-Hall.

Tarrow, Sydney, 2001, 'Transnational Politics, Contention and Institutions in International Politics', *Annual Review of Political Science*, 4: 1–20.

Taylor, Brian D., 2003, *Politics and the Russian Army. Civil–Military Relations, 1680–2000*, Cambridge University Press.

Thaa, Winifred, 2001, ' "Lean Citizenship": the Fading Away of the Political in Transnational Democracy', *European Journal of International Relations*, 7(4): 503–23.

The Northern Dimension, 2003, http://europa.eu.int/comm/external relations/north dim/.

Theiler, Tobias, 2003, 'Societal Security and Social Psychology', *Review of International Studies*, 29(2): 249–68.

Thomas, Daniel C., 2001, *The Helsinki Effect: International Norms, Human Rights, and the Demise of Communism*, Princeton University Press.

Tocci, Nathalie, 2002, 'Cyprus and the European Union Accession Process: Inspiration for Peace or Incentive for Crisis?', *Turkish Studies*, 3(2): 104–38.

Trajlinková, Katarína, 2001, 'A Review of Slovakia's Accession to the OECD', *BIATEC*, 3(9): 35–7.

Trenin, Dmitri, 2002, *The End of Eurasia: Russia on the Border Between Geopolitics and Globalization*, Carnegie Endowment for International Peace.
Turner, John, 1987, *Rediscovering the Social Group*, Basil Blackwell.
Underhill, Geoffrey, 2000, 'State, Market and Global Political Economy: Genealogy of an (Inter?) Discipline', *International Affairs*, 76(4): 805–24.
United Nations Development Programme (UNDP), 1994, *Human Development Report*, Oxford University Press.
Vachudova, Milada, 2001, 'The Leverage of International Institutions on Democratizing States: Eastern Europe and the European Union', *EUI Working Papers RSC 2001/33*, European University Institute.
van Cranenburgh, Oda, 1999, 'International Policies to Promote Africa', in Jean Grugel (ed.), *Democracy without Borders: Transnationalization and Conditionality in New Democracies*, Routledge.
van der Pijl, Kees, 1995, 'The Second Glorious Revolution: Globalizing Elites and Historical Change', in Bjorn Hettne (ed.), *International Political Economy: Understanding Global Disorder*, Zed Press.
van der Stoel, Max, 1998, 'The Role of the OSCE High Commissioner on National Minorities in Enhancing the Process of Integration', *Romanian Journal of International Affairs*, 4(3–4): 293–305.
van Ham, Peter, 2001, 'Security and Culture, or, Why NATO Won't Last', *Security Dialogue*, 32(4): 39–406.
Vanhanen, T., 1997, *Prospects of Democracy: a Study of 172 Countries*, Routledge.
Vasilev, Stefan, 1999, 'The HCNM Approach to Conflict Prevention', *Helsinki Monitor: Quarterly on Security and Cooperation in Europe*, 10(3): 45–58.
Velšic, Marián, 2001, 'Spoločenská Atmosféra', in Olga Gyárfášová, Vladimír Krivý, Marián Velšic et al., *Krajina v Pohybe: Správa o Politických Názoroch a Hodnotách L'udí na Slovensku*, Inštitút pre Verejné Otázky.
Verdoodt, A., 1964, *Naissance et Signification de la Declaration Universelle des Droits de l'Homme*, Lovain Editions Nauwelaerts.
*Výběr z výzkumů veřejného mínění v České republice*, MZV, 20, 1997.
Waltz, Susan, 2002, 'Reclaiming and Rebuilding the History of the Universal Declaration of Human Rights', *Third World Quarterly*, 23(3): 437–48.
Wendt, Alexander, 1999, *Social Theory of International Relations*, Cambridge University Press.
White, Nigel D., 2002, *The United Nations System: Toward International Justice*, Lynne Rienner.
White, Stephen, 1984, 'Soviet Political Culture Reassessed', in Archie Brown (ed.), *Political Culture and Communist Studies*, Macmillan.
White, Stephen and Richard Rose, 2001, *Nationality and Public Opinion in Belarus and Ukraine*, University of Strathclyde, No. 346.
Whitehead, Lawrence, 1996, *The International Dimension of Democratization*, Oxford University Press.
Whitehead, Lawrence, 2002, *Democratisation Theory and Practice*, Oxford University Press.
Williams, Michael C. and B. Neumann, Iver, 2000, 'From Alliance to Security Community: NATO, Russia and the Power of Identity', *Millennium*, 29(2): 357–87.
Wilson, Andrew, 1980, *The Aegean Dispute*, Adelphi Paper 155, International Institute for Strategic Studies, London.

Wolf, C., 1991, *Promoting Democracy and Free Markets in Eastern Europe*, RAND.

Worchel, S. and W. G. Austin (eds), 1985, *Psychology of Intergroup Relations*, Nelson-Hall.

Yashar, Deborah, 2002, 'Globalization and Collective Action', *Comparative Politics*, 34(3): 355–62.

Yesilada, Birol, 2002, 'The Virtue Party', *Turkish Studies*, 3(1): 62–81.

Yost, David, 1998, *NATO Transformed: the Alliance's New Roles in International Security*, United States Institute for Peace Press.

Youngs, Richard, 2001, *Democracy Promotion: the Case of the EU Strategy*, CEPS Working Paper, No. 167, October.

Zellner, Wolfgang and Falk Lange (eds), 2001, 'Max van der Stoel: Peace and Stability Through Human and Minority Rights', *Speeches by the OSCE High Commissioner on National Minorities*, Nomos.

Zieleniec, Josef, 1995, 'Dárek pod stromeček', *Lidové noviny*, 12(4): 8.

Zielonka, Jan, 2001, 'Foreign Made Democracy', in Jan Zielonka and Alex Pravda (eds), *Democratic Consolidation in Eastern Europe. Vol. II: International and Transnational Factors*, Oxford University Press.

# Author Index

# Subject Index